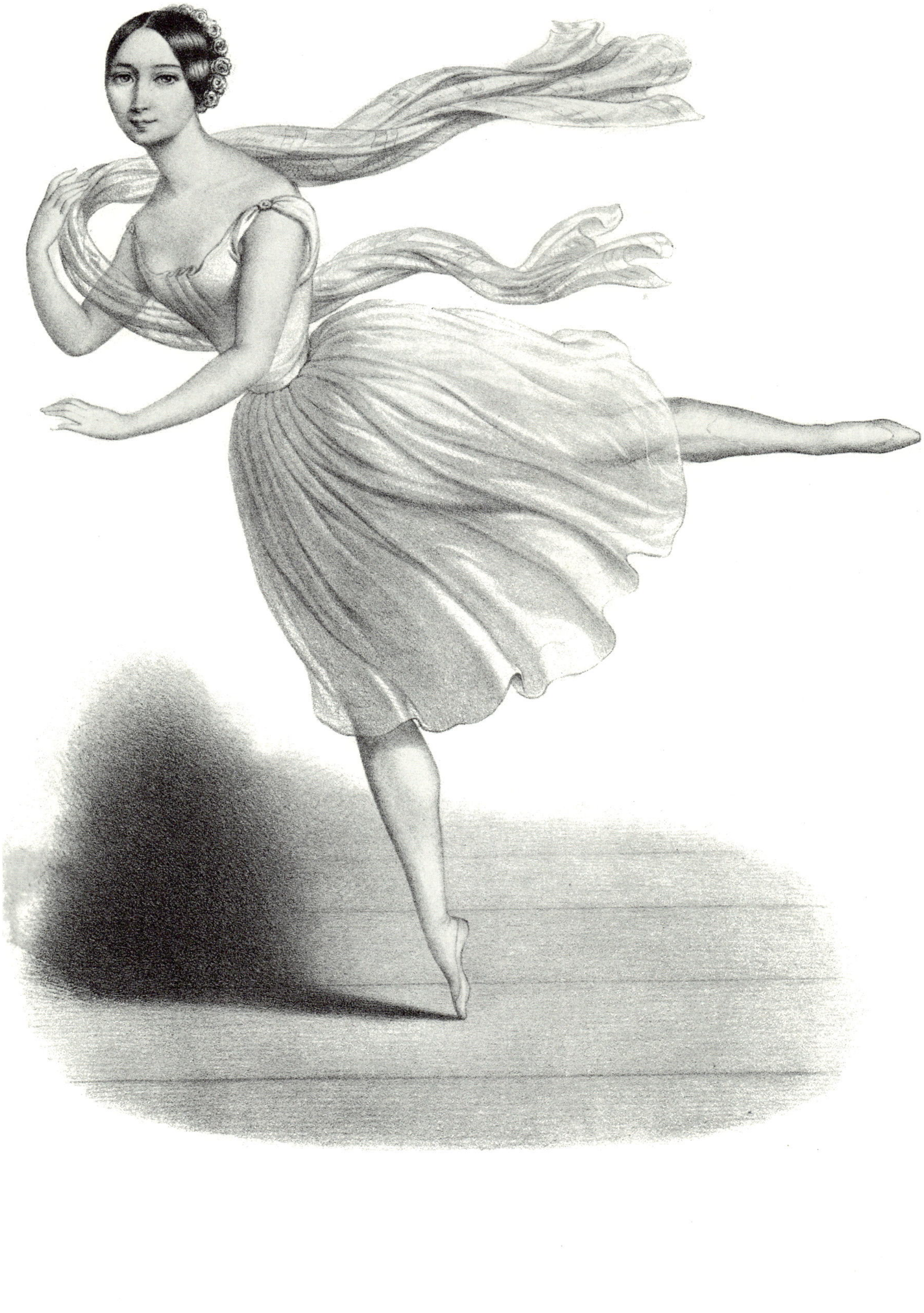

Great Ballet Prints of the Romantic Era

109 ILLUSTRATIONS

Parmenia Migel

DOVER PUBLICATIONS, INC.
NEW YORK

For "Pommier"
with gratitude, admiration and affection

COVER: Louise Fleury as Myrtha in *Giselle* (Her Majesty's Theatre, London, 1842).

FRONTISPIECE: Nathalie Fitzjames (née Fijan), portrait, Paris, ca. 1840.

Published in Canada by General Publishing Company, Ltd., 30 Lesmill Road, Don Mills, Toronto, Ontario.
Published in the United Kingdom by Constable and Company, Ltd., 10 Orange Street, London WC2H 7EG.

Great Ballet Prints of the Romantic Era: 109 Illustrations is a new work, first published by Dover Publications, Inc., in 1981.

International Standard Book Number: 0-486-24050-9
Library of Congress Catalog Card Number: 81-66802

Manufactured in the United States of America
Dover Publications, Inc.
180 Varick Street
New York, N.Y. 10014

Contents

Introduction

NOWADAYS, if we want to recapture something of the history and the atmosphere of the Romantic ballet, we must turn to the engravings and lithographs of the period. Since dance is an art of motion, it is obvious that these fixed images can convey only fleeting impressions of nineteenth-century performances; nevertheless pictures are more effective than verbal descriptions, considering that only in recent times have dance critics had much useful knowledge of technique or attempted to describe in anything except general terms or poetic hyperbole what they observed on the stage.

Although the heritage of dance prints includes masterworks such as Jean Berain's prodigious oeuvre for French court ballets and the exquisite eighteenth-century engravings of Jean-Baptiste Martin, it was during the Romantic era that prints were in greatest demand and achieved new standards of perfection.

Ballet was suddenly popular. It was no longer a pastime of privileged aristocrats, although it had originated in the courts of Italian Renaissance princes and then evolved at the Opéra founded by Louis XIV; it had become a favorite entertainment of the general public and even a main preoccupation of young men-about-town. Everyone wanted souvenirs of ballet idols, much as people today collect "pin-ups" or photographs of cinema stars.

At the same time, prints became more accessible. Aloys Senefelder, a Czech living in Munich, stumbled on a method of printing from slabs of stone. In 1818, he published a memorandum describing his "lithographs" and was rewarded by the king of Bavaria with a pension for life. The process, although it never entirely replaced engraving on copper plates, was enthusiastically adopted in Europe and America. For black-and-white it was faster and cheaper and separate stones could be prepared for various colors, thereby eliminating the long and tedious labor of coloring prints by hand. The new medium was also more sensitive and gave greater scope to artists, enabling them to suggest the diaphanous, floating qualities associated with the Romantic ballet.

Lithographs remained the vogue until people considered it more exciting to sit for photographers. These new likenesses seemed astonishingly realistic and an added attraction was that these pictures were so small that they could be carried about in wallets or ladies' reticules or mounted in little albums and handed around at parties between the inevitable recitations and bouts of homemade music. In 1839, the French Academy of Sciences announced the photographic discoveries of Louis-Jacques-Mandé Daguerre and he too received an annuity—6000 francs—and was decorated with the Legion of Honor. By the time another decade or so had passed, his invention, known as the "daguerreotype," had dealt a fatal blow to the portrait-print industry, which had flourished for some four hundred years and now would succumb along with the sad remnants of the Romantic ballet.

Before examining the prints, perhaps we should try to define the Romantic ballet, which was, no doubt, the supreme expression of the Romantic era. Nearly all cultural historians suggest that this era began with the near-riot at the premiere of Victor Hugo's play *Hernani*, 1830 (the battle of the Romantics versus the Classicists), the opera *Robert le Diable*, 1831 (with its eerie moonlight falling on the macabre ruined cloister and the dead nuns rising from their graves; Plate 7), and the revelation of Marie Taglioni dancing on *pointe* in *La Sylphide*, 1832—all of them Parisian events. The Dictionnaire Larousse explains Romanticism as the "intellectual and artistic movement which, from the end of the eighteenth century, placed feeling above reason and imagination above critical analysis as the esthetic principle in literature, in music and in the fine arts"—the early date being that of the appearance of the first German literary fairy tales. Indeed these stories by Tieck, Novalis, Brentano and E. T. A. Hoffmann, which began to emerge in 1796, really launched Romanticism. "The point," says a Tieck character, "is to find a way of looking at everyday life as a fairy tale; in that way we can become acquainted with the most wonderful things as if they were the most common things." It was the escapist, the exotic, the mysterious which were to dominate as themes of the period.

In the ballet in France, despite the strictures of Pierre Gardel, the Opéra's reactionary, tyrannical ballet master from 1787 to 1829, there were intimations of Romanticism as early as Emilie Bigottini's emotional portrayal of *Nina, ou la Folle par amour* in 1813. This ballet was not only the epitome of sentimentality, but also its "succession of incidents," said Cyril Beaumont, "is so similar to those in the first act of *Giselle* as to suggest that Vernoy de Saint-Georges received inspiration from *Nina* for some of his situations." After a second histrionic triumph in *Clari, ou la Promesse de mariage*, 1820, in which she was partnered by Paul, "l'aérien" (Plate 2), Mlle Bigottini appeared in a real fairy tale, *Cendrillon*, 1823 (Plate 1), with Albert (François Decombe) as both choreographer and the Prince. The music was by Fernando Sor, a brilliant Spanish harpist and guitarist, about whom little is known except that he married the ballerina Félicité Hullin and lived in London, where *Cendrillon* was produced a year before it reached the Paris Opéra.

When Spontini's opera *Fernand Cortès*, 1809, was restaged in 1817, Mlle Gosselin (Constance, later known professionally as Madame Anatole) danced in the ballet *divertissements* (Plate 3). The name of this ballerina evokes the never-ending controversy as to who was the first exponent of dancing on *pointe*, because her elder sister Geneviève is a main contender for the honor. Eminent historians have proposed half a dozen candidates, basing their choice on prints that depict dancers on, or nearly on, *pointes*. But here, for once, reports of contemporary authors seem more valid than pictures. Reviewing Taglioni's dancing, the *Journal des Débats* of August 3, 1827, remarked: "It reminds one of the elder Mlle Gosselin . . . and her muscular strength which enabled her to remain poised for one minute on the very tip of her toes . . ." Note well the "one minute." And two years later the magazine *I Teatri* said of Amalia Brugnoli that she had learned from Armand Vestris "the sort of dancing which was lost with the celebrated Mlle Gosselin and which places upon the extreme point of the toe the weight that others sustain by the entire foot." Taglioni reminisced that, in 1822 in Vienna, she had seen Brugnoli presenting "a new kind of dancing; she did extraordinary things on the point of her foot," but added disparagingly: "I did not find her graceful because, in order to rise on *pointe*, she had to make great efforts with her arms." Quite the contrary was the impression of Lady Blessington, who saw Brugnoli in Italy only months later and observed that she "advances rapidly across the stage on the extreme point of her toes, cuts into the air, and alights again on the point of her feet, as if she were no heavier than gossamer." And so, if Geneviève Gosselin, who died in 1818, was a pioneer, remaining on *pointe* "for one minute," then surely it was Brugnoli who perfected the technique and was the model for Taglioni and her successors.

We have dwelt at length on this because dancing on *pointe* was to become the distinguishing feature of the Romantic ballerinas, who achieved their effect wearing only a soft slipper. The dancers themselves merely reinforced their slippers by stiching and darning the toes; the first boxed ballet slipper only came into use with Carlotta Grisi around 1841. It is certain, in spite of the artistic license of several painters of the period, that none of them ever appeared barefoot on the stage.

In 1823, at the Théâtre de la Porte-Saint-Martin, Antoine Titus staged *La Laitière suisse* with Louise Pierson (Plate 5). The mists of time have veiled this charming dancer's all-too-brief career, but her associations here are of special interest: the theater was the proving ground of many performers and choreographers who later became famous at the Paris and other opera houses; her partner was "l'incomparable" Charles-François Mazurier (Color Plate A), described by Marian Hannah Winter as "the most gifted comic dancer of France and probably in all Europe"; and the ballet itself was an object of contention. Titus had pirated it from Filippo Taglioni, who was accused of stealing it from Louis Henry, who himself had filched it from Gaetano Gioja. Although Taglioni admitted the theft, he restaged it as *Nathalie ou la Laitière suisse* for his daughter Marie in 1832 at the Opéra, where, in spite of its ridiculous plot, it had a considerable success and Pauline Montessu, Pauline Duvernay, Pauline Leroux (Plate 10), Fanny Elssler and Jules Perrot (Plate 11) all appeared in it.

Partly because of his proven plagiarisms, there is a tendency to denigrate Filippo Taglioni and not nearly enough credit has been given to him for his role in establishing the Romantic ballet. Finding his daughter's Paris training totally inadequate, it was he who taught her not only technique but especially the spirit of her dancing, which was to enshrine her as the symbol of Romanticism. Dr. Louis Véron, then director of the Opéra, observed in his *Mémoires:* "Taglioni *père* founded a new school of the dance, entirely different in its style and philosophic thought from the school of a Gardel or a Vestris . . . Vestris taught elegance, seduction; he was a sensualist; he insisted on provocative smiles, poses and attitudes that were almost immodest and shameless. I have often heard him say quite cynically to his pupils: 'My dears, be charming, coquettish, display the most alluring freedom in every move you make; you must inspire love both during and after your *pas* and make the audience and orchestra desirous of sleeping with you.' The school, style and language of Taglioni *père* were exactly the opposite. He demanded graceful ease of movement, lightness, elevation and especially *ballon;* but he did not allow his daughter a single gesture or pose which might be lacking in decency or modesty. He told her: 'Women and young girls must be able to watch you dance without blushing.'"

As a choreographer Filippo was equally influential. Besides his earlier Vienna and Stuttgart productions, he created for the Opéra the ballets *La Sylphide*, 1832 (Color Plate B, Plates 12 & 13); *Nathalie*, 1832; *La Révolte au sérail*, 1833 (Plate 21); *La Tempête*, 1834; *Brézilia*, 1835; and *La fille du Danube*, 1836 (Plates 30 & 31); as well as the ballet *divertissements* for the operas *Le Dieu et la Bayadère*, 1830 (Color Plate F—it was known in the United States as *The Maid of Cashmere*—and Plate 9); *Robert le Diable*, 1831; *Gustave*, 1833 (Plate 20); *La Juive*, 1835; and *Les Huguenots*, 1836—in addition to all the ballets that followed in St. Petersburg such as *La Gitana*, 1838 (Plate 34), and *L'Ombre*, 1839. Though he worked primarily for his daughter, his ballets became vehicles for most of the ballerinas of the period, who thus diffused Romanticism all over Europe and the United States.

Londoners had hardly recovered from the excitement of seeing Brugnoli's by now accomplished dancing on *pointe* in *L'Anneau magique* at the King's Theatre, March 1832 (Plate 15), when they were even more captivated by *La Sylphide* in July, only four months after the Paris premiere. Taglioni in this role was a revelation, and though she went on to sensational and unremitting acclaim in Paris, St. Petersburg and elsewhere, she remained a special idol of the British until her retirement in 1847.

Even the arrival of Fanny Elssler contained no threat to Taglioni in London. Elssler was the second of the four great Romantic ballerinas (Taglioni, Elssler, Grisi, Cerrito) but she had only a modest success when she first appeared at the King's Theatre in 1833–34. It was enough, however, to convince Dr. Véron that he should lure her to Paris and introduce her as a rival to Taglioni, who was becoming a far too demanding star at the Opéra.

Taglioni and her partner, Jules Perrot, had been rewarded with an ovation in 1830 when they appeared in the continuing revivals of Spontini's *Fernand Cortès*. The Spanish-Mexican exoticism of this opera appealed to the audience, whose enthusiasm redoubled on seeing authentic and outstanding dancers from Spain: Mariano Camprubì, Francisco Font, Dolores Serral and Manuela Dubinon (Plates 22–25). Elssler, for whom no ballets had been produced in Paris that made the most of her particular gifts, was quick to take advantage of the new craze. By 1836, she was able to perform her finished and thrilling *pas*, La Cachucha, in *Le Diable boiteux* (Plate 27). Almost overnight Paris was divided into two fanatical camps—the Taglionists, who opted for Taglioni's spirituality, and the Elsslerists, who were seduced by Elssler's physical beauty, sensuality and verve. Calm was only restored among the balletomanes when Taglioni decided to spend her next five winters in Russia and the summers in London, Vienna and Stockholm.

Elssler lingered in Paris until 1840 (Color Plate C, Plate 32), when she asked the Opéra for a year's leave of absence in order to accept an engagement in New York. Her Cachucha had meanwhile inspired a host of imitators (Plates 28 & 29). She needed new fields to conquer and perhaps it was her turn to fear the rivalry of another ballerina. Lucile Grahn was almost ten years younger, she was ravishingly pretty and her dancing seemed to combine elements of Taglioni's grace and Elssler's technique. She was the pupil and protégée of August Bournonville, who himself had been trained by Vestris and Gardel and did a brief stint at the Opéra before eventually becoming ballet master of the Royal Danish Ballet. As Grahn outstayed her leave from Copenhagen and could never return there, so Elssler, dazzled by her reception in America, broke her Opéra contract and could never return to Paris.

This left the way clear for the sudden triumphs of Carlotta Grisi, for whom the Opéra staged *Giselle*, 1841 (Plates 41 & 43). The best efforts of Adolphe Adam as composer, Théophile Gautier and Vernoy de Saint-Georges as librettists (basing their work on a folklore study by Heinrich Heine), Pierre Ciceri as designer and Giovanni Coralli (Plate 40) as choreographer were united in the production of an enduring masterpiece, and as its first interpreter, Carlotta Grisi was exquisite. *La Péri*, 1843 (Plates 48 & 49),was the next collaboration of Gautier and Coralli, with the latter devising some spectacular *pas*, especially the famous Leap, in which Grisi dropped from the sky into the outstretched arms of Lucien Petipa, who sometimes caught her and sometimes did not.

Soon Elssler, Grahn and Grisi all gravitated to London, making it for a while the heart and center of the Romantic ballet. Perrot had preceded them there, having suffered at the Opéra from unjust treatment, the jealous aspersions of Marie Taglioni and offense, no doubt, at receiving no credit for the dances he created in *Giselle* for Carlotta Grisi, whose "husband" and teacher he had been for many years. In England, though he continued dancing (Color Plate H), he flourished mainly as a choreographer, producing, in conjunction with the composer Cesare Pugni, twenty-one ballets, many of which were first-rate works of art and one, at least, a masterwork—*La Esmeralda*, which can still be seen in Russia at the present time (Color Plate D).

With Fanny Cerrito, Perrot's galaxy of ballerinas acquired added brilliance (Color Plate D, Plates 50, 52, 53, 65, 71). Cerrito herself choreographed several of the ballets in which she sparkled and some were composed for her by her dancing partner, Arthur Saint-Léon, whom she married in 1845, the year when Perrot had his most resounding success, presenting Taglioni, Grisi, Grahn and Cerrito together in his *Pas de Quatre* (Plate 55).

This was also the high moment of the Romantic ballet, whose progress now began a slow descending curve. Other new and younger dancers would arrive from faraway places—Carolina Rosati, Flora Fabbri, Sofia Fuoco, Amalia Ferraris, each one talented and enchanting—but in Italy the emphasis was to be more and more on technical feats and spectacular shows rather than the art of dancing. Berlin, with Marie's brother, Paul Taglioni, as ballet master, was a dead end; and after the departure of Lucile Grahn and the early retirement of Augusta Nielsen, Copenhagen's ballet became an enclave unto itself, jealously guarded by Bournonville until 1877. In America a spark had been kindled by visiting European dancers, but after Augusta Maywood no real ballerina would be forthcoming until the twentieth century. Paris had a white hope in young Emma Livry and when reports about her reached Marie Taglioni at her villa in Como, she came out of retirement to teach Livry and choreograph a ballet for her. Alas, there was to be no new Sylphide, because Mlle Livry's tutu caught fire and in 1863, at the age of twenty-one, she perished of burns. There was even a faint echo of ballet's golden era when Arthur Saint-Léon returned from Russia to the Opéra to choreograph *Coppélia* in 1870. Giuseppina Bozzacchi was only sixteen when she created the role of his lively heroine but she died that same year, as did Saint-Léon. Only Russia, future world center of dance, was able to preserve a part of the tradition through the unchanging discipline of its two great ballet schools and through the long memory of ballet master Marius Petipa, who presided in St. Petersburg from 1847 to 1905.

What then, if anything, remains today of the Romantic ballet? There are revised versions of *La Sylphide*, *Giselle*, *La Esmeralda* and a very fabricated *Pas de Quatre*. As recently as four years ago, a charming old lady in Paris was reminiscing about her grandfather, Jules Perrot. Teachers have been an important link. The precepts of nineteenth-century Carlo Blasis have come down to us in a direct line through Enrico Cecchetti and his many disciples; and Catarina Beretta, who danced at the Opéra in 1855, lived to teach Pavlova, Trefilova and Karsavina and imbue them with something of the spirit of Romanticism.

And there is the gallery of Romantic ballet prints.

List of Plates

THE TITLES as they appear on the original prints are supplied here within quotation marks; the captions on the plate pages furnish more correct forms of proper names where necessary. The entries indicate whether the same artist did both the original drawing (or painting) and the lithograph, or whether the lithography was done by an artist or firm other than the original draftsman (or painter). Entries of the type "after a print by . . ." indicate that the item illustrated is a pirated print; such piracies were typical of Haguental in Paris and Currier in New York. Dimensions are given in inches, height before width. The dates are those of the prints. All prints are from the collection of the author.

COLOR PLATES

The color plates follow black-and-white Plate No. 16.

COVER: "The Favorites of the Ballet. No. 9. Mad^{lle} Fleury [as] Myrtha in Giselle." Drawn and lithographed by William C. Steer, London, 1844. 11¼ × 7.

A. "Mazurier/Artiste du Théâtre de la Porte St. Martin/Rôle de Beterse dans La Laitière Suisse." Drawn by Marin, lithographed by C. Motte, Paris, 1823. 12¾ × 7.

B. "Marie Taglioni als Sylphide." Drawn by Johann Nepomuk Geiger; lithographed by F. Herr, Vienna, n.d. 16½ × 9½.

C. "Gloires de l'Opéra. No. 5. Fanny Elssler/La Cracovienne dans Gipsy." Lithographed (after a print by Joseph Bouvier) by Haguental, Paris, n.d. 12¼ × 9¼.

D. "Fanny Cerrito St. Leon als Esmeralda" [in *La Esmeralda;* avant la lettre]. Drawn by Bürde, lithographed by C. Mittag, Berlin, 1847. 16½ × 12¼.

E. "Clara Vestris Webster/Nancy, in Lady Henrietta or the Statute Fair." Drawn and lithographed by Thomas Herbert Maguire, London, 1845. 17¼ × 9¾.

F. "Celeste as the Maid of Cashmere." Drawn by Edmund Thomas Parris, lithographed by A. Picken, London, 1837. 16¾ × 11.

G. "La Petite Augusta/Aged 12 years/In the Character of Zoloe, in the Bayadere." Drawn by "EWC," lithographed by H. R. Robinson, N.Y., 1838. 13 × 9¾.

H. "Gloires de l'Opéra. No. 11. Carlotta Grisi & Perrot Dansant la Polka." Lithographed (after a print by Joseph Bouvier) by Haguental & Fagonde, Paris, n.d. 12½ × 9¼.

BLACK-AND-WHITE PLATES

FRONTISPIECE: "Mlle Nathalie Fitz-James." Drawn by Alexandre Lacauchie, lithographed by J. Rigo et Cie, Paris, n.d. 9⅝ × 6.

1. "Costumes d'Albert rôle du Prince Ramir, et de Mlle Bigotini rôle de Cendrillon, dans Cendrillon. Ballet pantomime. Th. de l'Acad^{e} Roy^{le} de Musique." Martinet No. 524, engraved by Maleuvre, Paris, n.d. 8¼ × 5¼, color.
2. "Galerie Théâtrale/Mr Paul (dans Clary Ballet Pantomime)." Drawn by Coeuré, engraved by Prud'hon, Paris, n.d. 9½ × 5⅝, color.
3. "Galerie Théâtrale/Mlle Gosselin (Rôle d'Anatole dans Fernand Cortes)." Drawn by Coeuré, engraved by Prud'hon, Paris, n.d. 9 × 5⅝, color and gold.
4. "Mlle Noblet In the Ballet of La Paysanne Supposée." Painted by F. Waldeck, engraved by R. Cooper, London, 1822. 10½ × 5¾, color.
5. "Mlle Louise Pierson/Artiste du Théâtre de la porte St Martin/Rôle d'Ida dans le Ballet de la laitière suisse." Drawn by A. Colin, lithographed by F. Noël, Paris, n.d. 11 × 7½.
6. "Galerie Théâtrale/Mme Montessu/Ballet de la somnambule." Drawn by Alexandre Lacauchie, engraved by E. Rouargue, Paris, n.d. 8¾ × 5¾, color.
7. "Académie Impériale de Musique (Théâtre de l'Opéra)" [cloister scene from *Robert le Diable*]. Drawn and lithographed by J. Arnout, Paris, n.d. 8½ × 9⅞, color.
8. "Mademoiselle Taglioni" [in *Flore et Zéphire*]. Drawn by Alfred Edward Chalon, lithographed by Richard James Lane, London, n.d. 14 × 9⅛, color.
9. "La Bayadère—Portrait of Mademoiselle Taglioni." Drawn by Alfred Edward Chalon, lithographed by Richard James Lane, London, n.d. 22¼ × 14⅛, color.

Great Ballet Prints of the Romantic Era

A Note on the Captions

THE SELECTION and arrangement of plates in this volume form a brief conspectus of the history of ballet in the Romantic era. The reference material supplied within parentheses in the captions represents in each case the place and date of the first performance of the particular role by the particular dancer, which are *not* necessarily the place and date of the prints. The information about the prints themselves is supplied in the List of Plates.

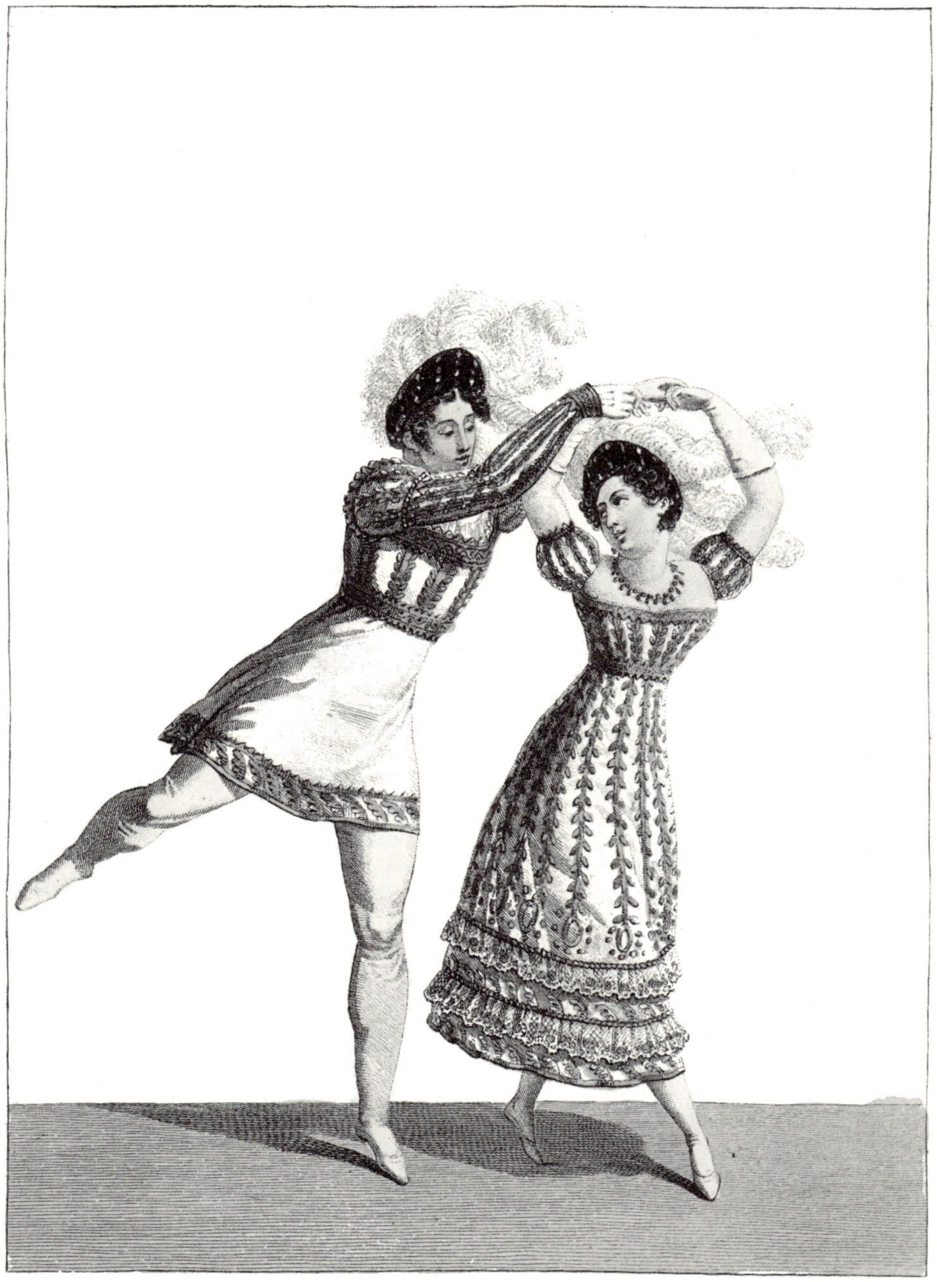

1. Albert (François Decombe) and Emilie Bigottini in *Cendrillon* (Opéra, Paris, 1823).

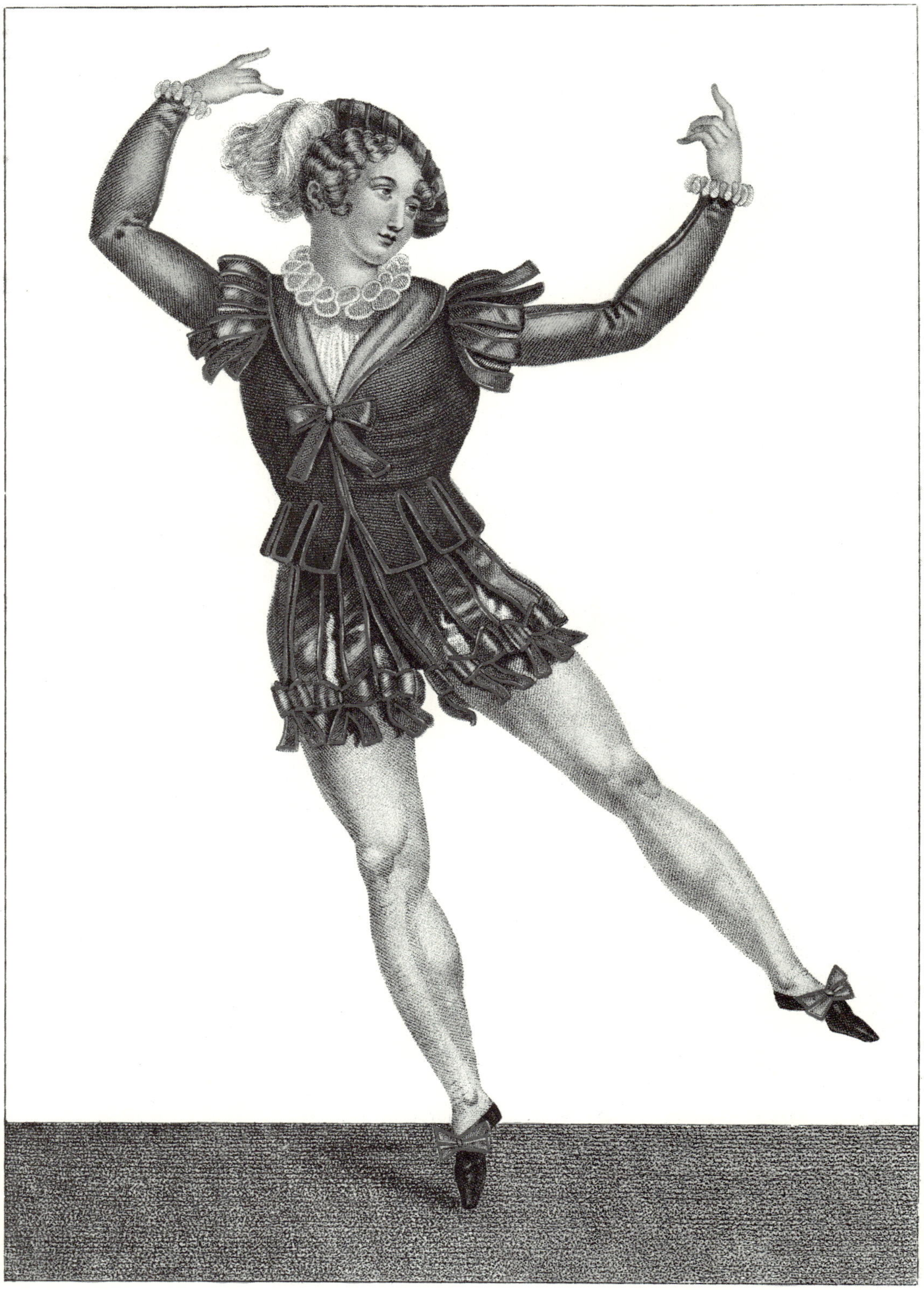

2. Paul (Antoine Paul) in *Clari* (Opéra, Paris, 1820).

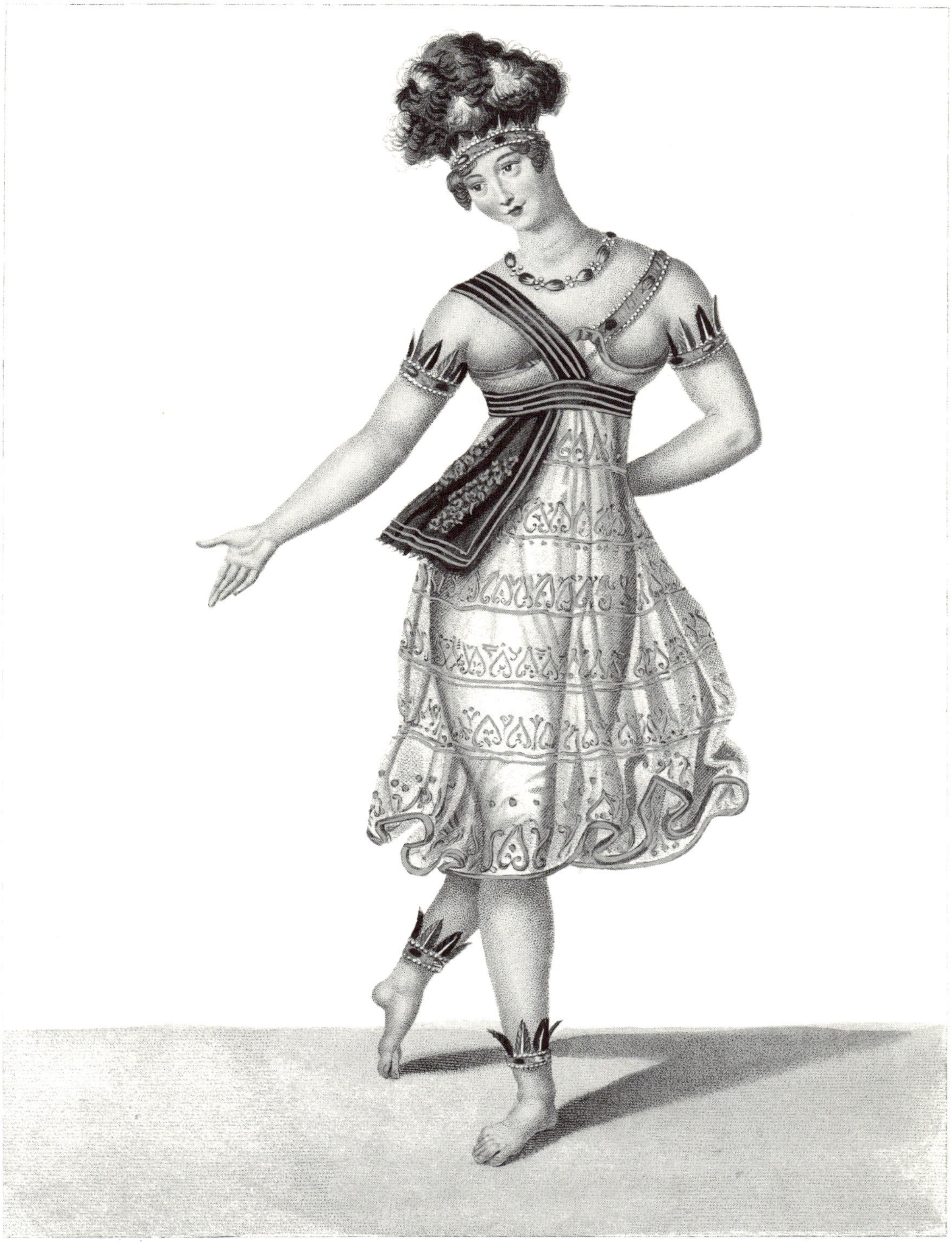

3. Constance Gosselin in *Fernand Cortès* (Opéra, Paris, 1817 revival).

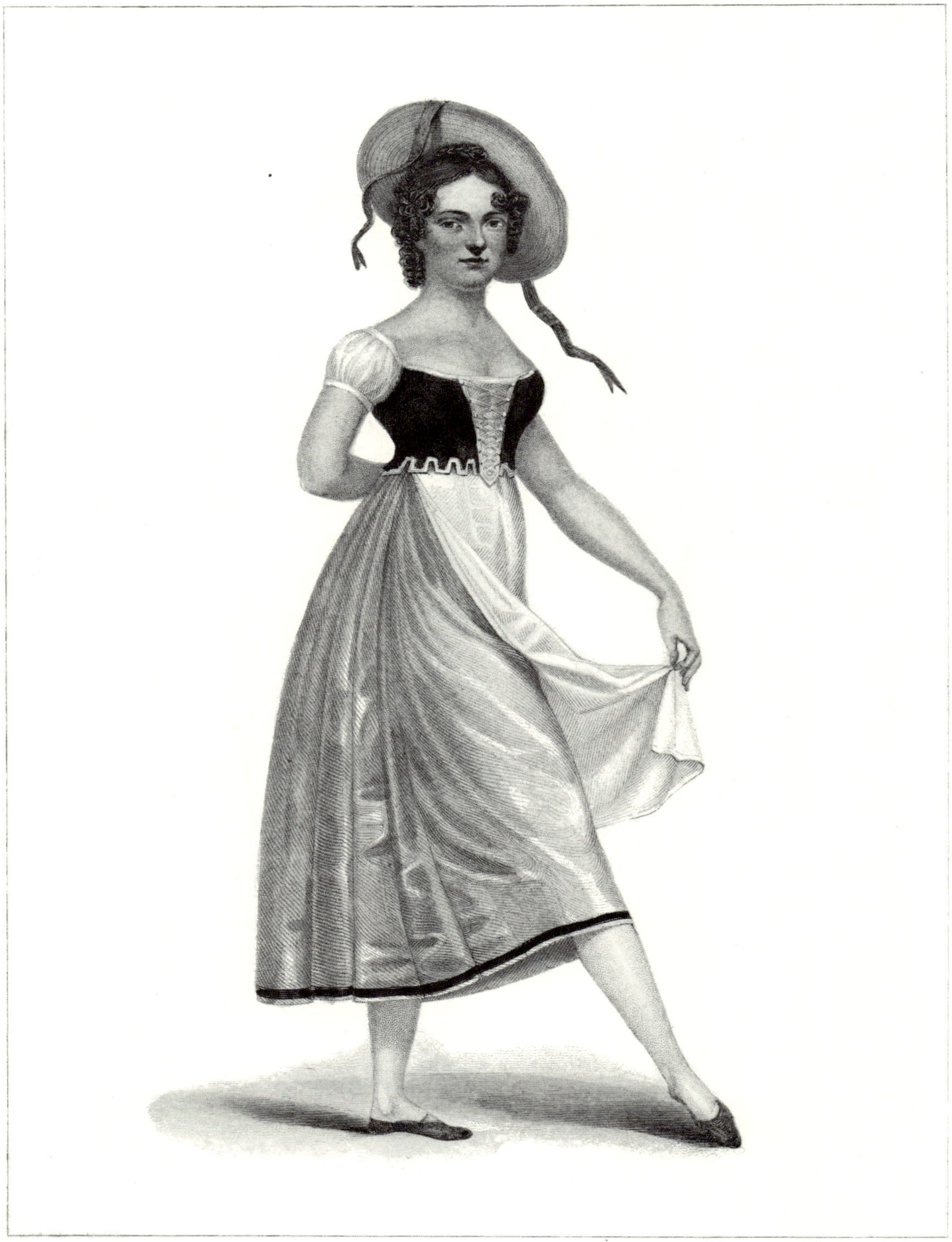

4. Lise Noblet in *La Paysanne Supposée* (King's Theatre, London, 1821).

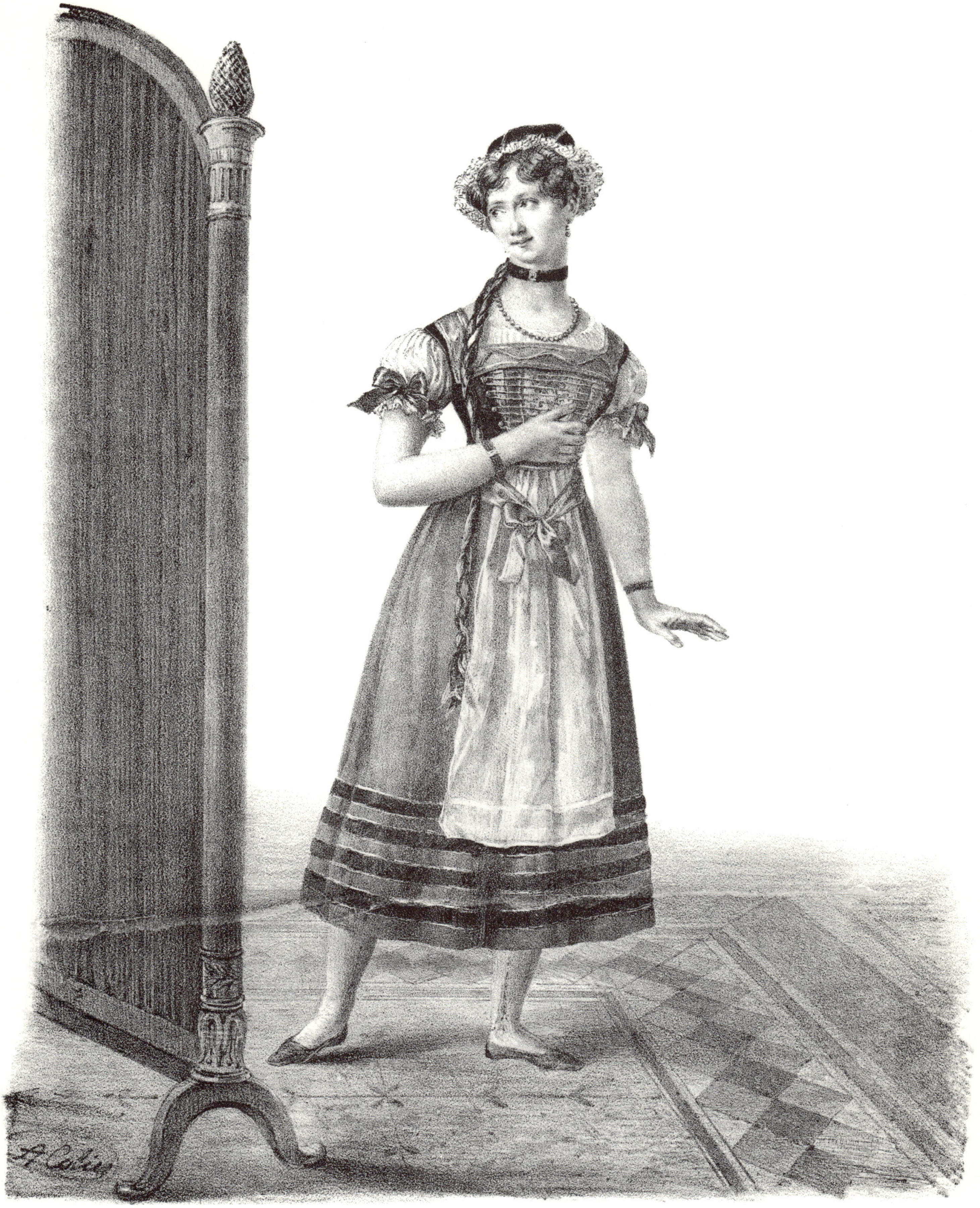

5. Louise Pierson in *La Laitière suisse* (Théâtre de la Porte-Saint-Martin, Paris, 1823).

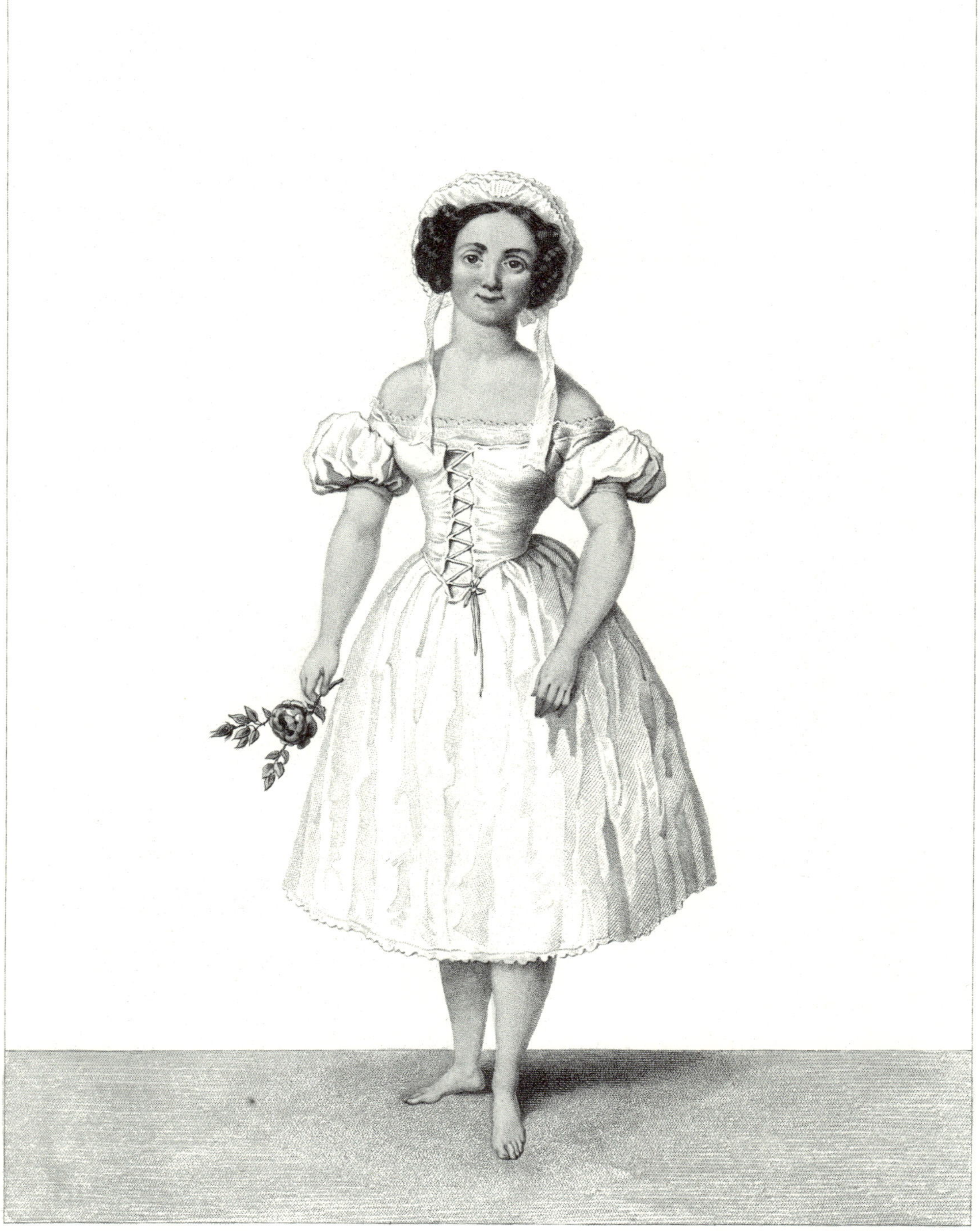

6. Pauline Montessu in *La Somnambule* (Opéra, Paris, 1827).

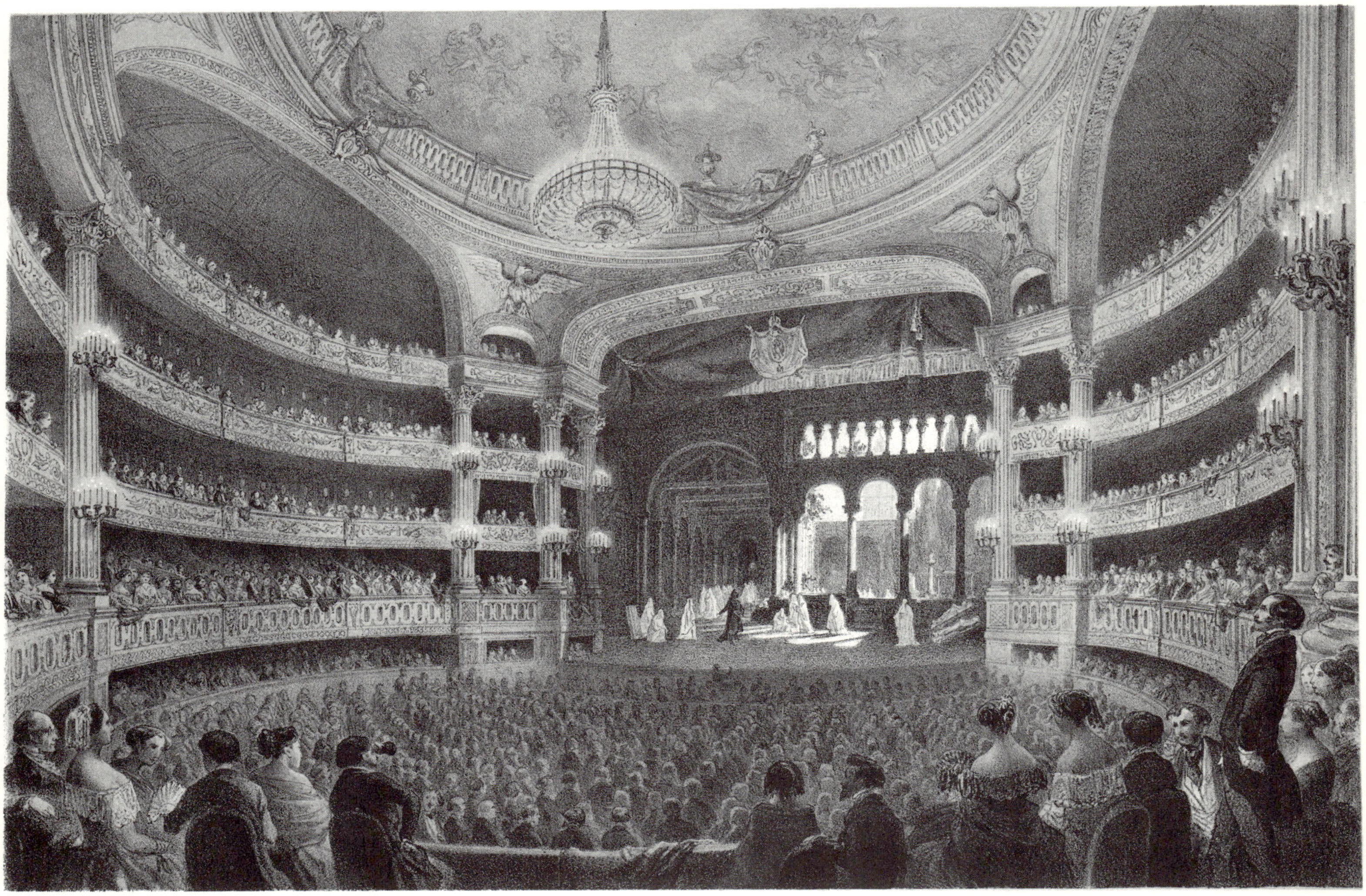

7. Cloister scene in *Robert le Diable* (Opéra, Paris, 1831).

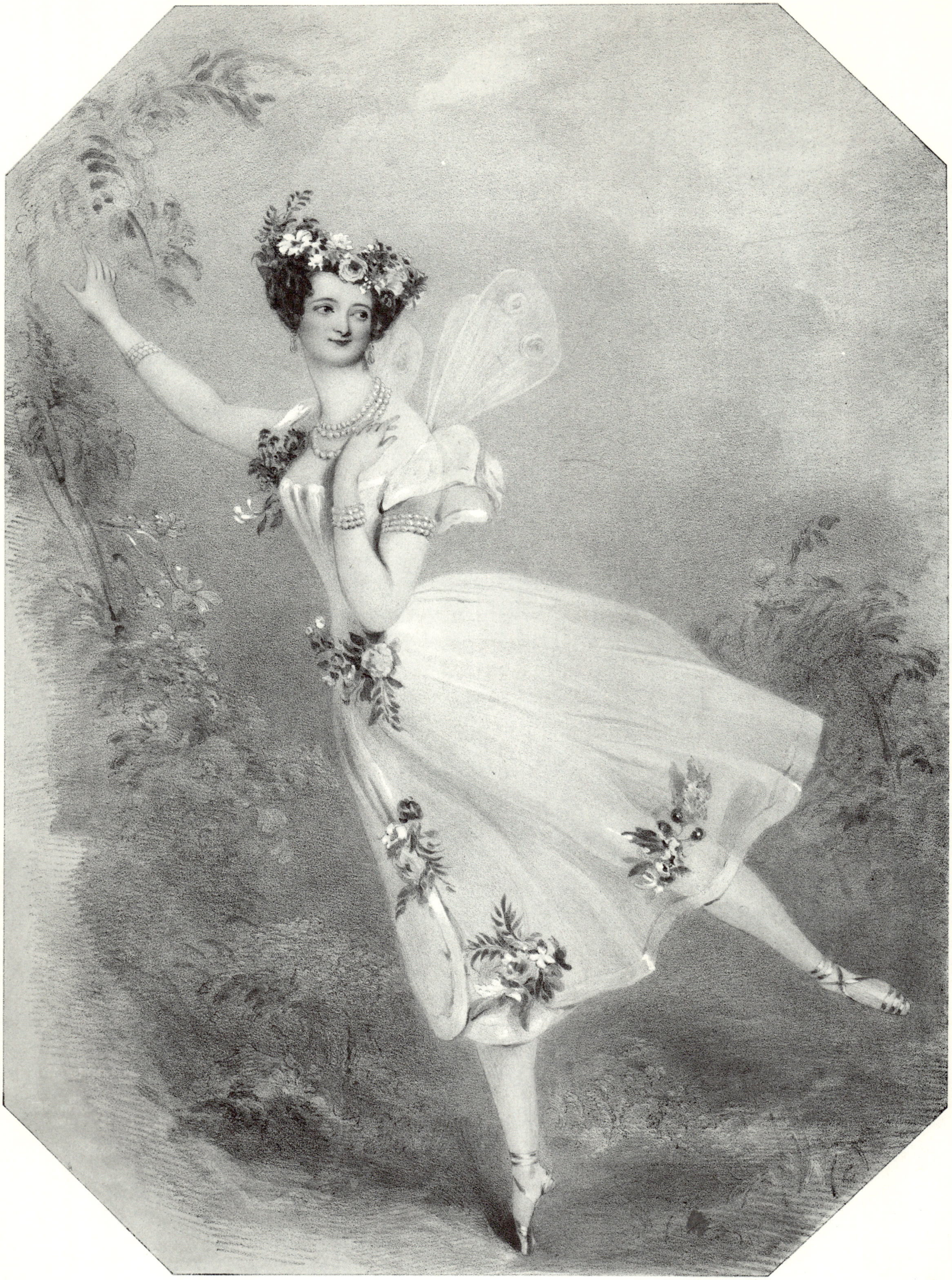

8. Marie Taglioni in *Flore et Zéphire* (King's Theatre, London, 1830).

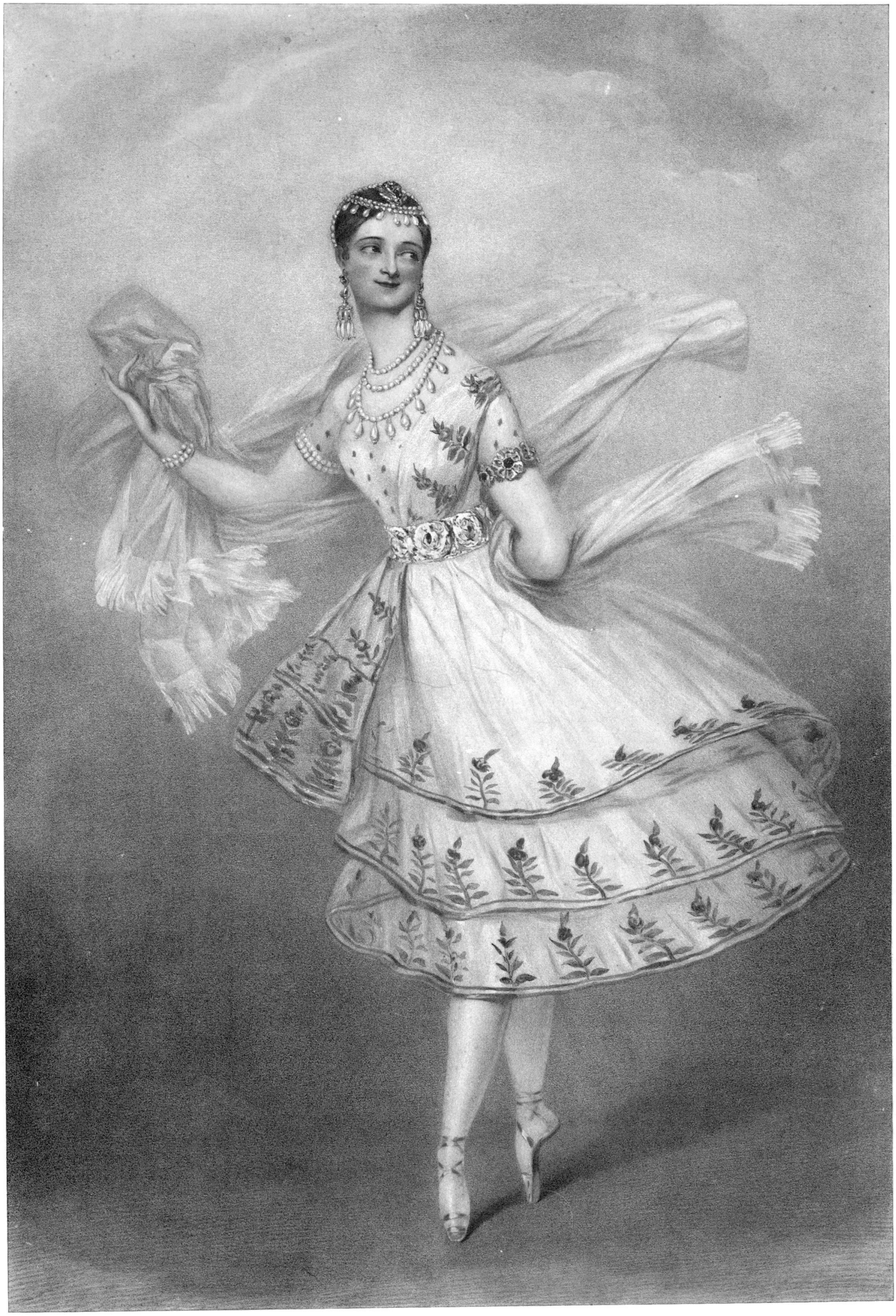

9. Marie Taglioni in *La Bayadère* (King's Theatre, London, 1831).

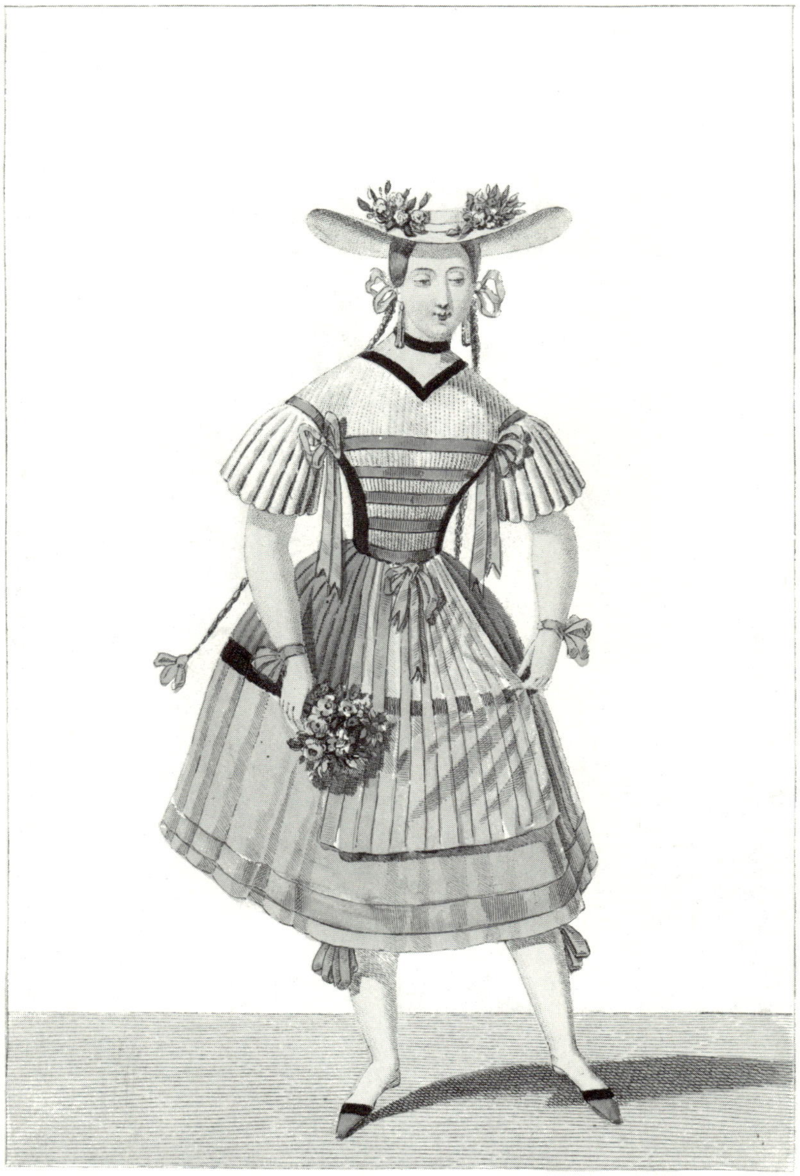

10. Pauline Leroux in *Nathalie ou la Laitière suisse* (Opéra, Paris, 1832).

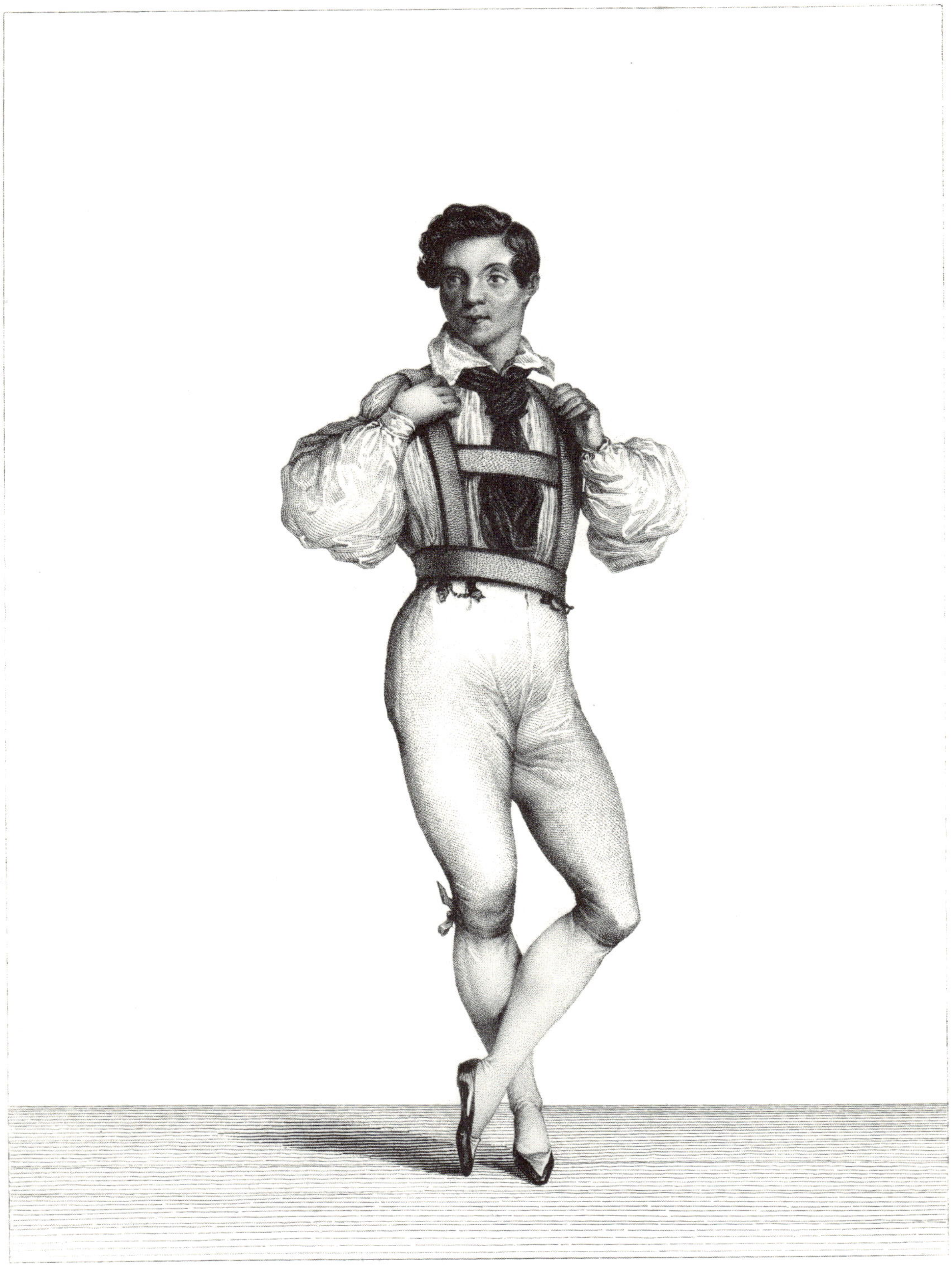

11. Jules Perrot in *Nathalie ou la Laitière suisse* (Opéra, Paris, 1832).

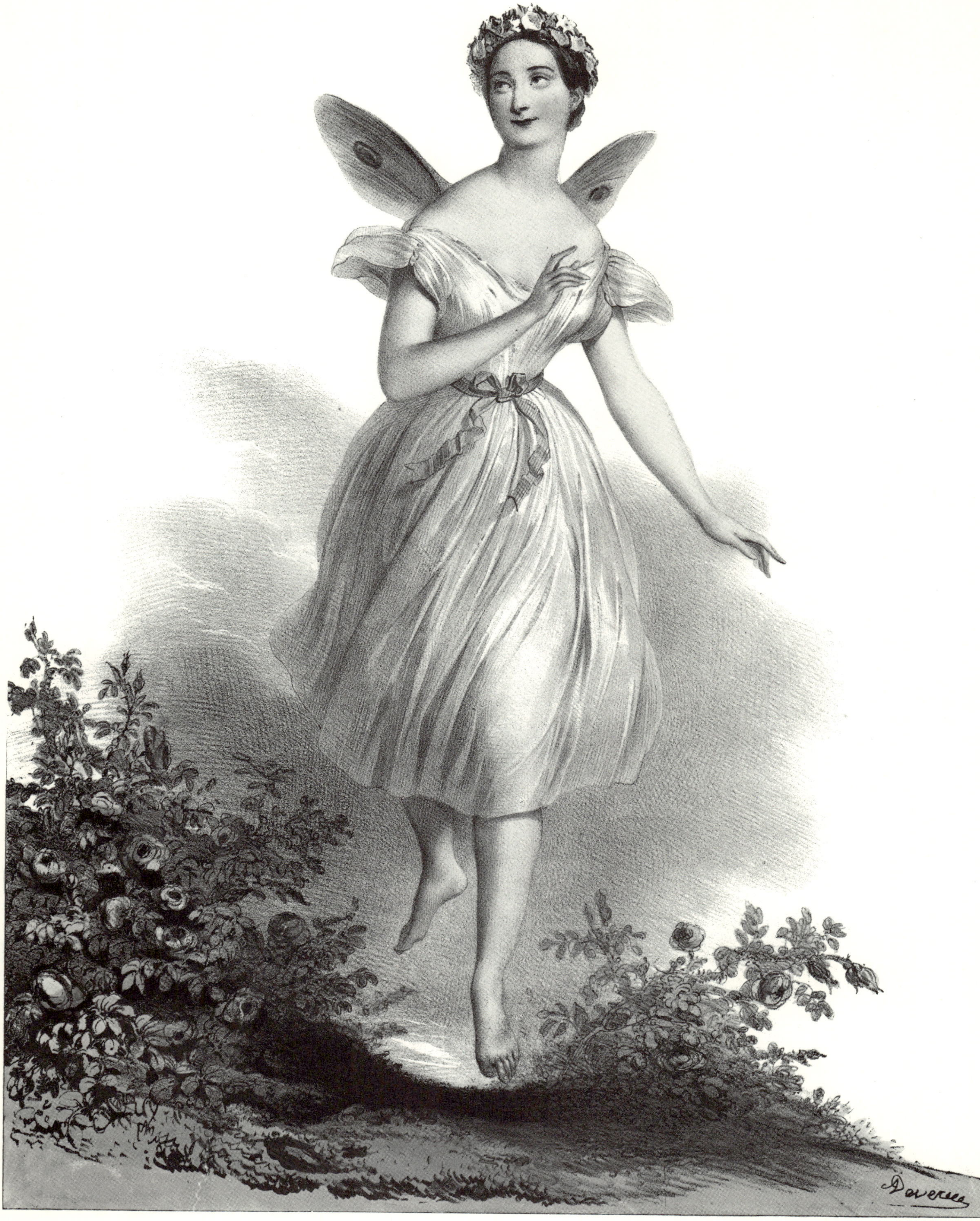

12. Marie Taglioni in *La Sylphide* (Opéra, Paris, 1832).

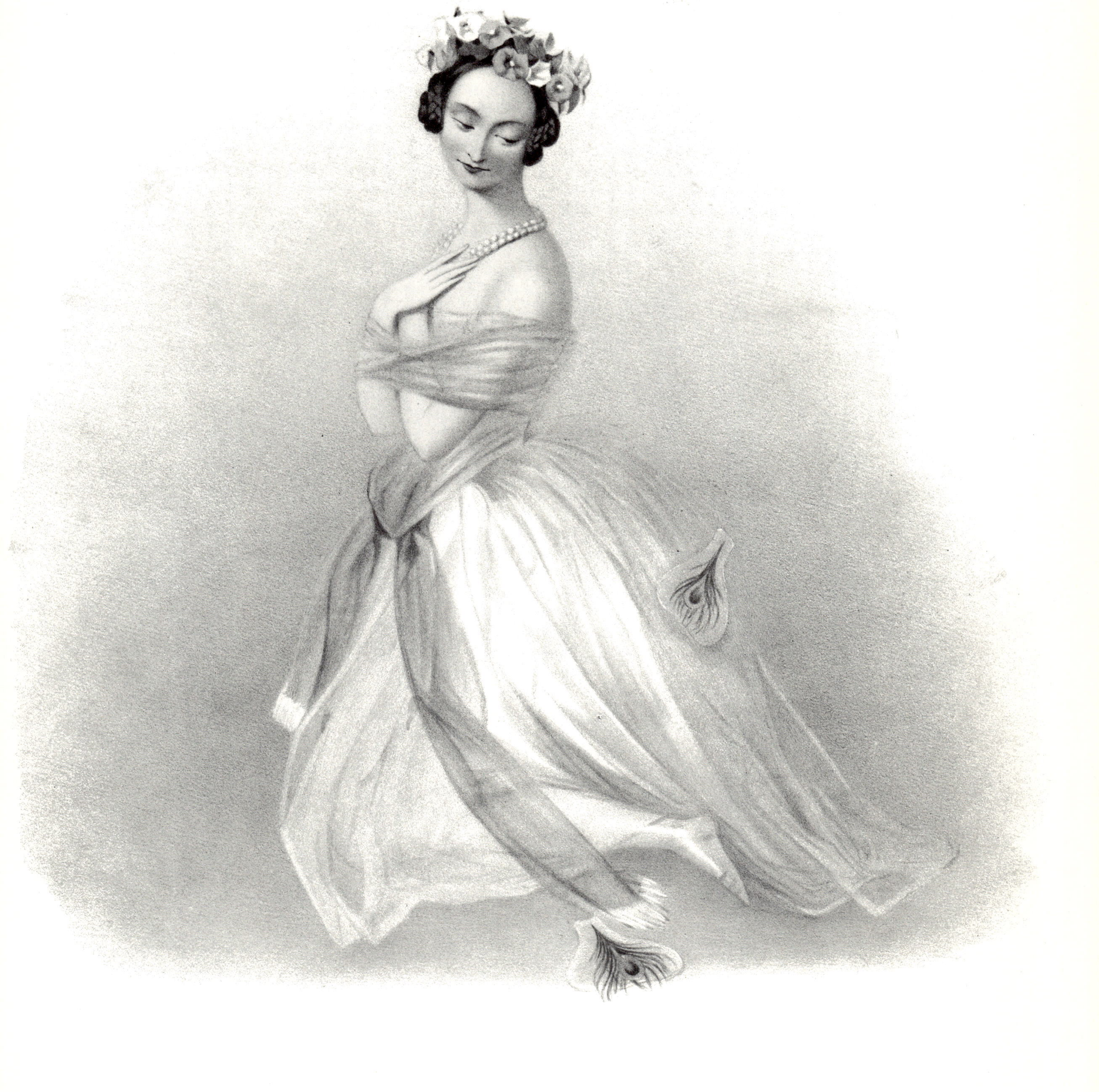

13. Marie Taglioni in *La Sylphide* (Opéra, Paris, 1832).

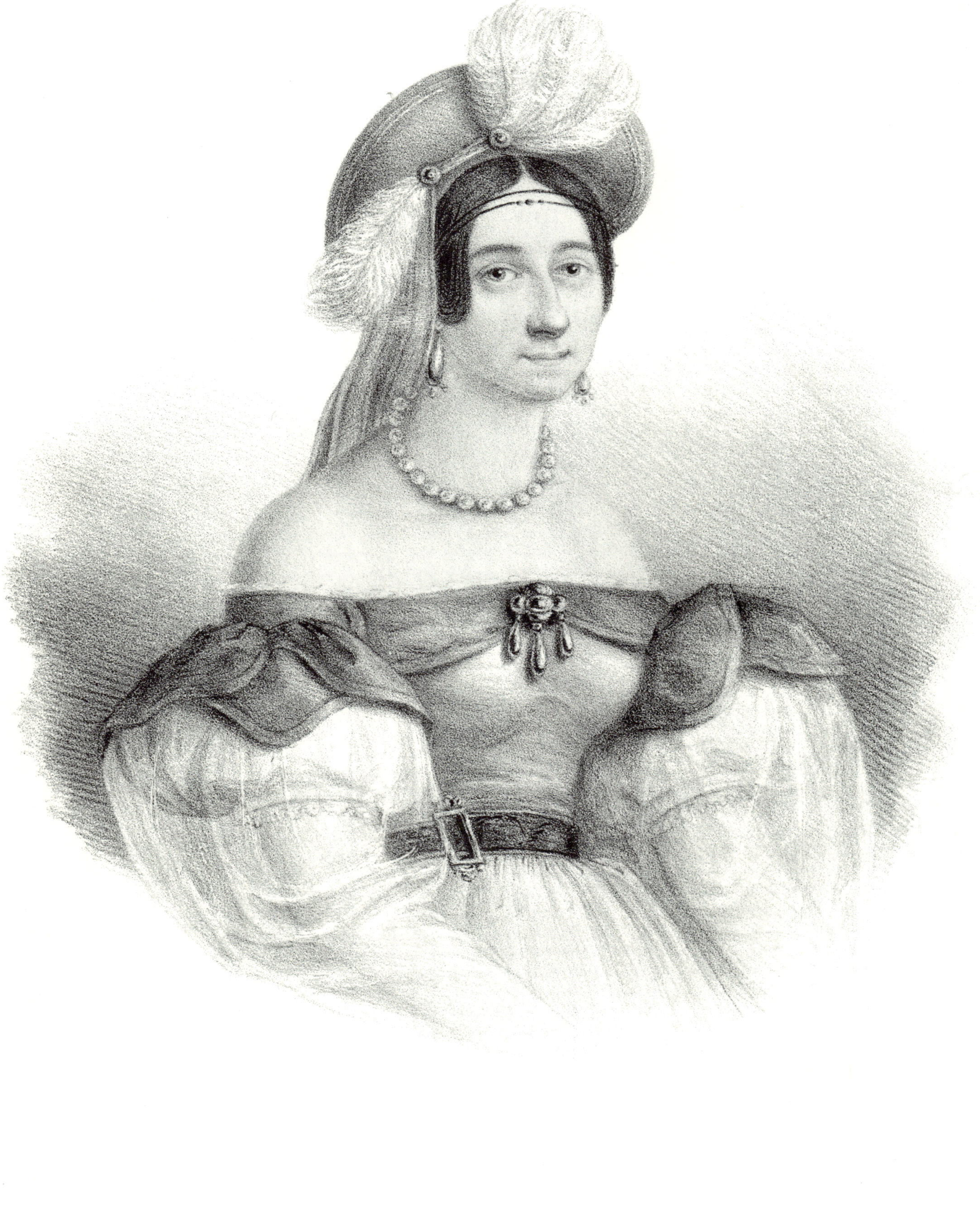

14. Amalia Brugnoli, portrait, Venice, 1834.

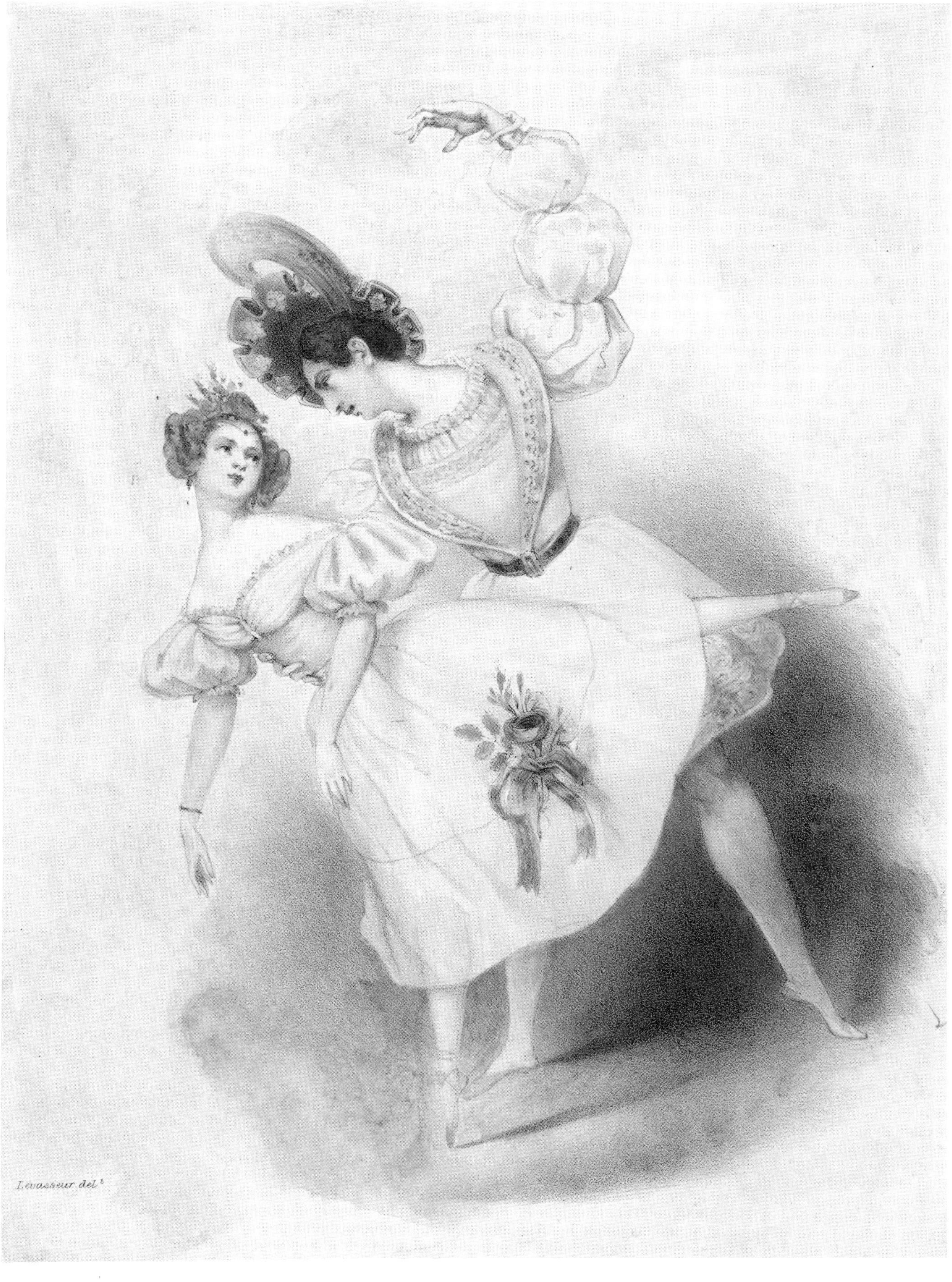

15. Amalia Brugnoli and Paolo Samengo in *L'Anneau magique* (King's Theatre, London, 1832).

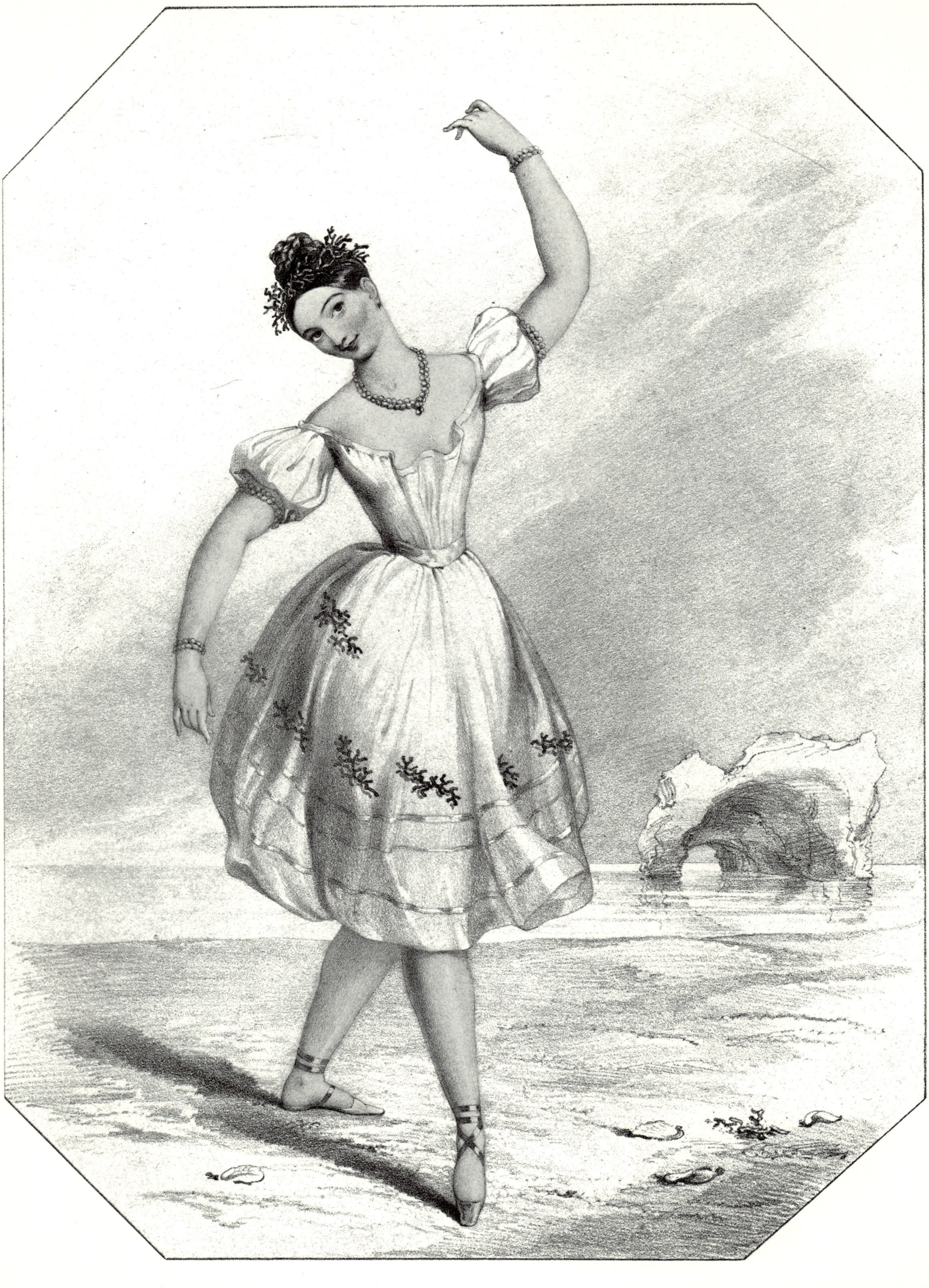

16. Pauline Duvernay in *The Sleeping Beauty in the Wood* (Drury Lane Theatre, London, 1833).

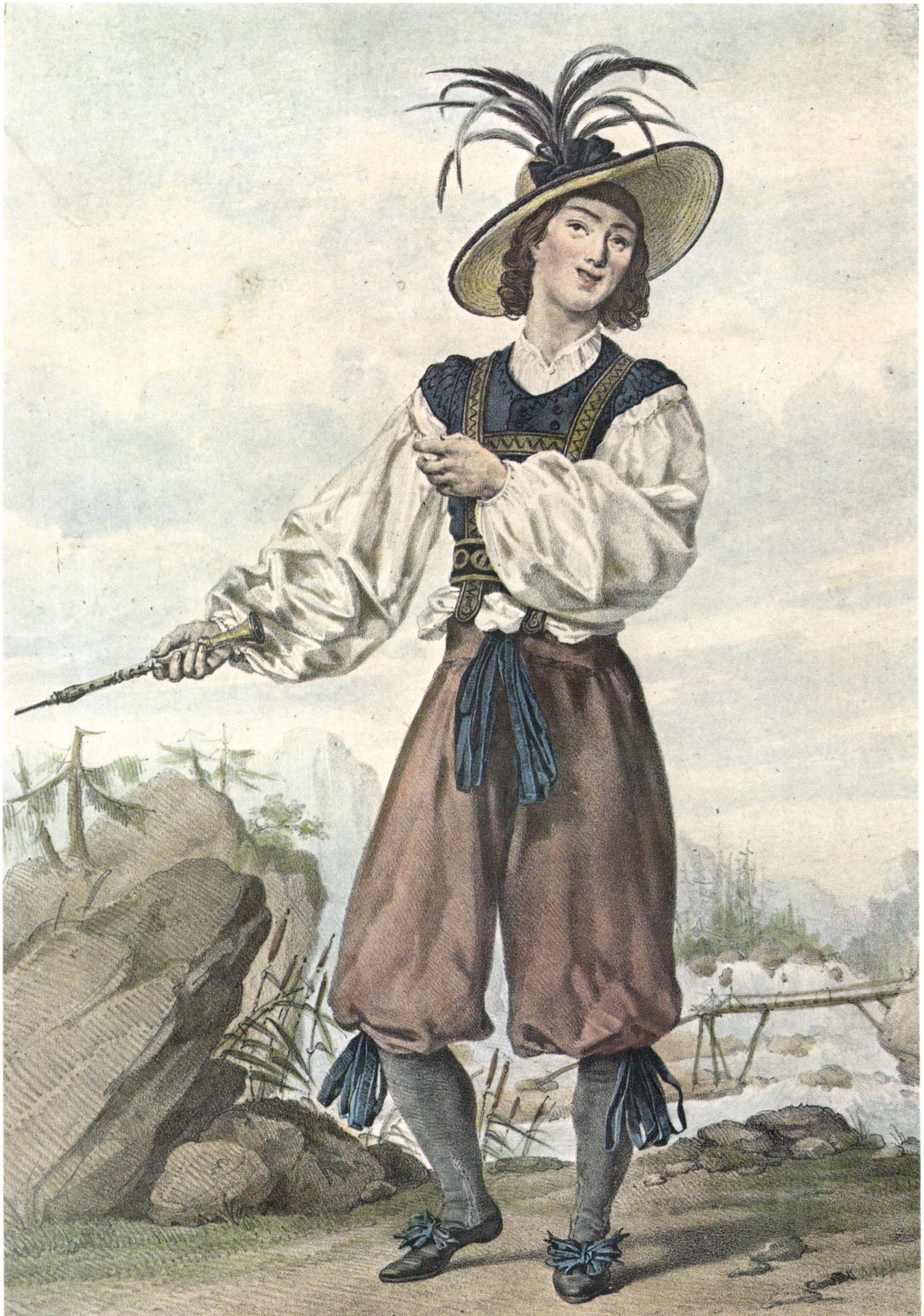

A. Charles Mazurier in *La Laitière suisse* (Théâtre de la Porte-Saint-Martin, Paris, 1823).

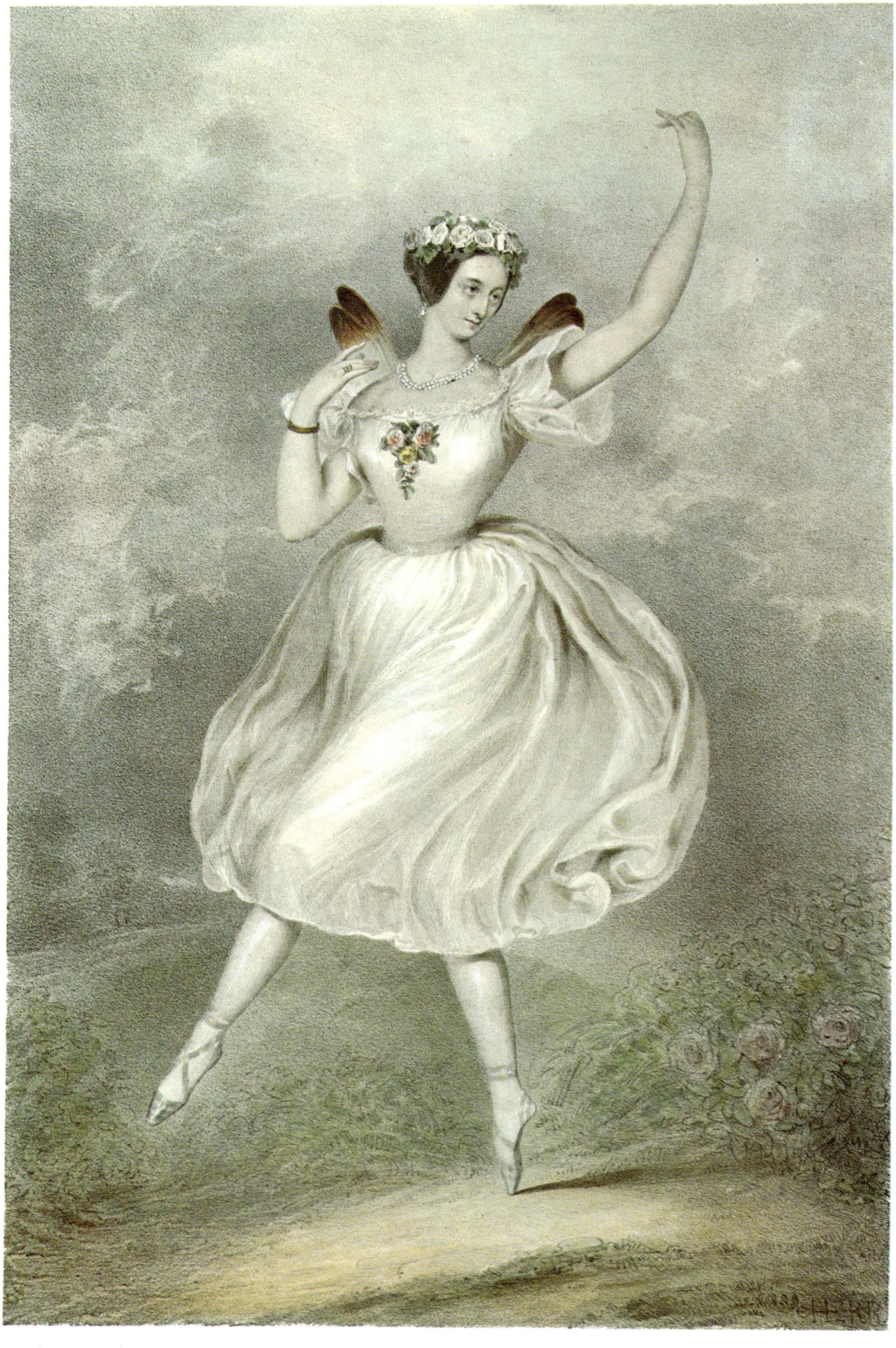

B. Marie Taglioni in *La Sylphide* (Opéra, Paris, 1832).

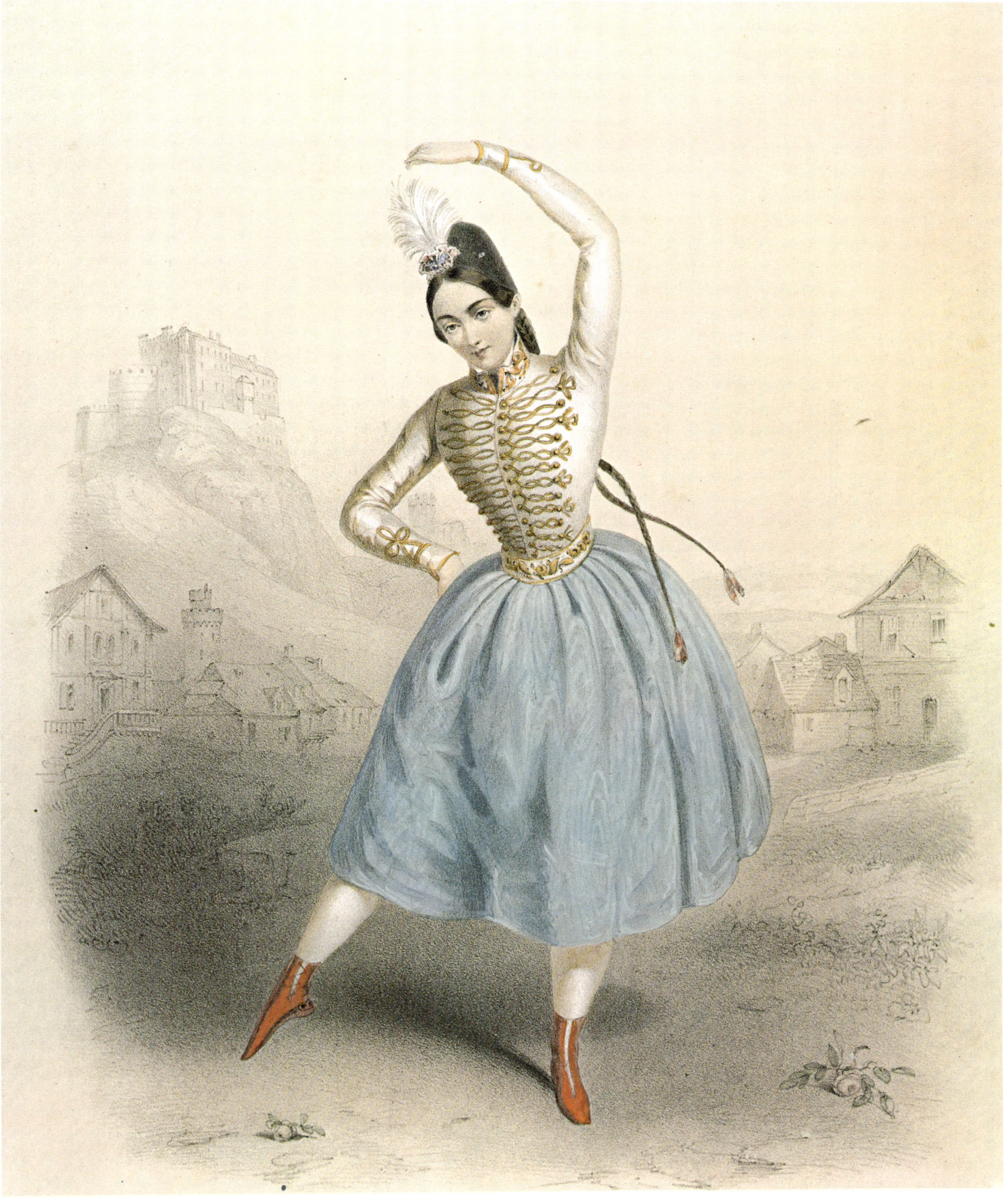

C. Fanny Elssler in the Cracovienne in *La Gipsy* (Opéra, Paris, 1839).

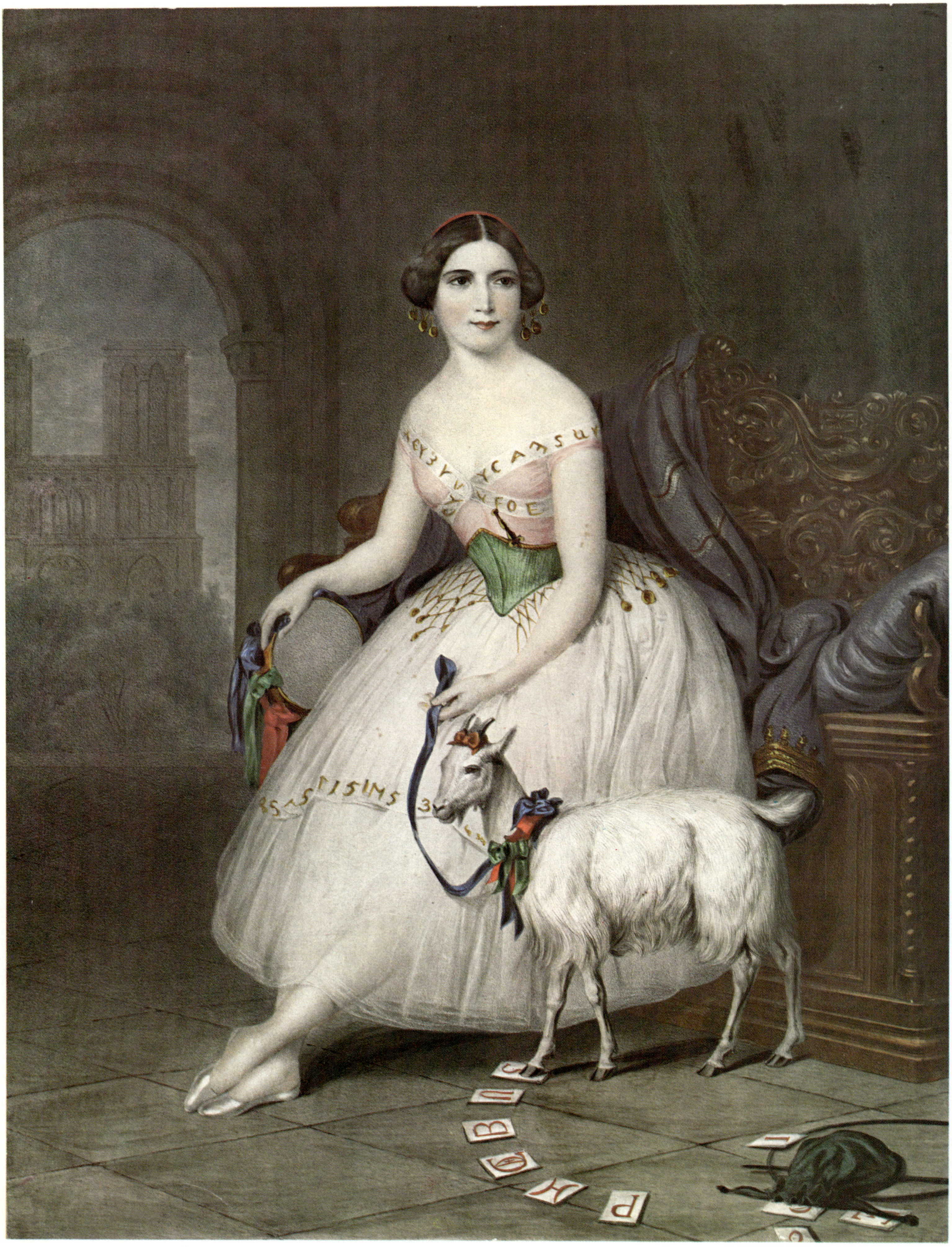

D. Fanny Cerrito in *La Esmeralda* (Berlin, 1847).

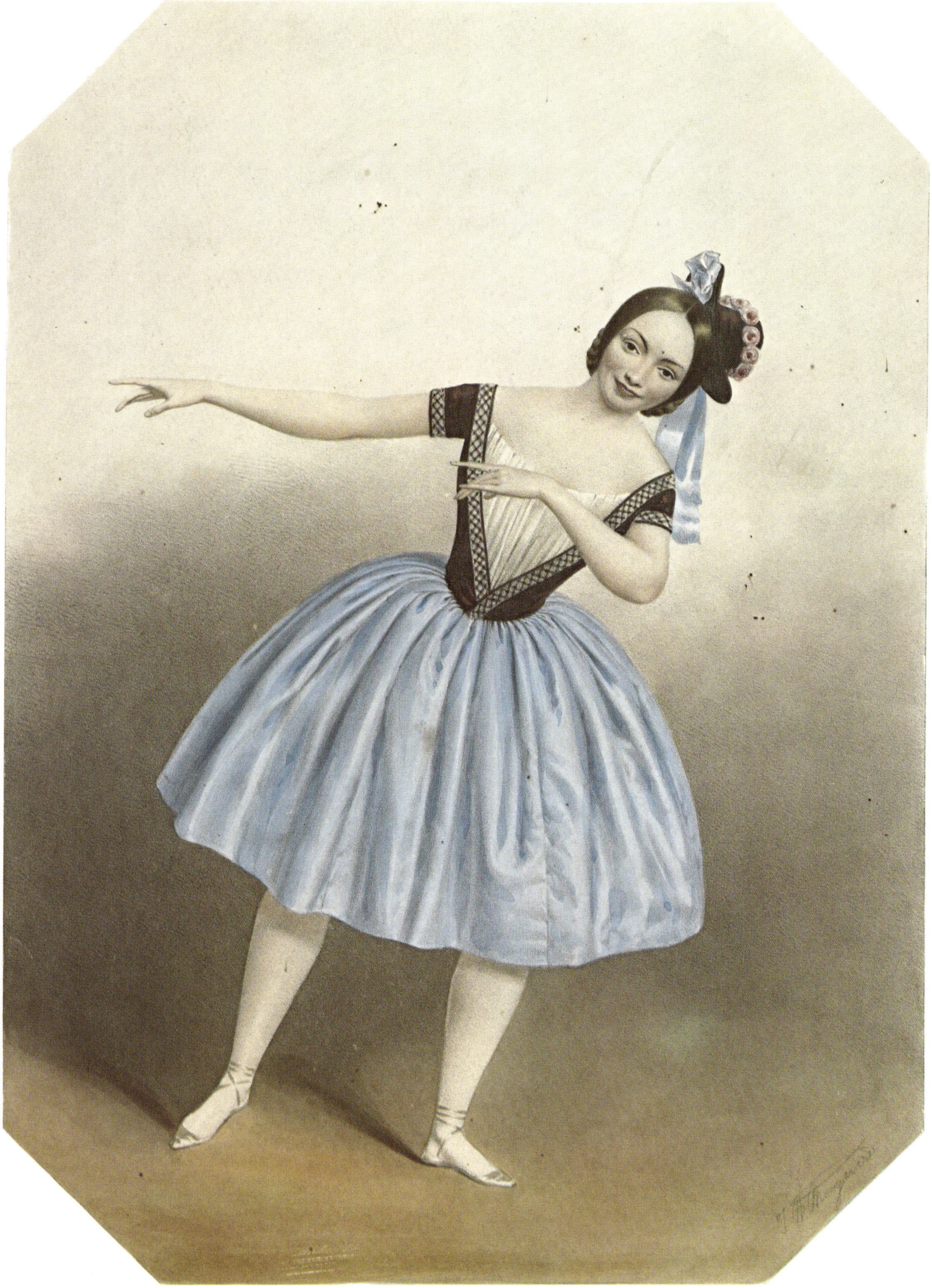

E. Clara Vestris Webster in *Lady Henrietta* (Drury Lane Theatre, London, 1844).

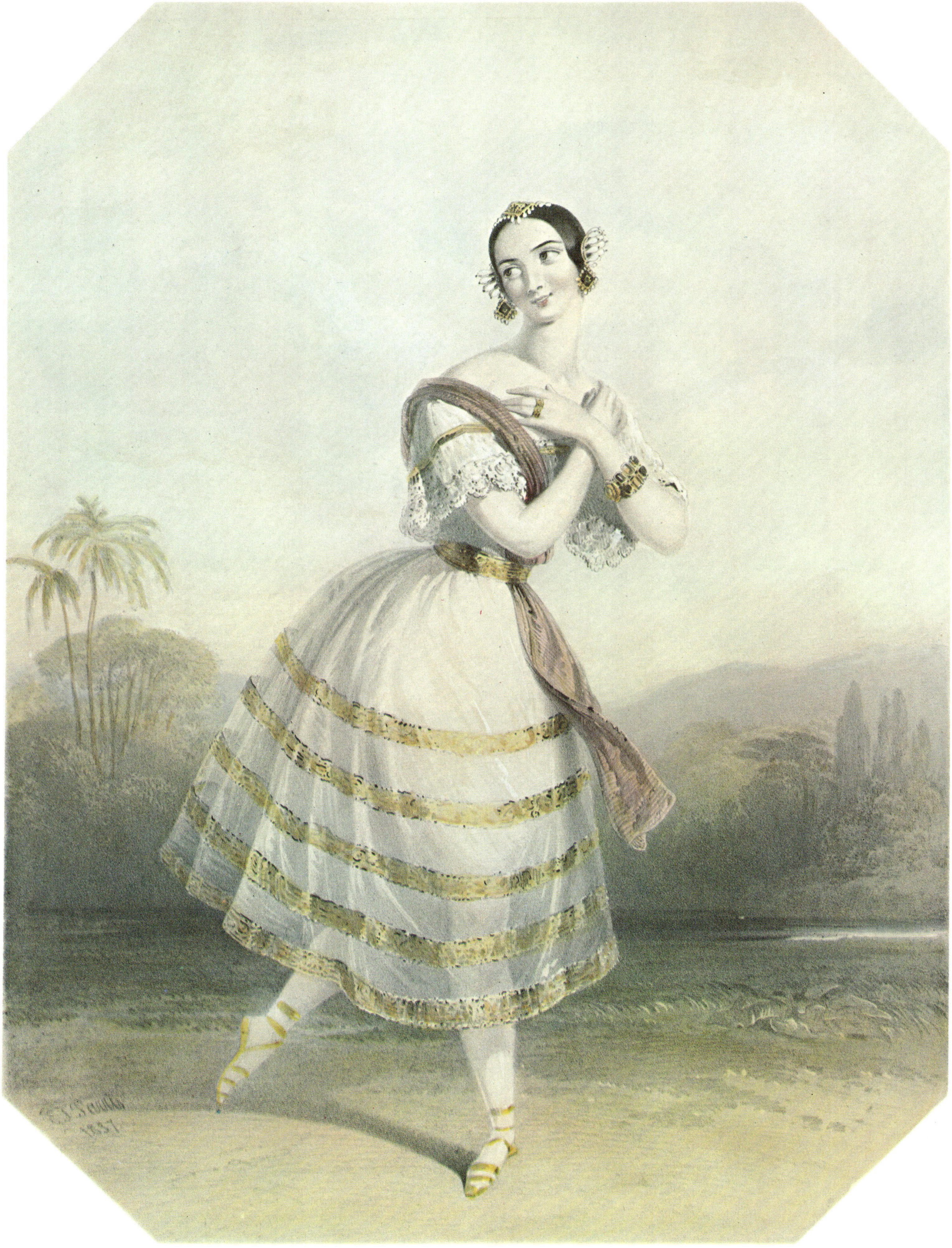

F. Céline Céleste (née Keppler) in *The Maid of Cashmere* (National Theatre, N.Y., 1836).

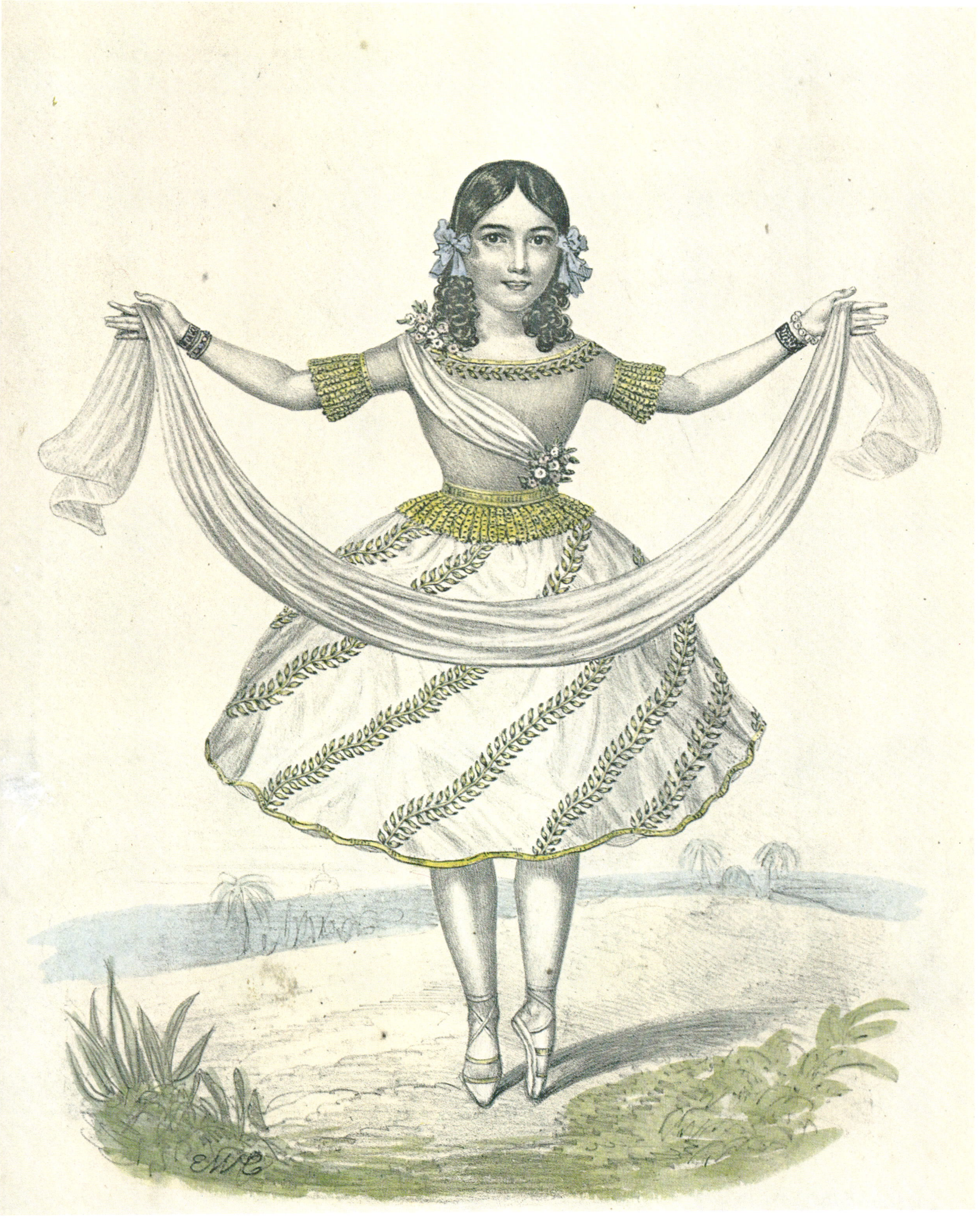

G. Augusta Maywood in *The Bayadère* (Park Theatre, N.Y., 1838; first staged Chestnut Street Theatre, Philadelphia, 1837, as *Maid of Cashmere*).

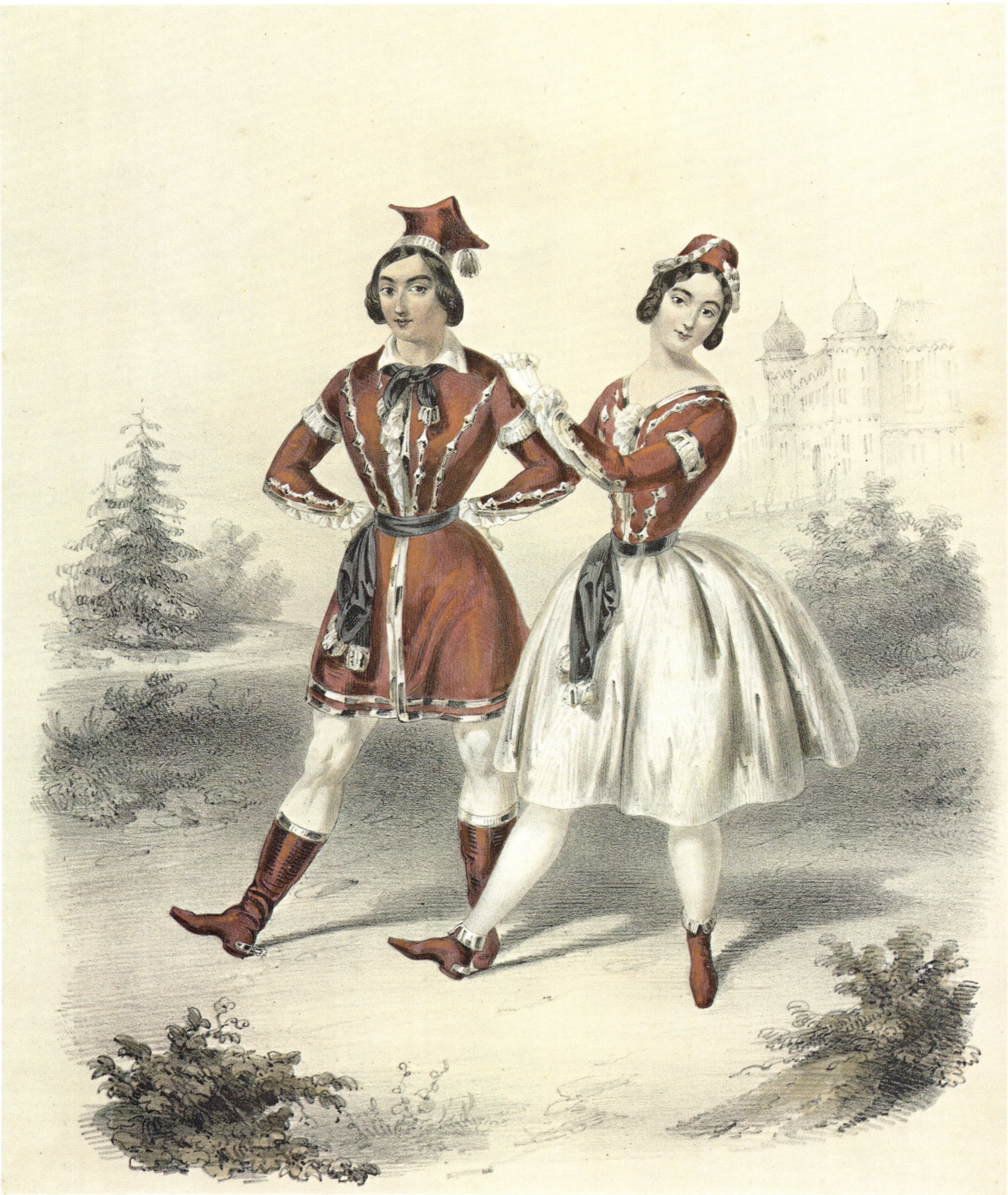

H. Carlotta Grisi and Jules Perrot in *La Polka* (Her Majesty's Theatre, London, 1844).

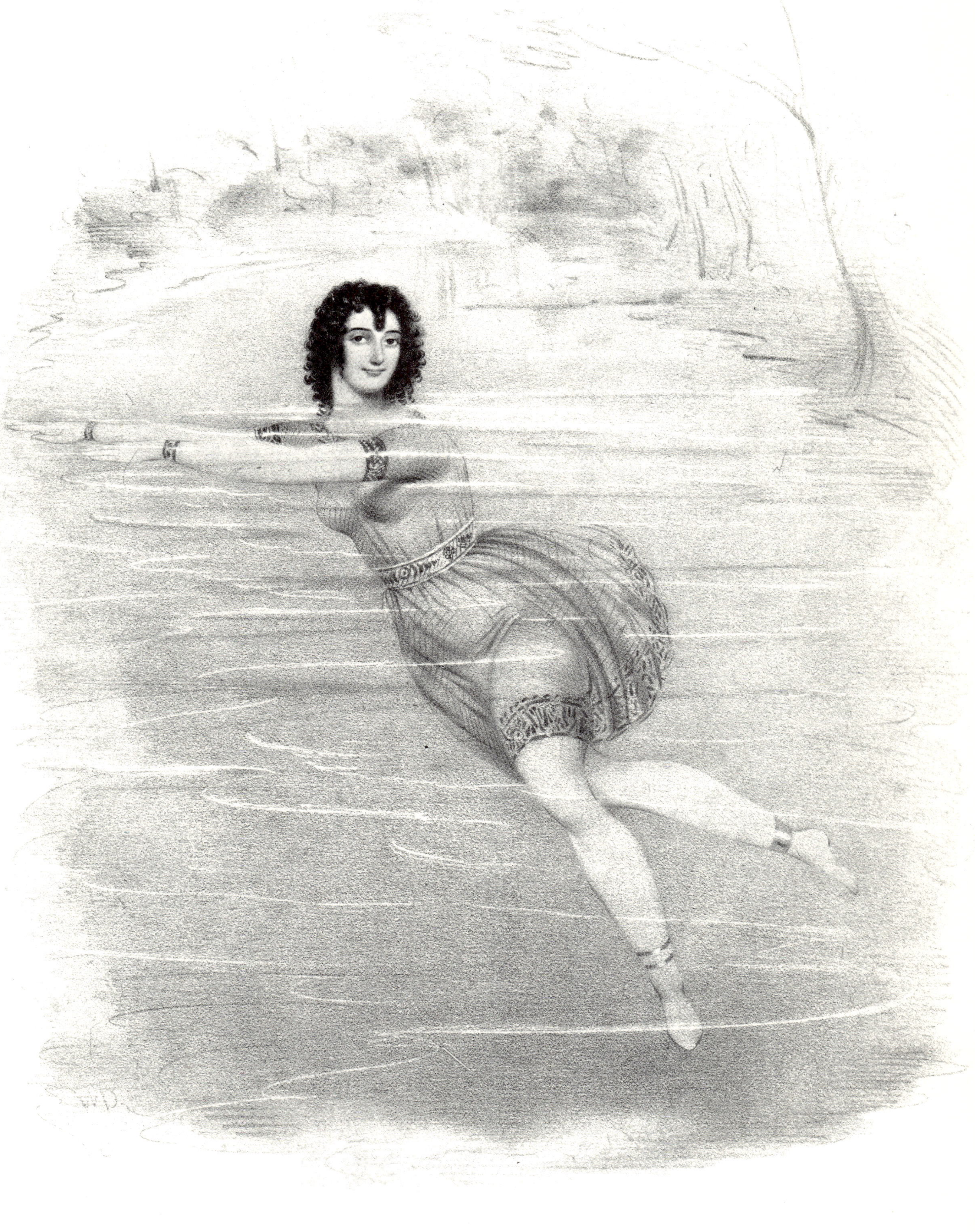

17. Madame Vestris in *Olympic Devils* (Royal Olympic Theatre, London, 1832).

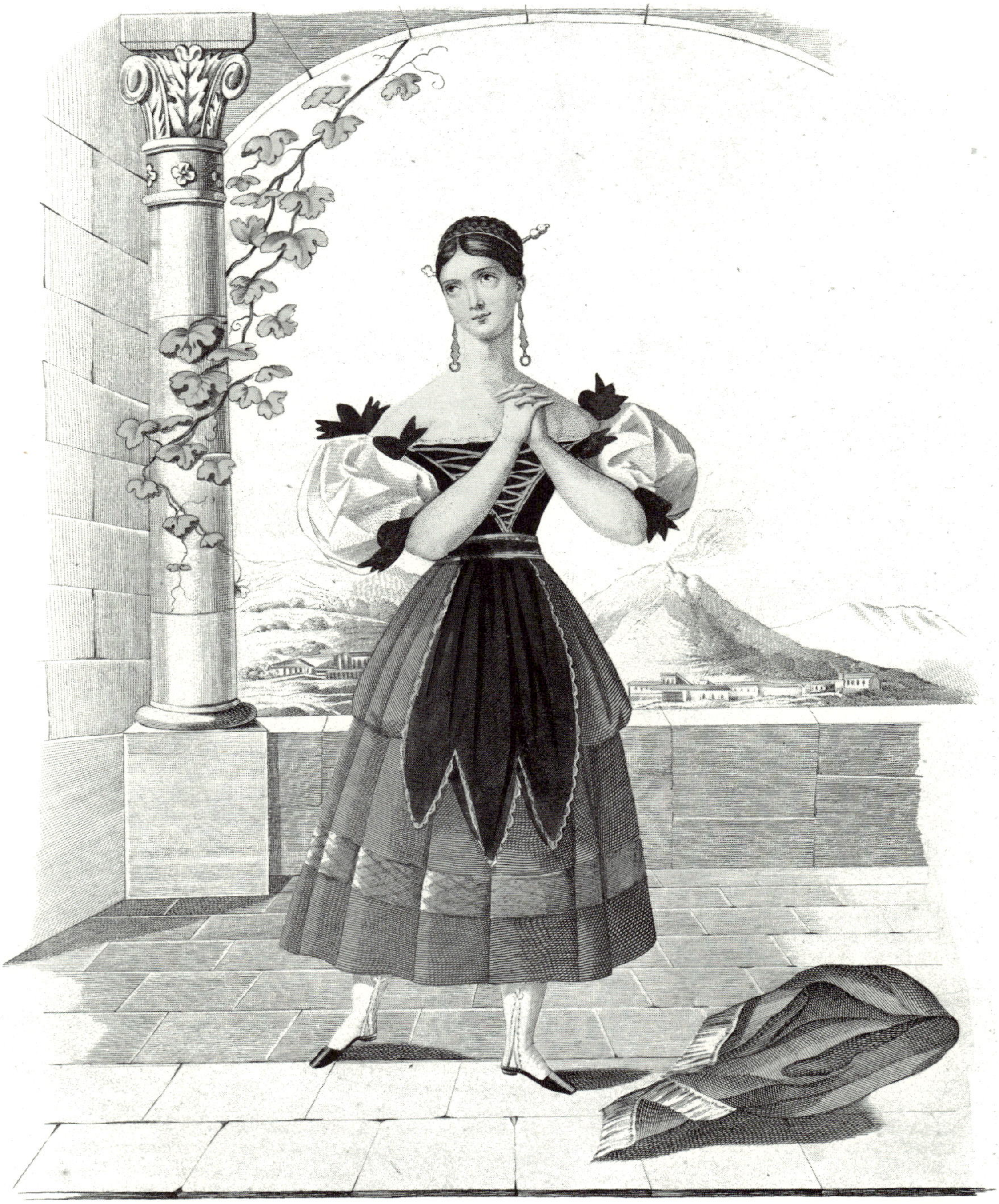

18. Fanny Elssler in *La Muette de Portici* (Kärntnertortheater, Vienna, 1832).

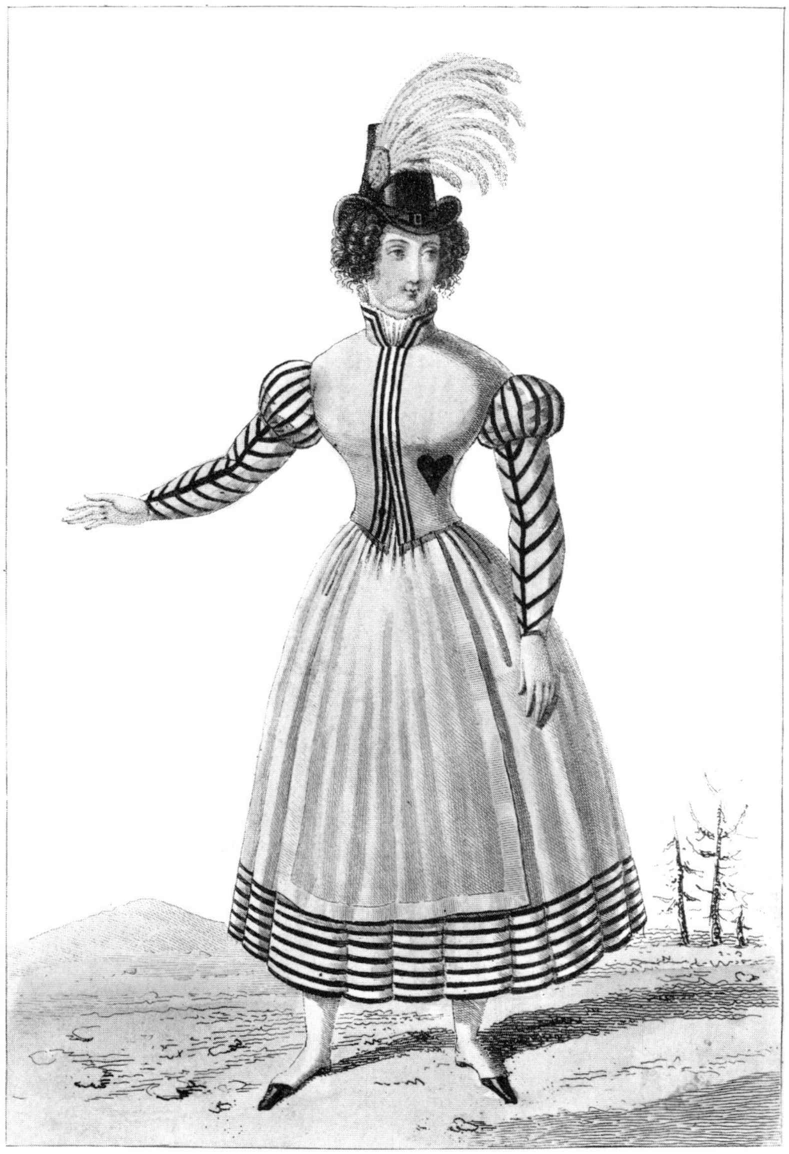

19. Pauline Duvernay in *La Tentation* (Opéra, Paris, 1833).

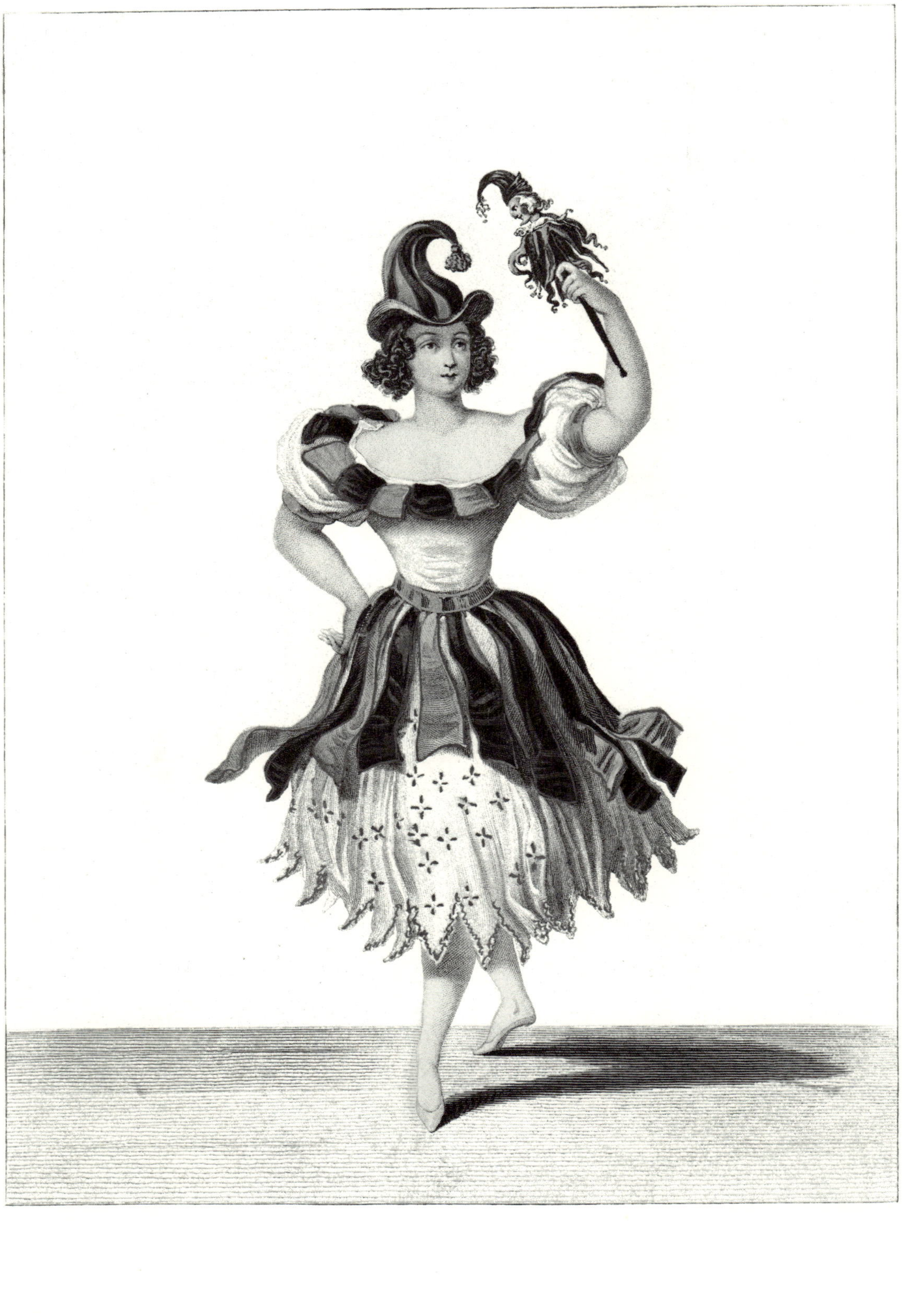

20. Lise Noblet in *Gustave III ou le Bal masqué* (Opéra, Paris, 1833).

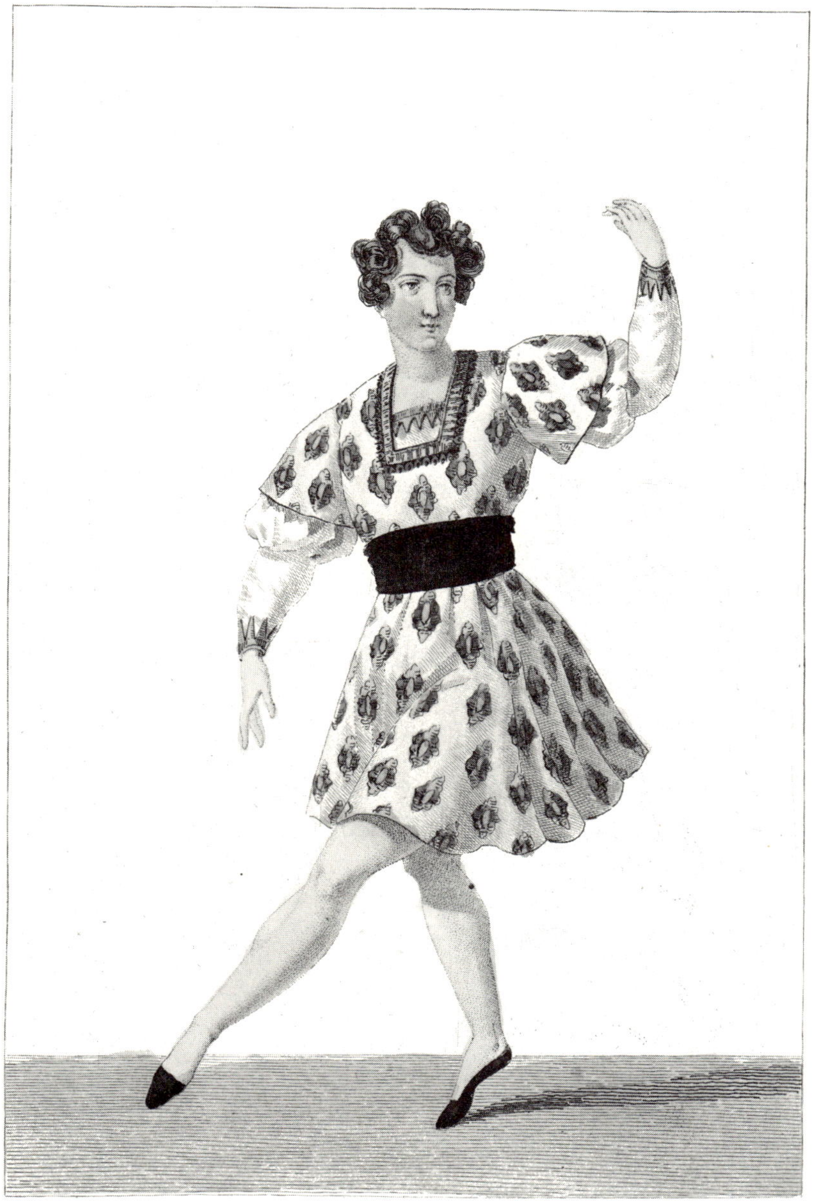

21. Jules Perrot in *La Révolte au sérail* (Opéra, Paris, 1833).

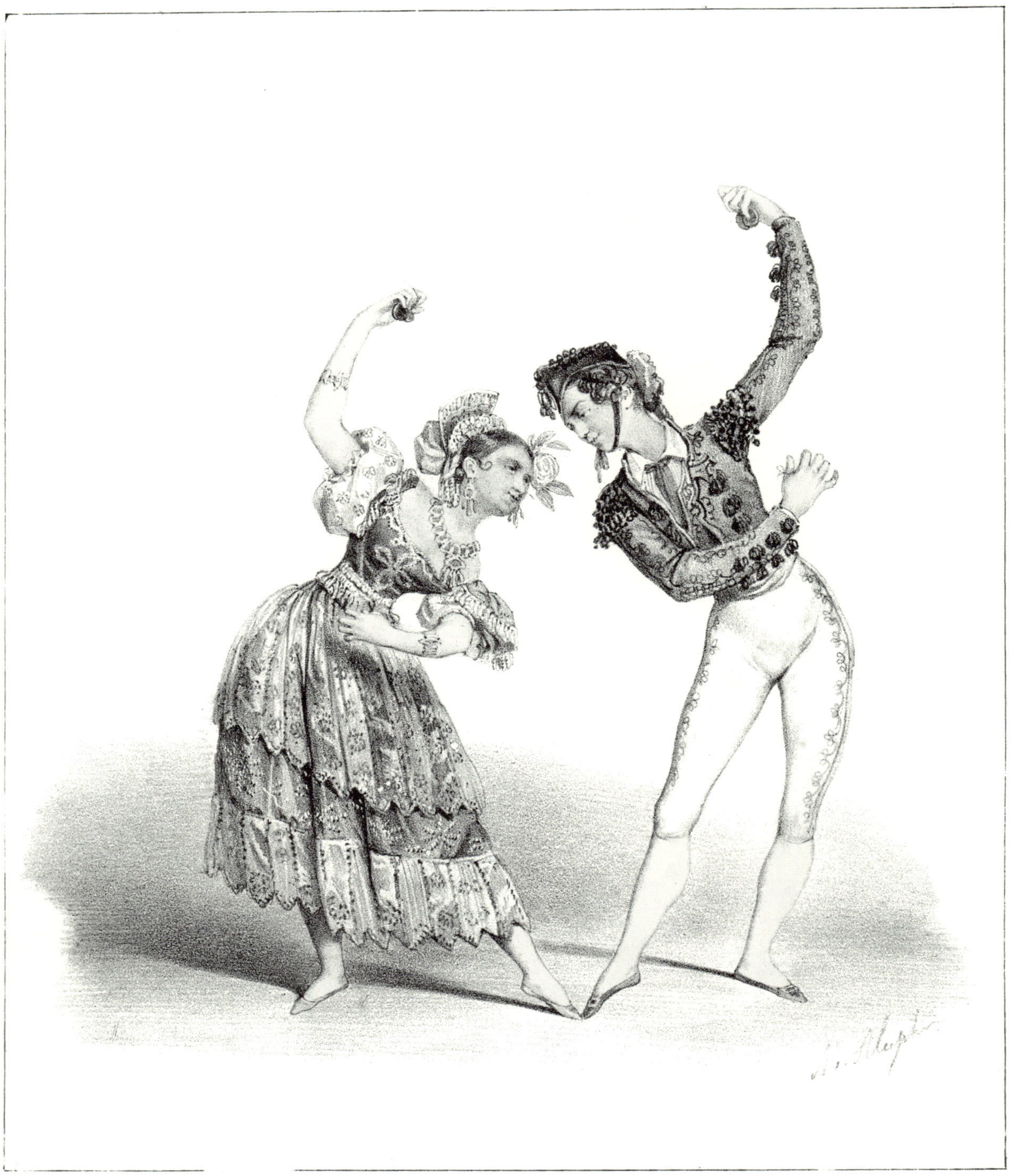

22. Mariano Camprubì and Dolores Serral in "Le Bolero" (Bals de l'Opéra, Paris, 1834).

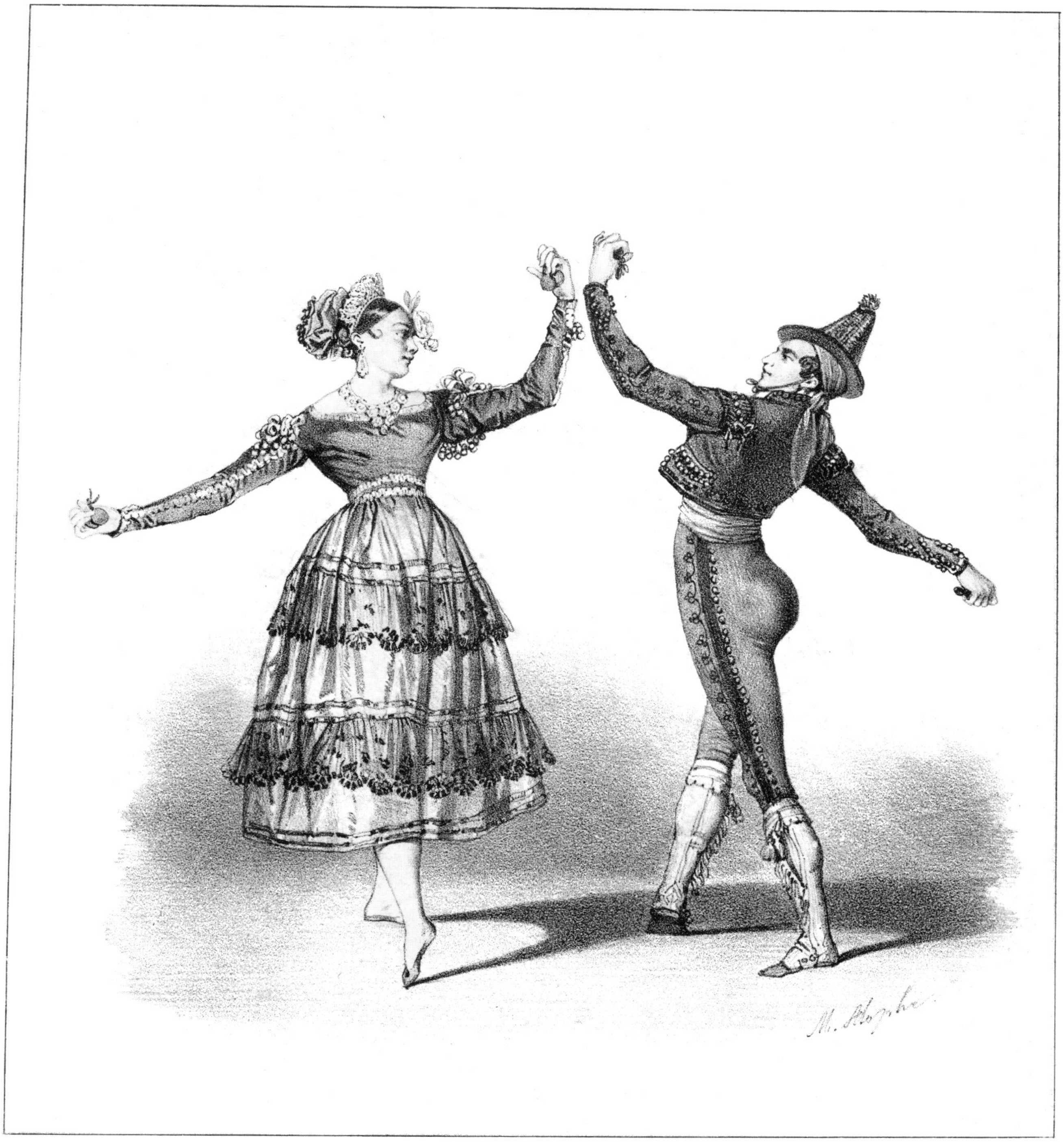

23. Francisco Font and Manuela Dubinon in "Corraleros de Séville" (Bals de l'Opéra, Paris, 1834).

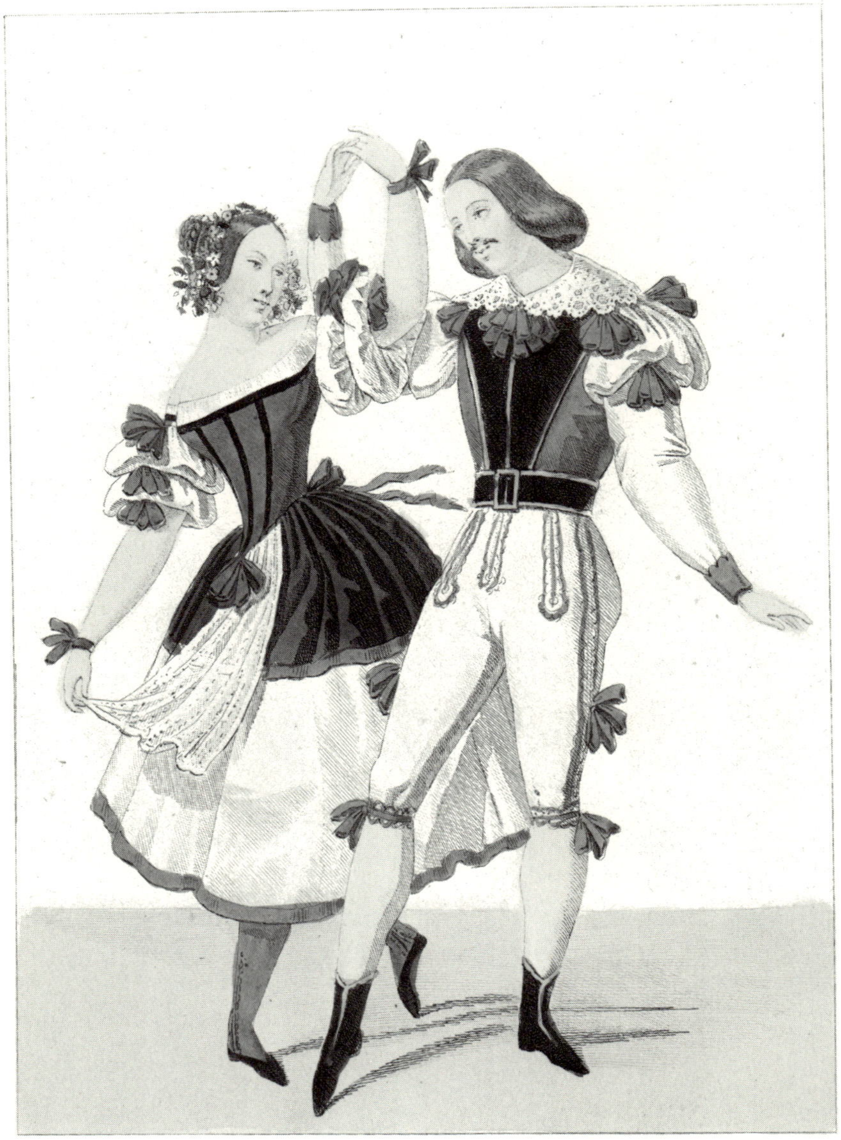

24. Mariano Camprubì and Dolores Serral in "Pas Styrien" (Palais Royal, Paris, ca. 1834).

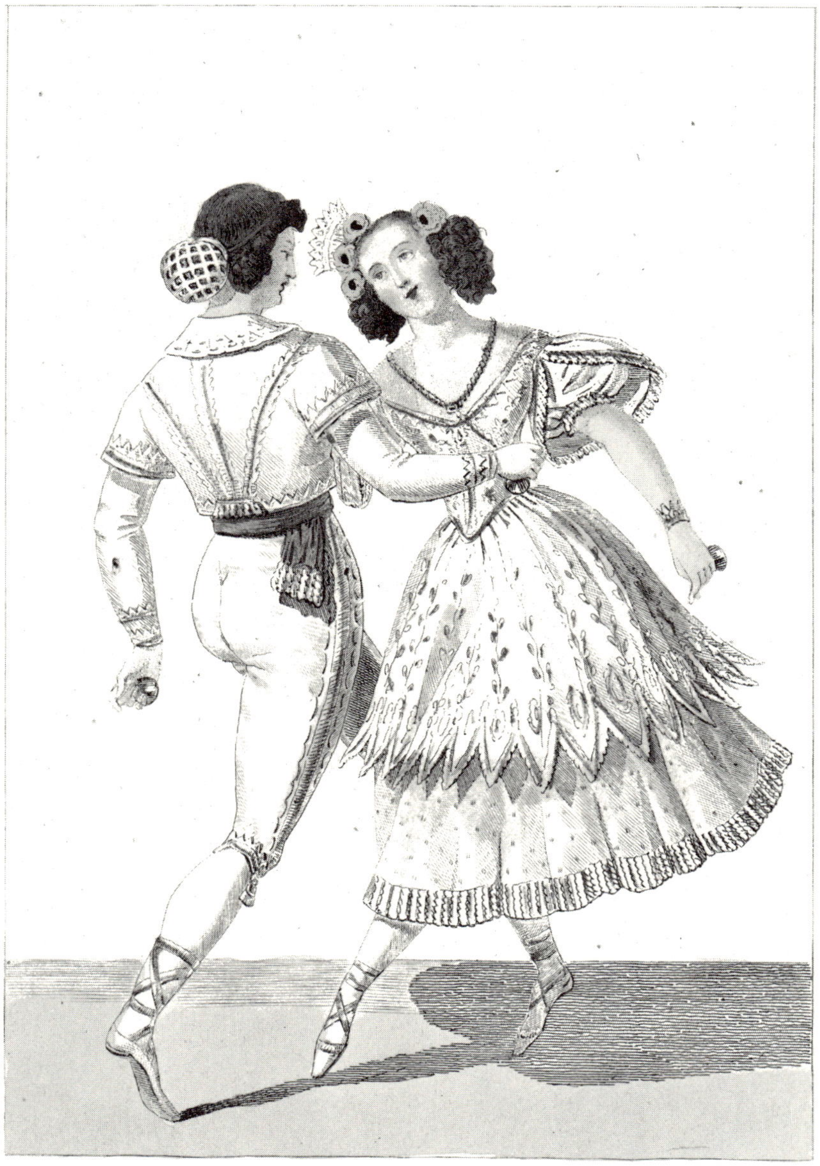

25. Mariano Camprubì and Dolores Serral in "La Cachucha" (Théâtre de la Gaîté, Paris, n.d.).

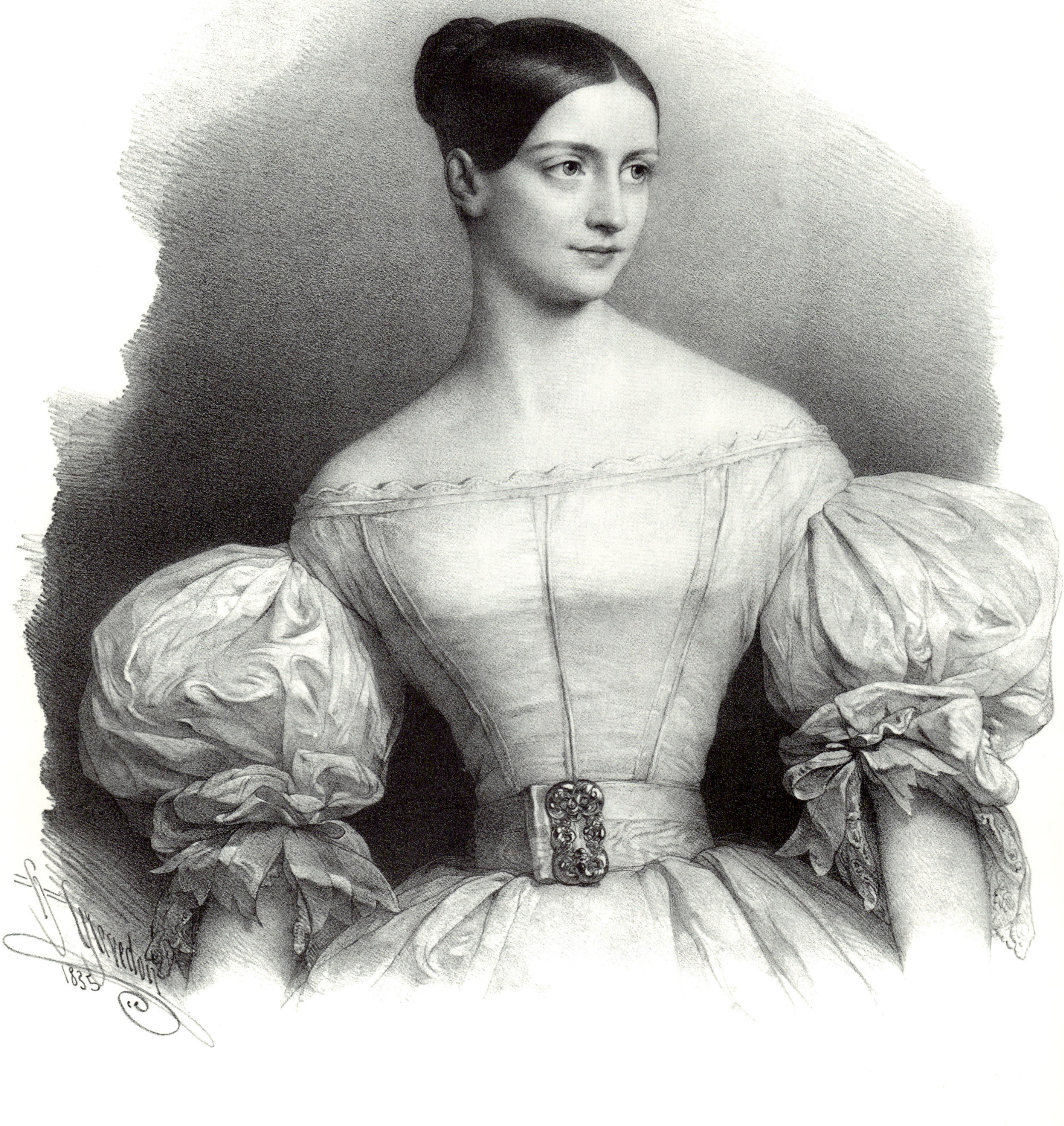

26. Fanny Elssler, portrait, Paris, 1835.

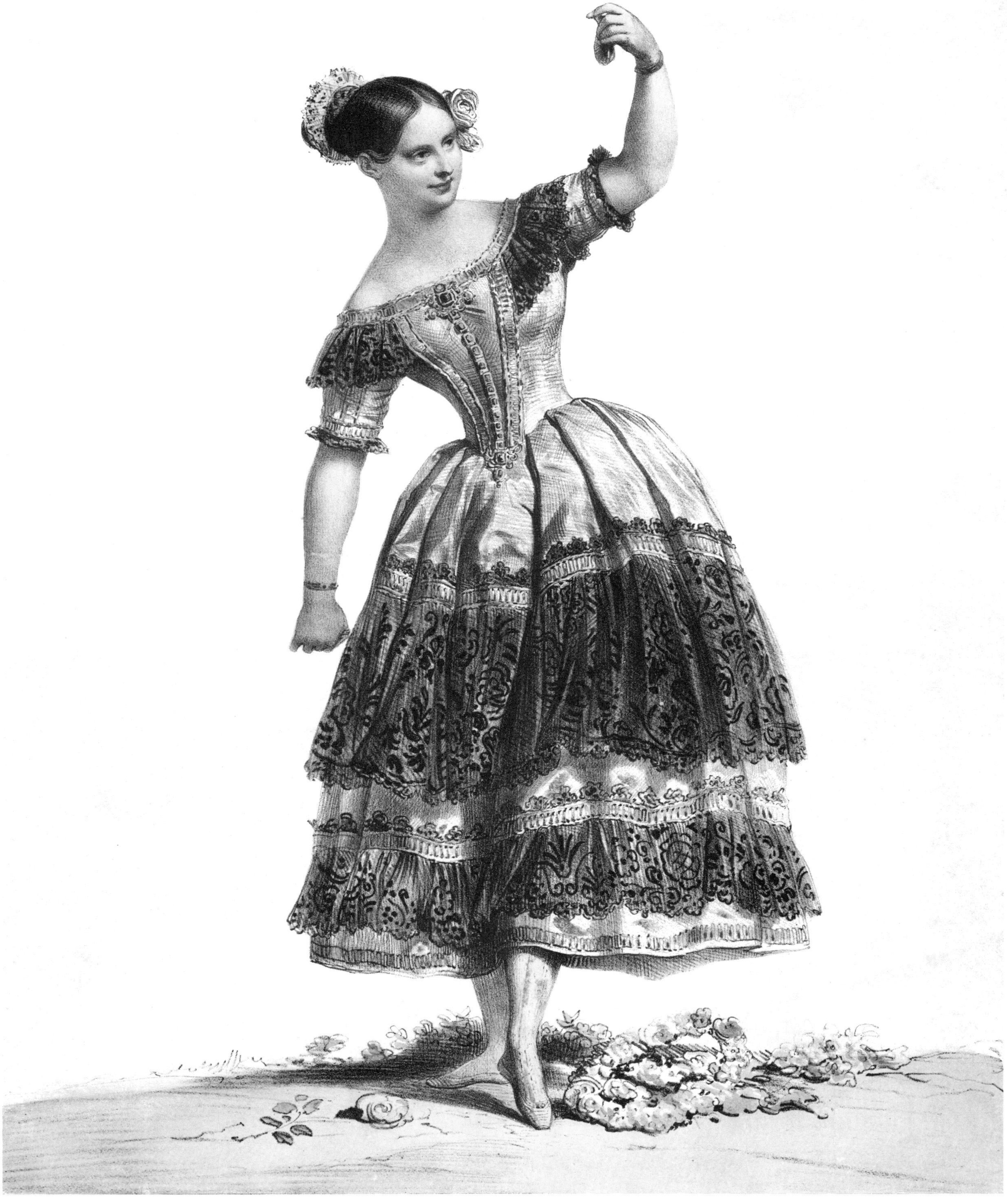

27. Fanny Elssler in the Cachucha in *Le Diable boiteux* (Opéra, Paris, 1836).

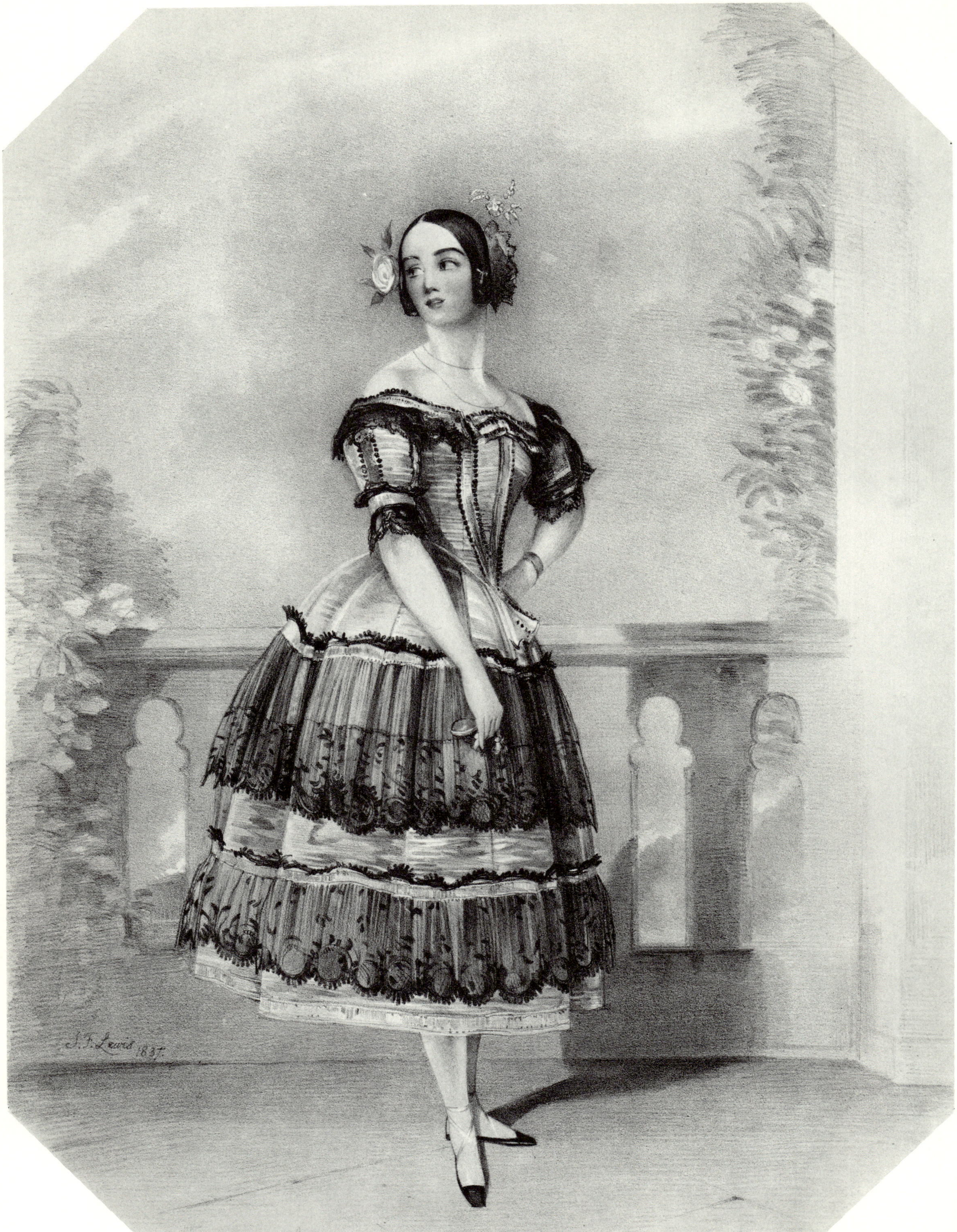

28. Pauline Duvernay in the Cachucha in *The Devil on Two Sticks* (Drury Lane Theatre, London, 1836).

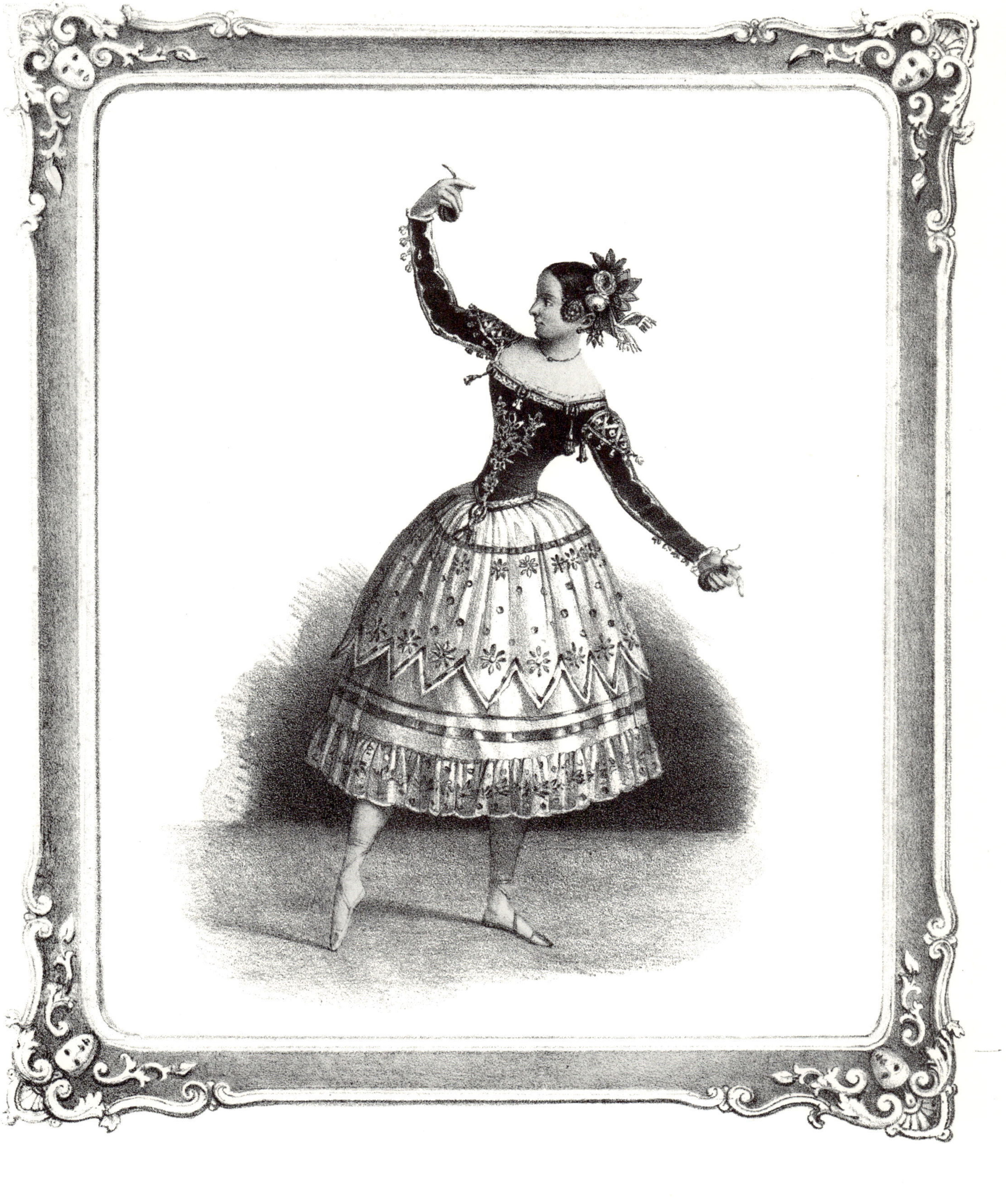

29. Lucile Grahn in "El Jaleo de Xeres" (Hamburg, 1838).

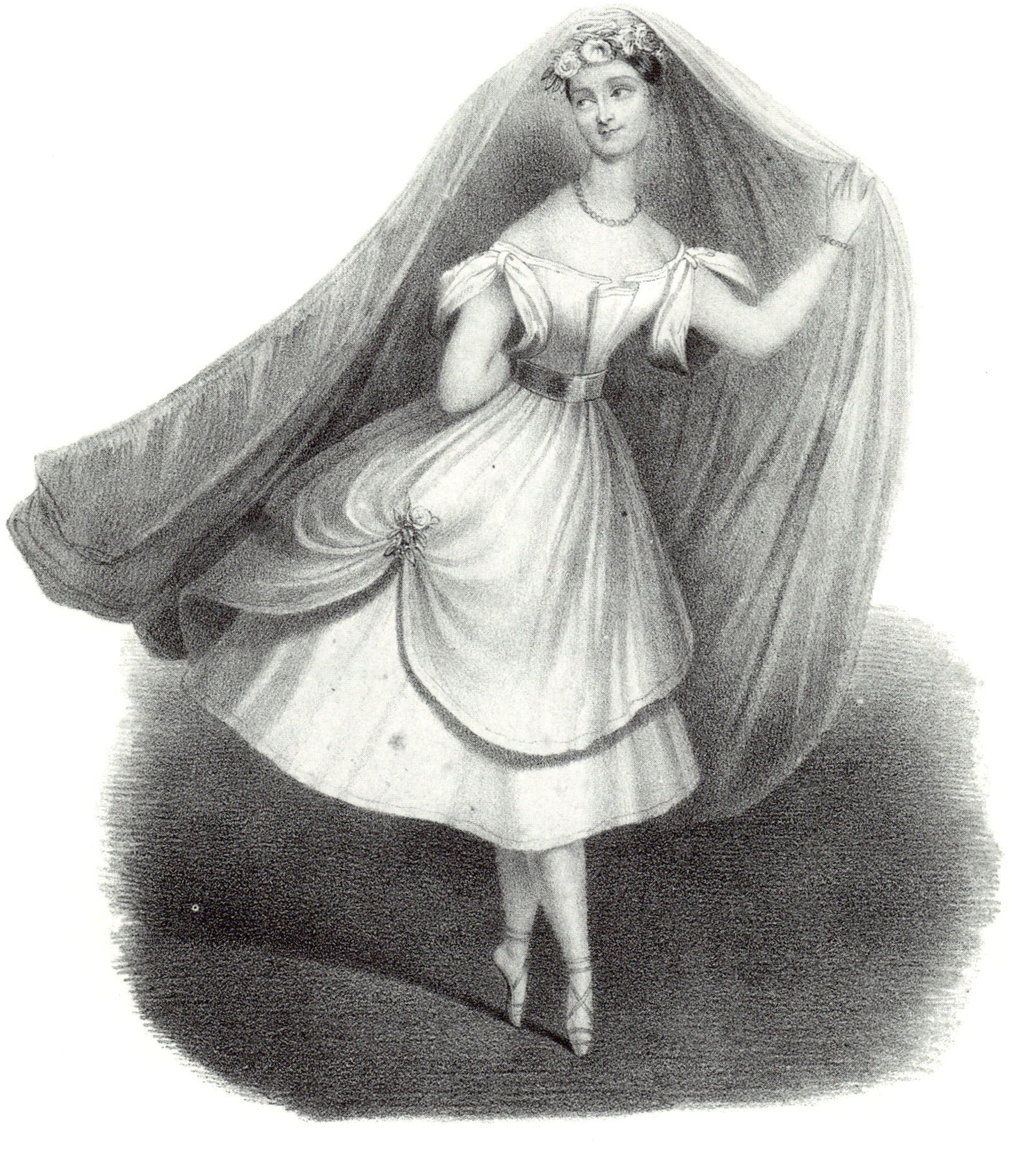

30. Marie Taglioni in *Donaumädchen* [La Fille du Danube] (Vienna, ca. 1838).

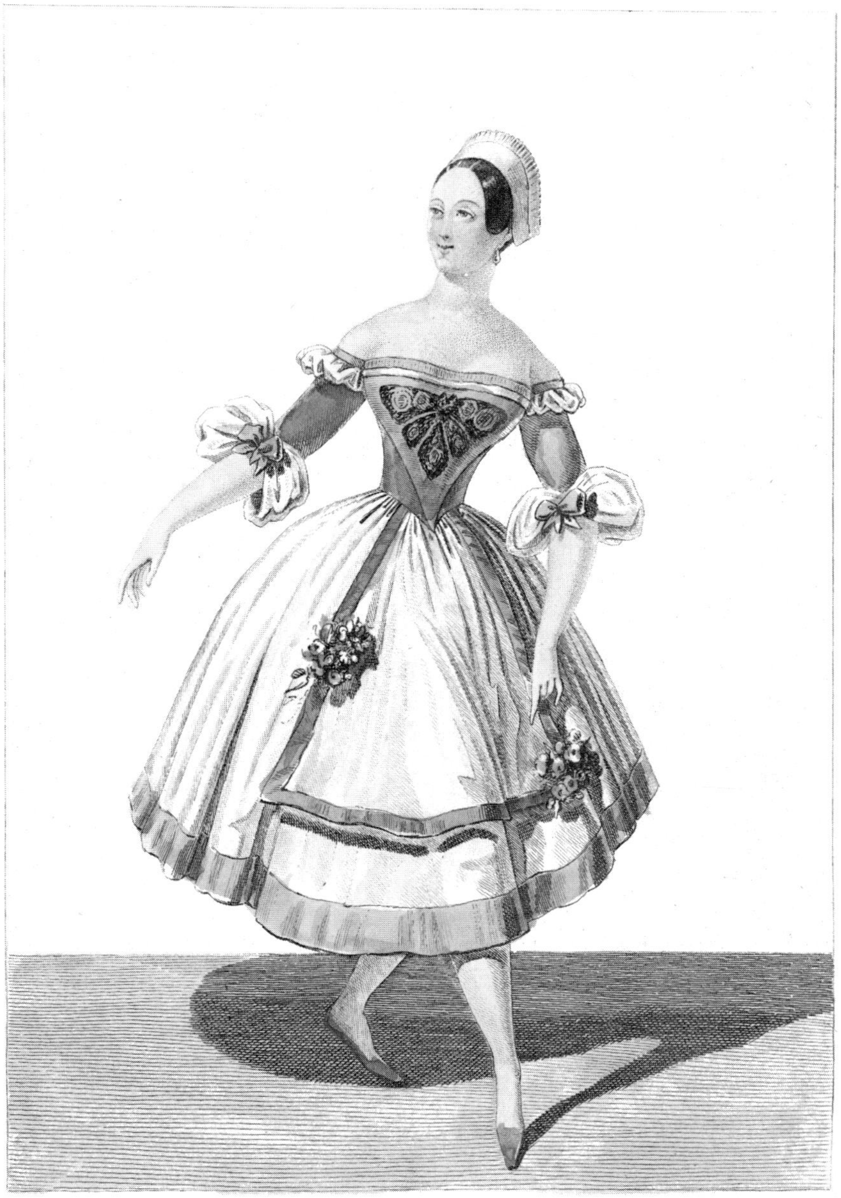

31. Marie Taglioni in *La Fille du Danube* (Opéra, Paris, 1836).

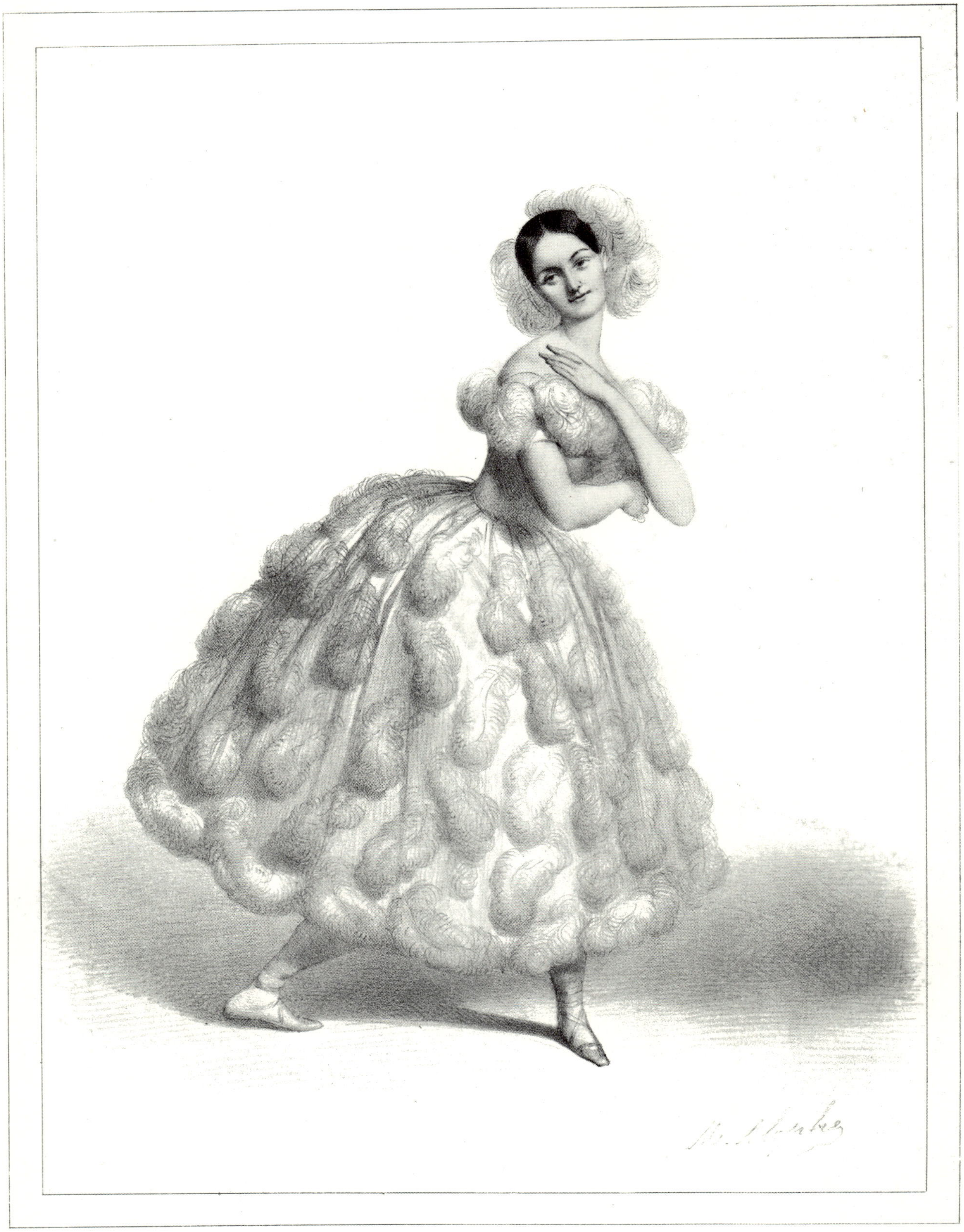

32. Fanny Elssler in *La Chatte métamorphosée en femme* (Opéra, Paris, 1837).

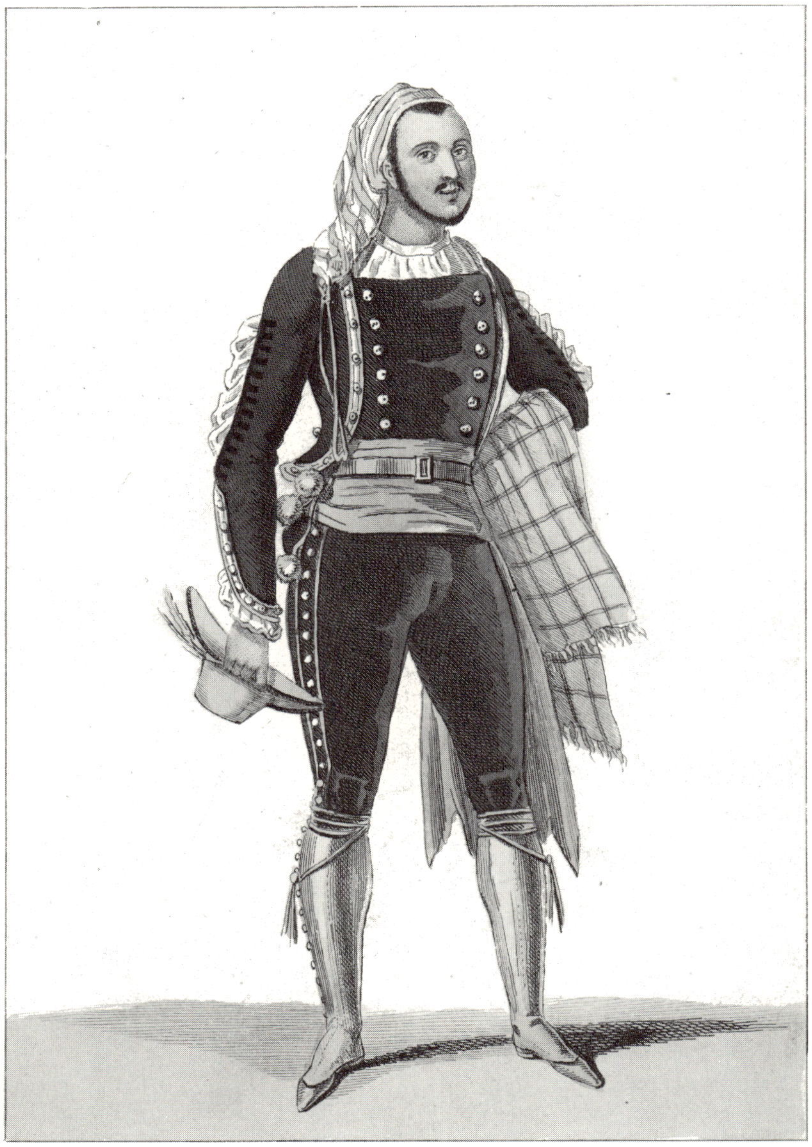

33. Paul (Antoine Paul) in the vaudeville *La Gitana* (Théâtre du Gymnase, Paris, n.d.).

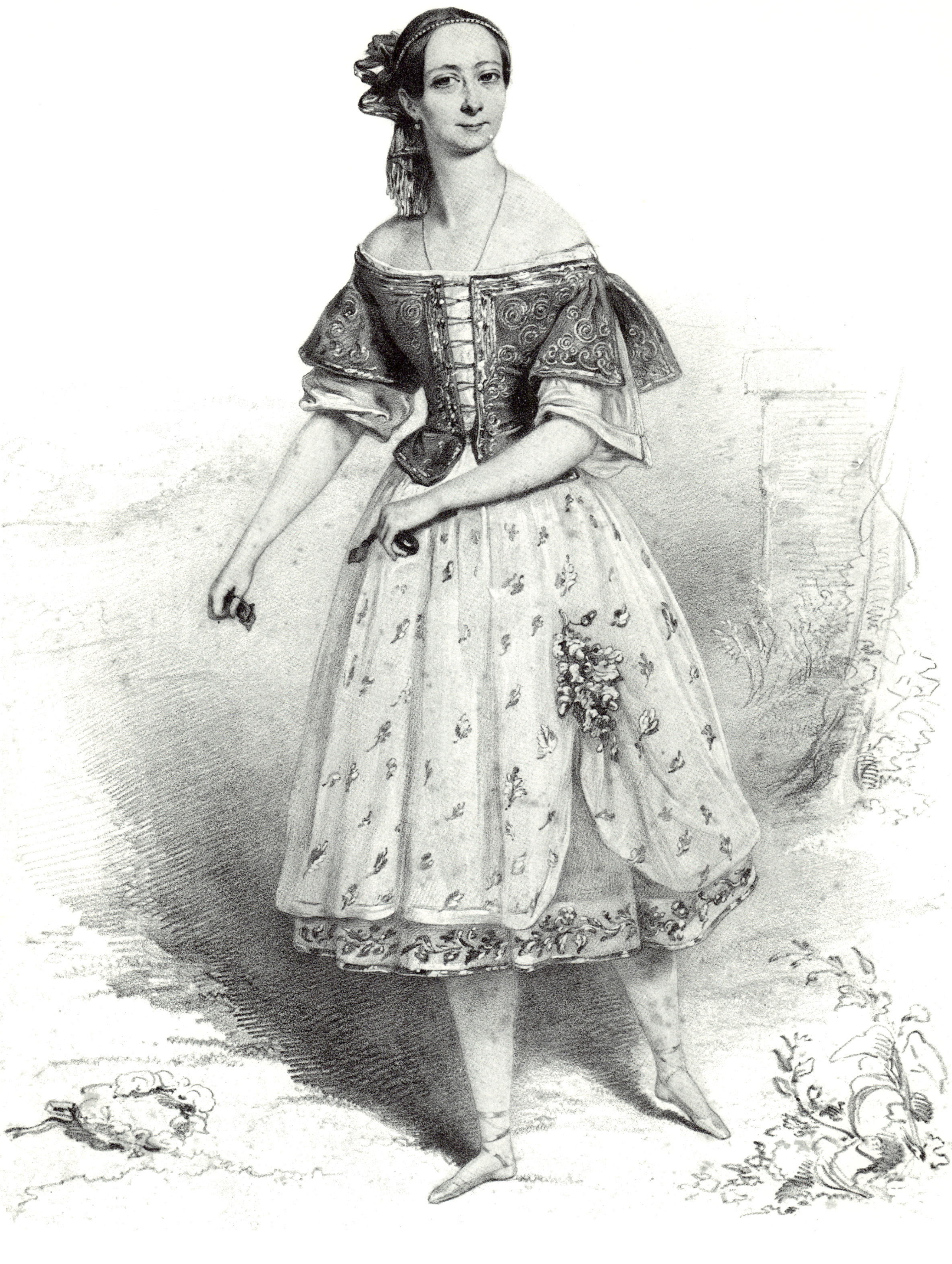

34. Marie Taglioni in the ballet *La Gitana* (Bolshoi Theatre, St. Petersburg, 1838).

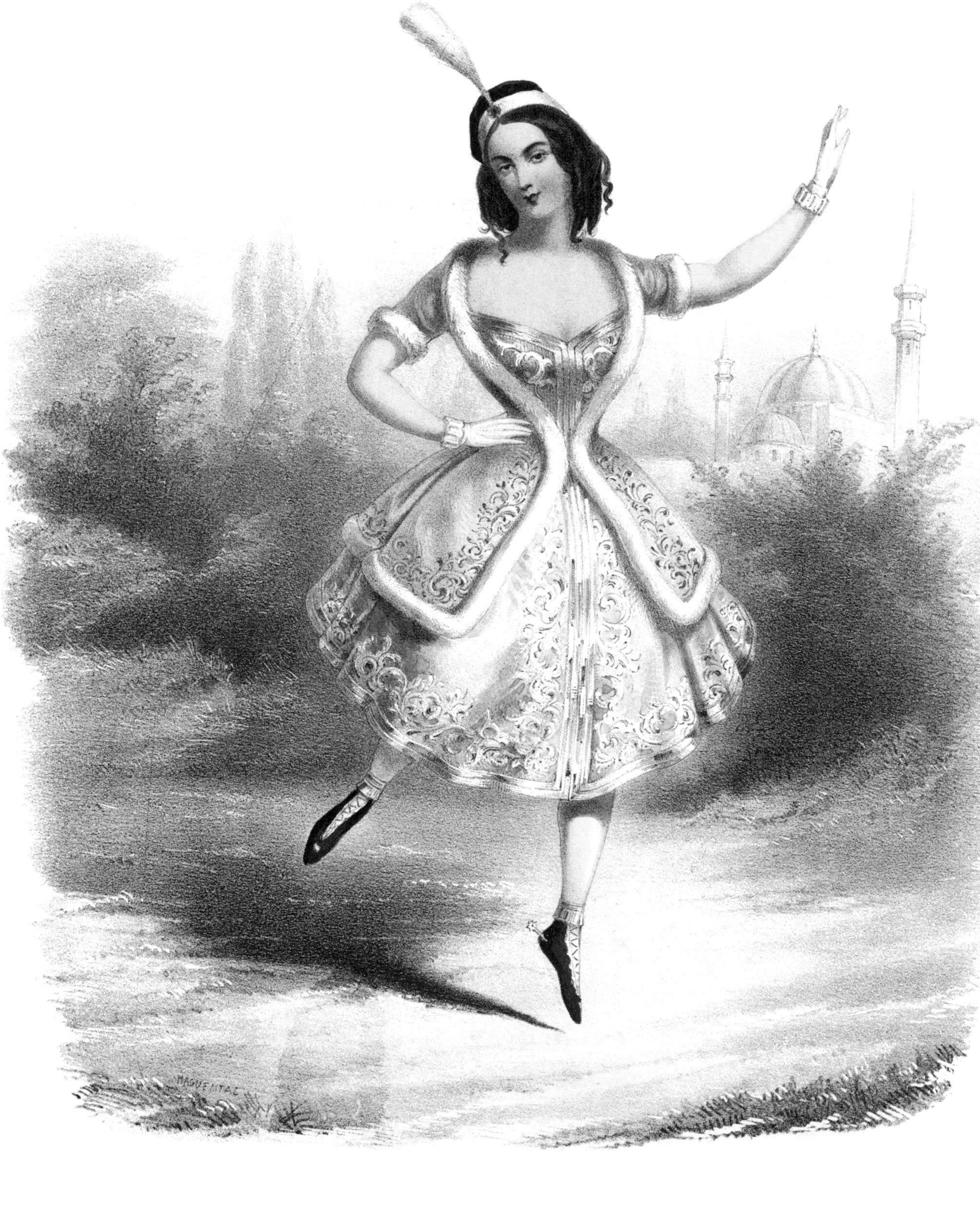

35. Fanny Cerrito in the Lituana in *Une Nuit de bal* (Her Majesty's Theatre, London, 1839).

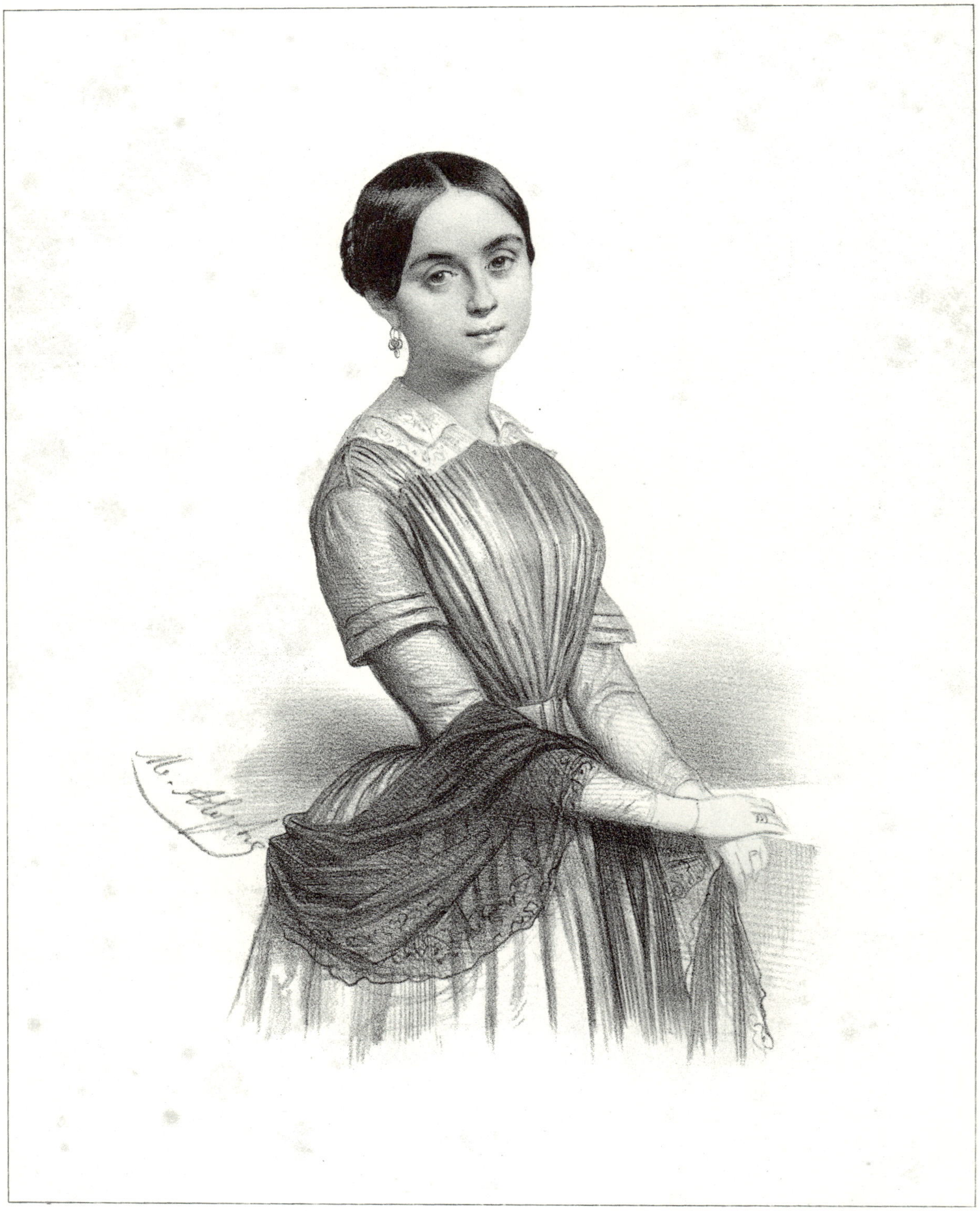

36. Maria Jacob, portrait, Paris, ca. 1841.

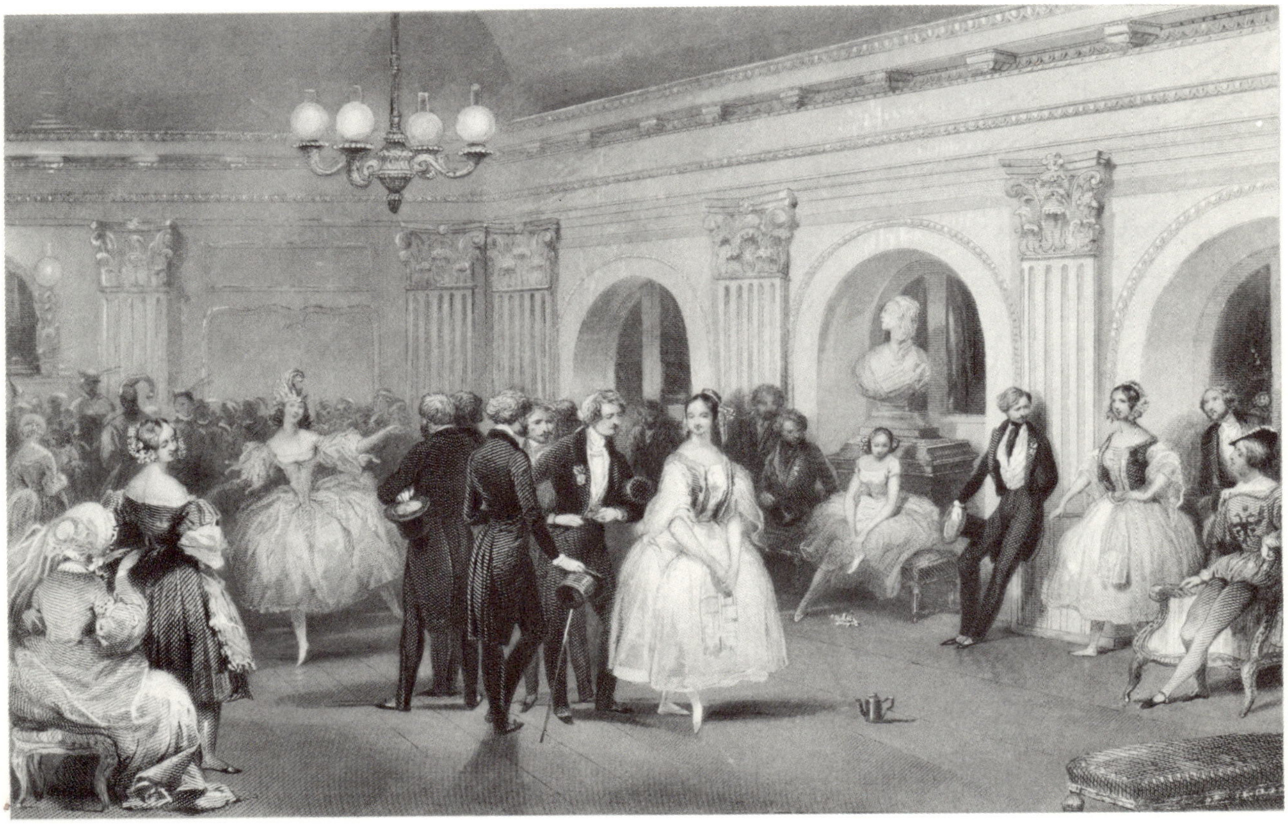

37. The Foyer de la Danse, Paris, 1841 (Maria Jacob on *pointe* in center).

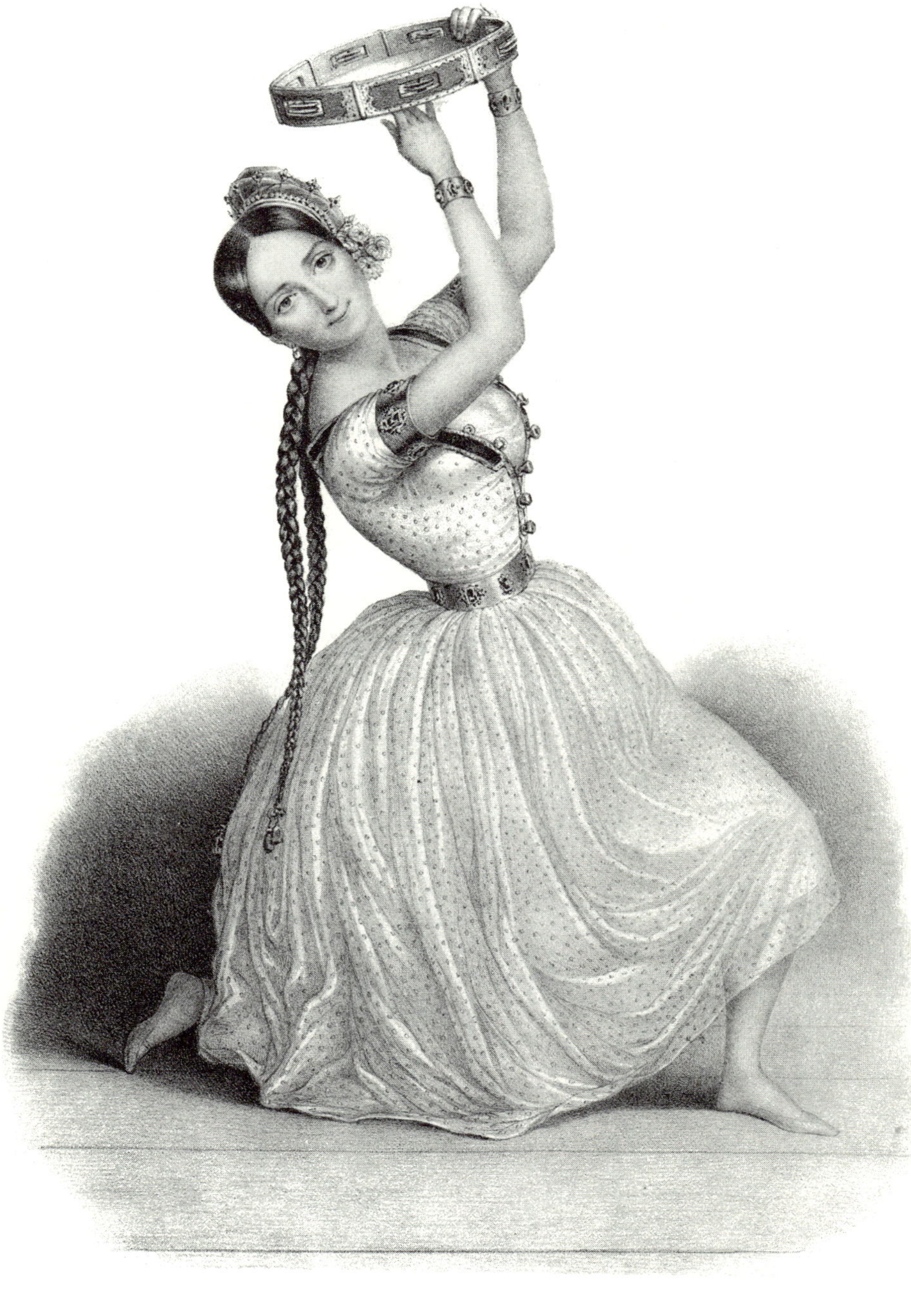

38. Pauline Leroux in *Le Diable amoureux* (Opéra, Paris, 1840).

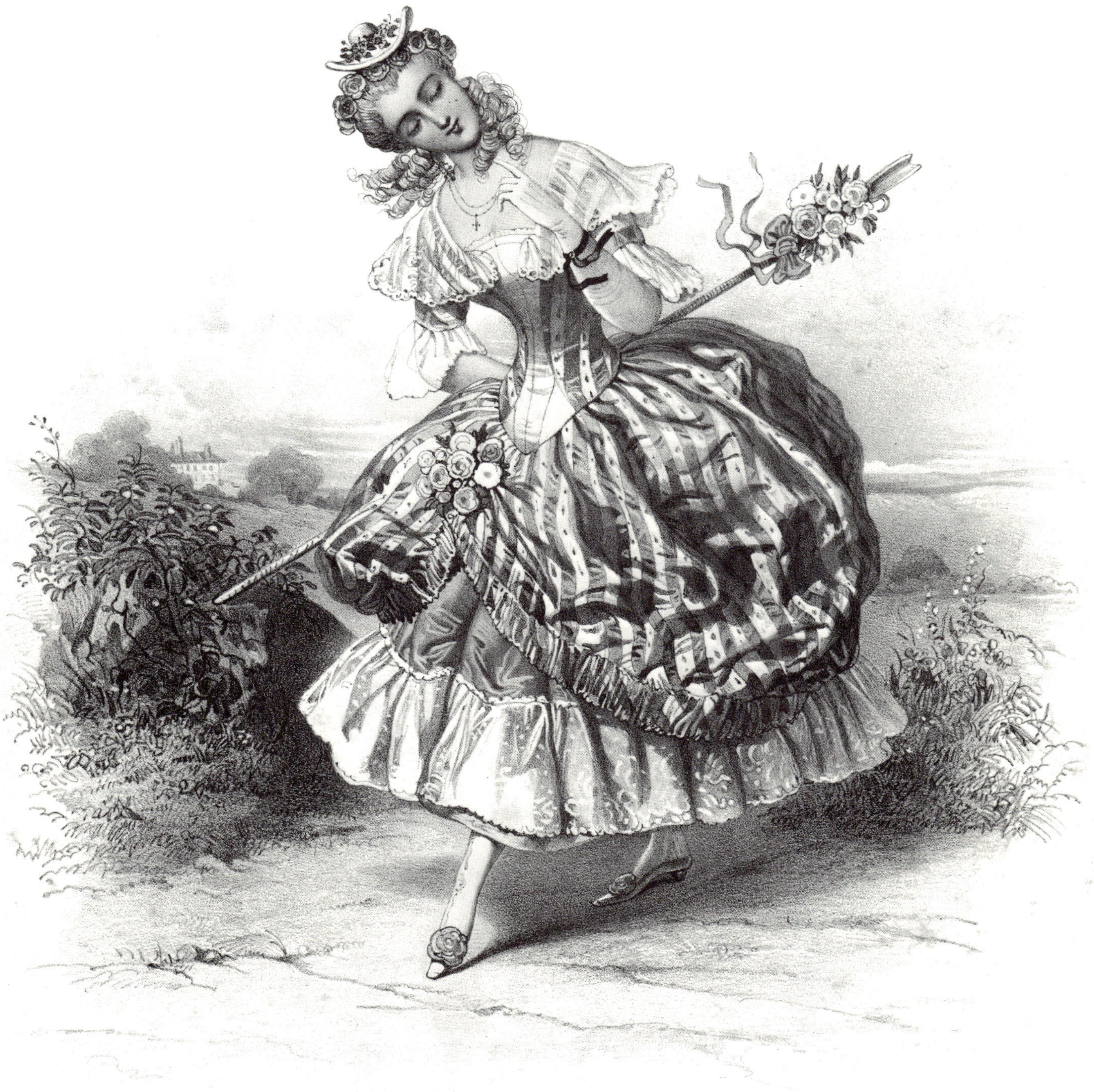

39. Pauline Leroux in "Pas Villageois" (Opéra, Paris, n.d.).

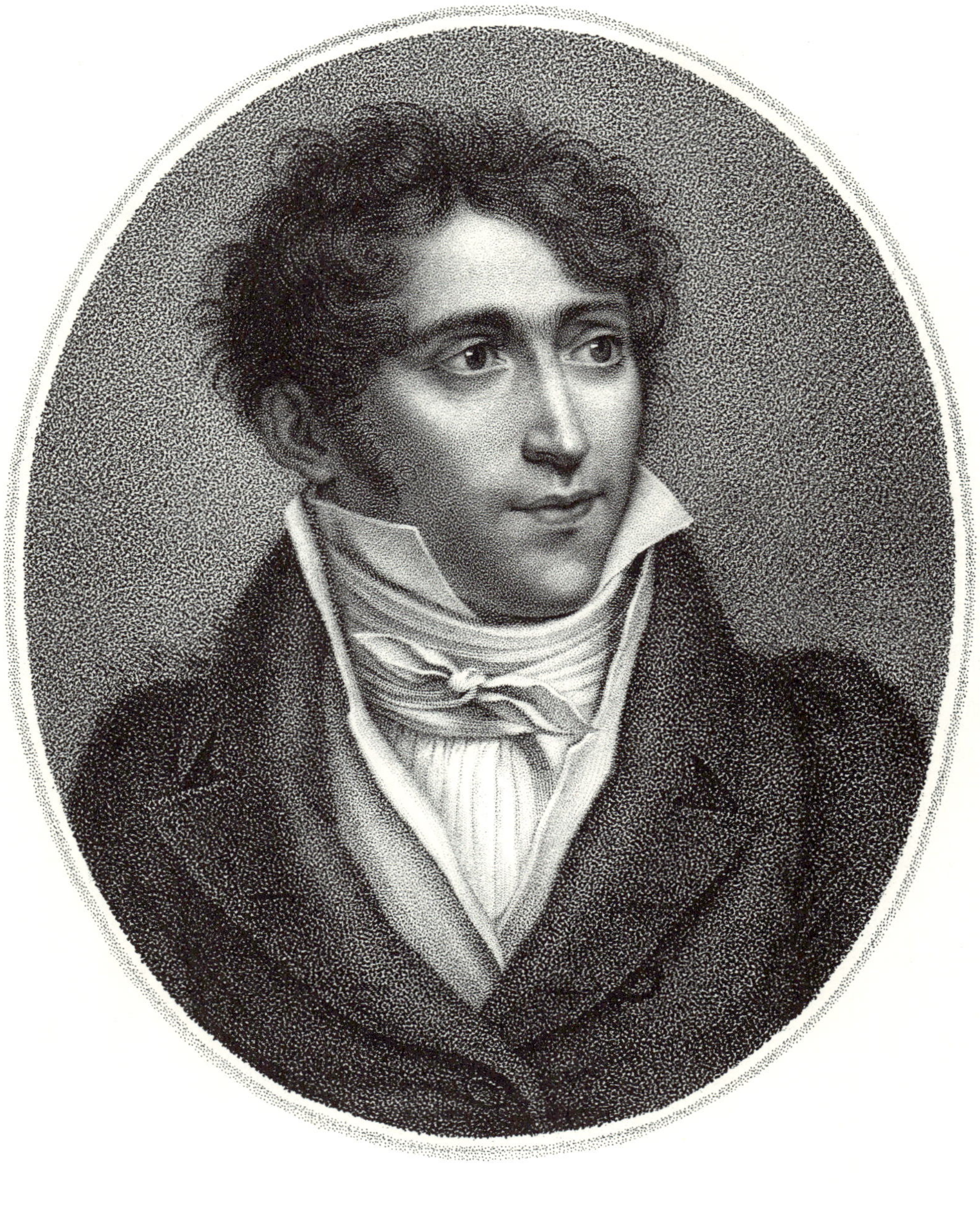

40. Giovanni Coralli, portrait, Milan, n.d.

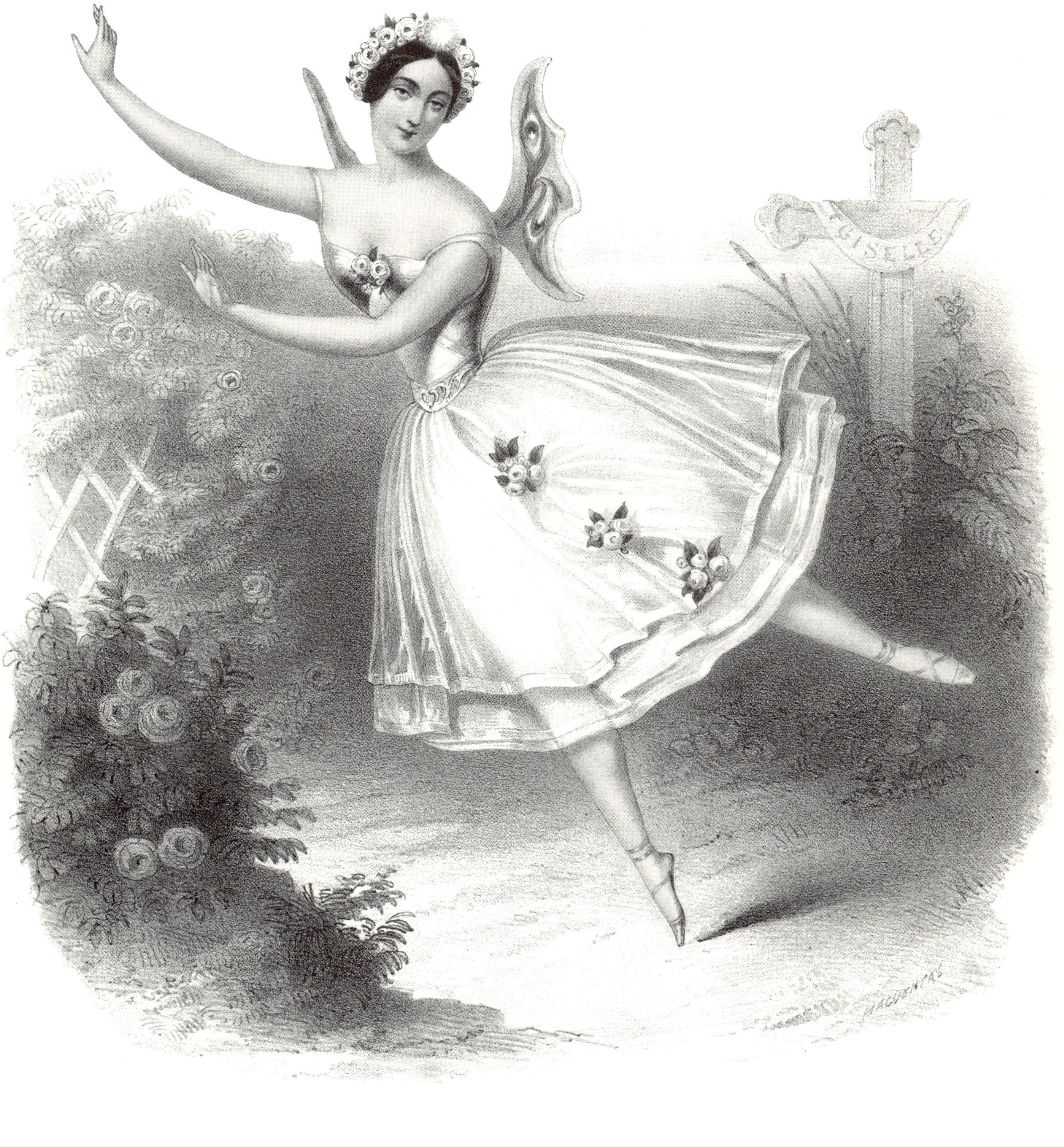

41. Carlotta Grisi in *Giselle* (Opéra, Paris, 1841).

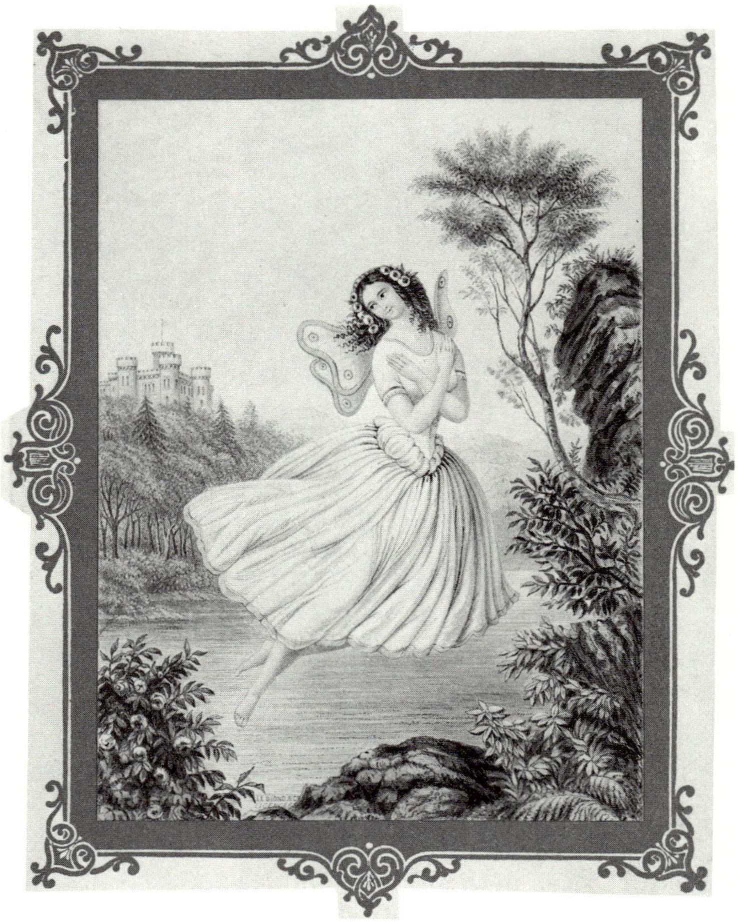

42. Carlotta Grisi in *La Sylphide* (Opéra, Paris, 1840s).

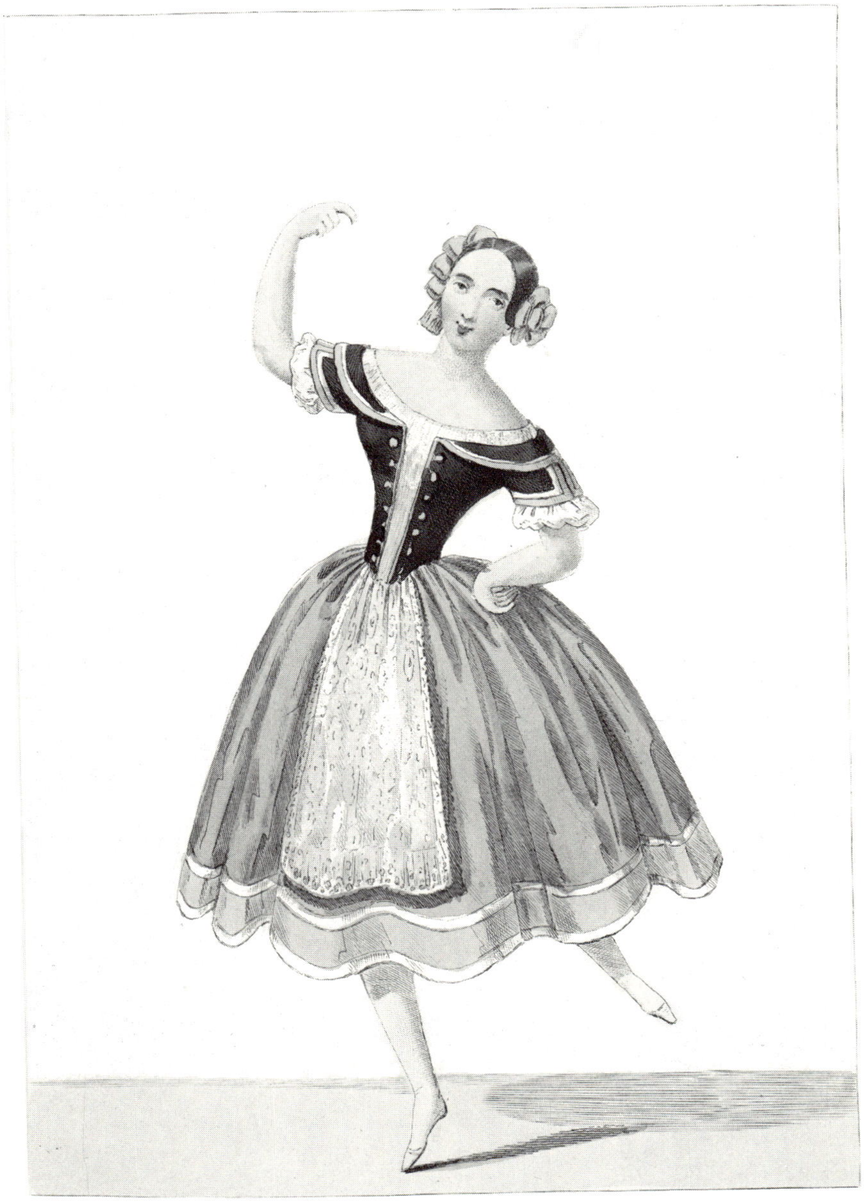

43. Carlotta Grisi in *Giselle* (Opéra, Paris, 1841).

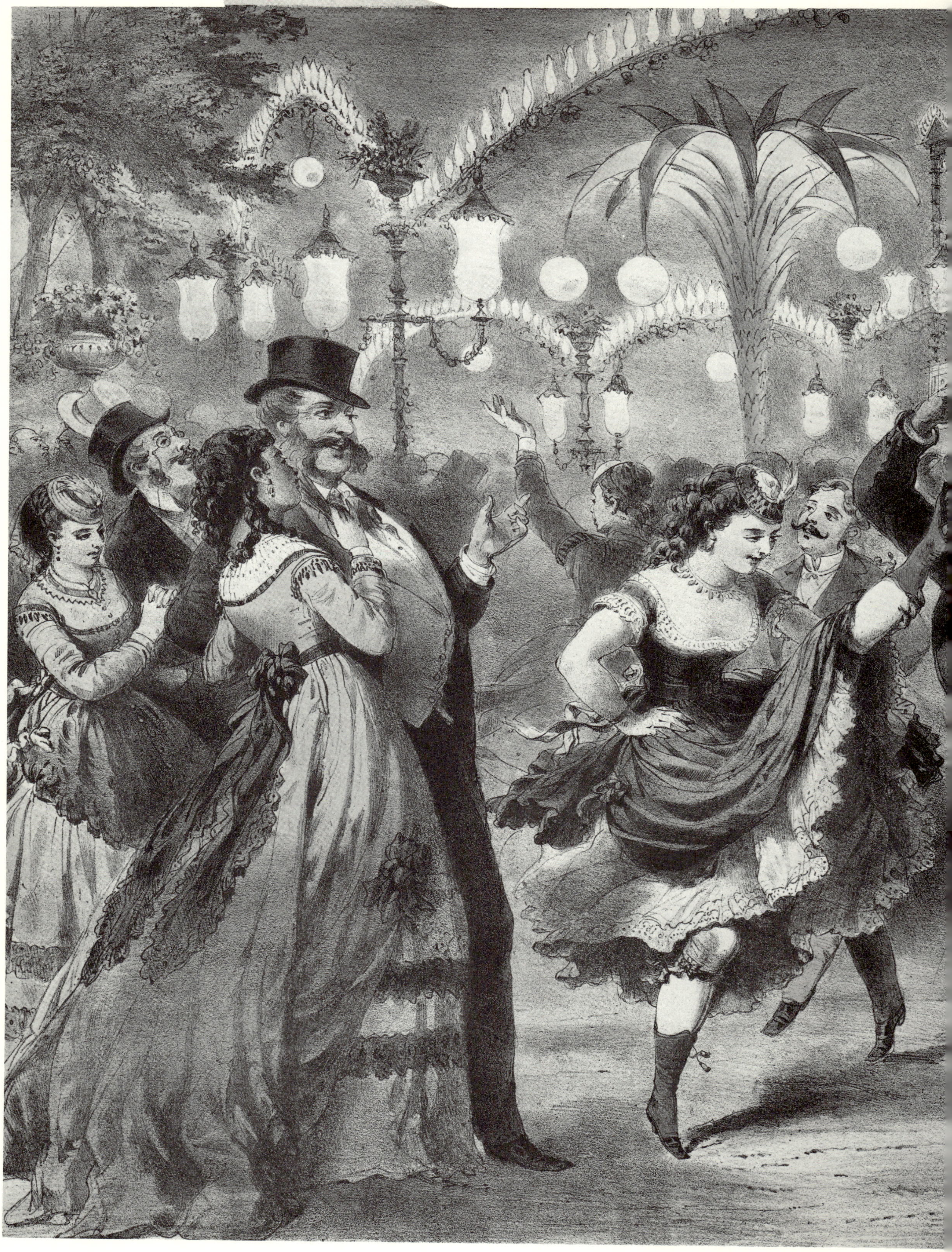

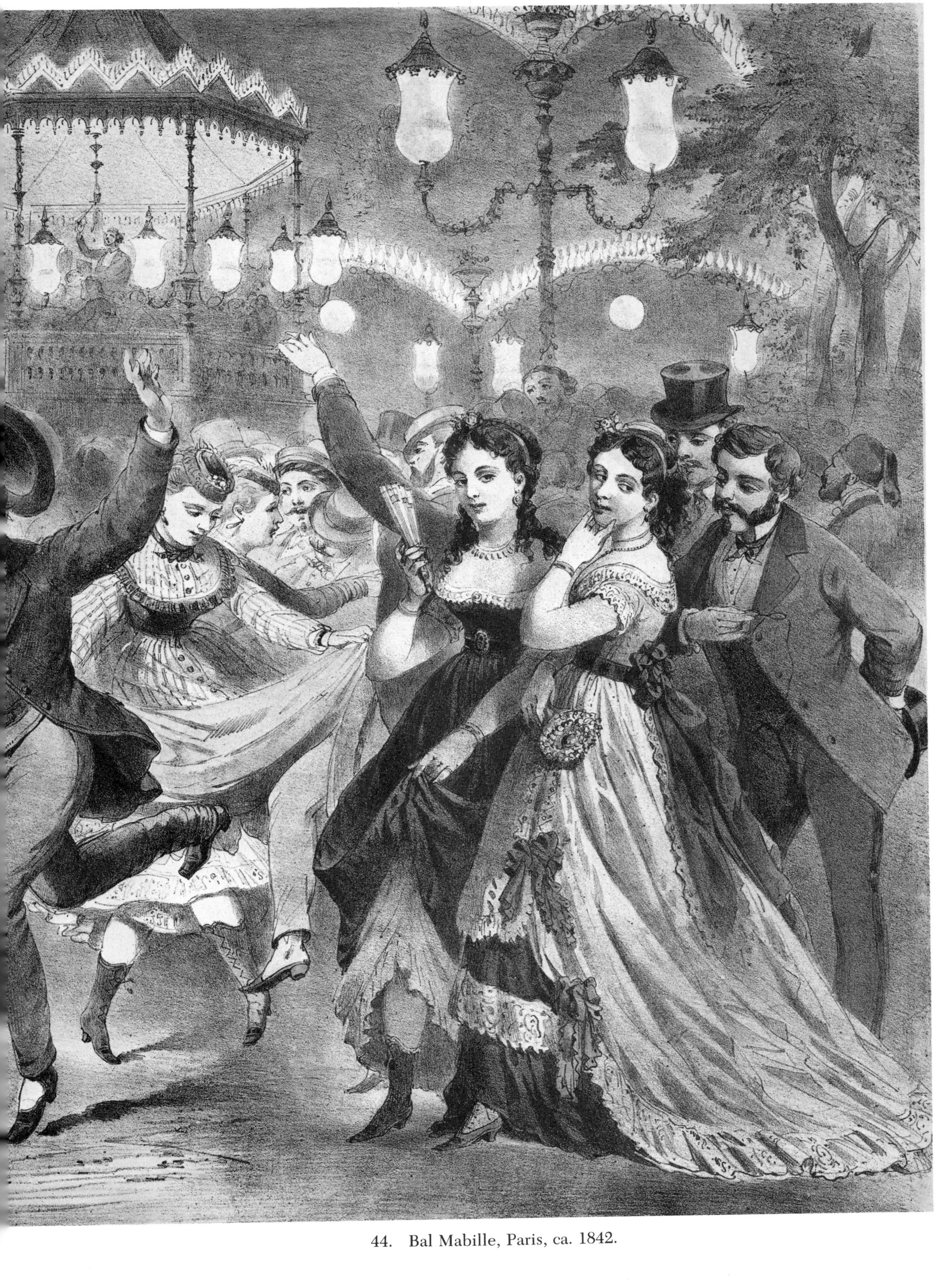

44. Bal Mabille, Paris, ca. 1842.

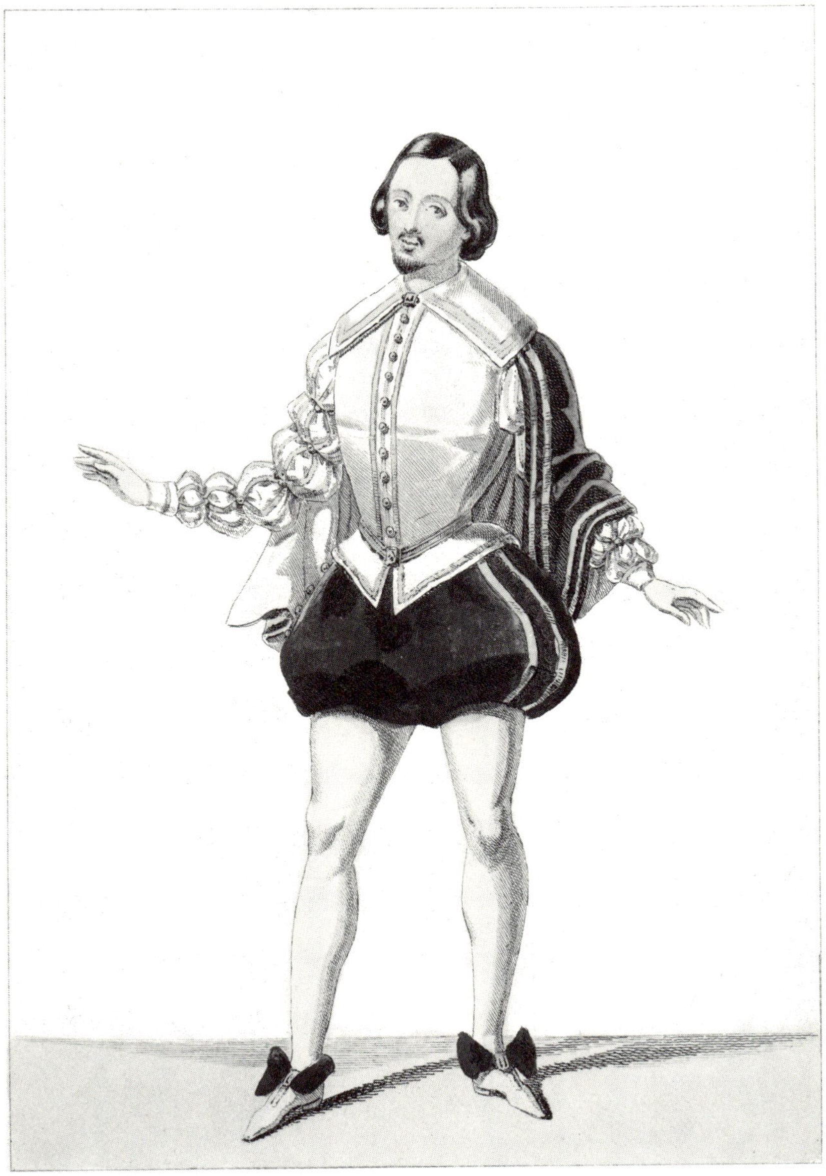

45. Albert (François Decombe) in *La Jolie Fille de Gand* (Opéra, Paris, 1842).

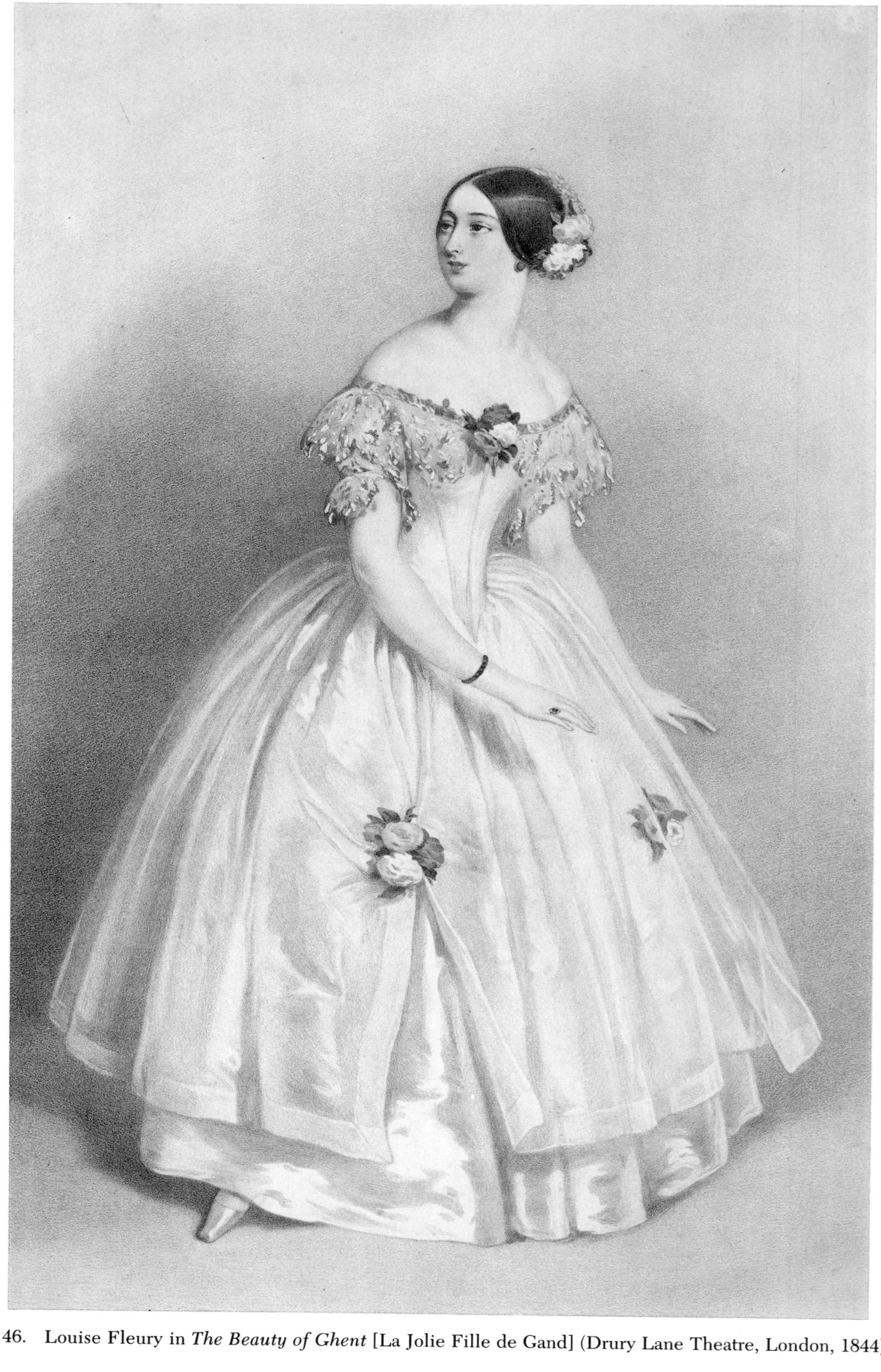

46. Louise Fleury in *The Beauty of Ghent* [La Jolie Fille de Gand] (Drury Lane Theatre, London, 1844).

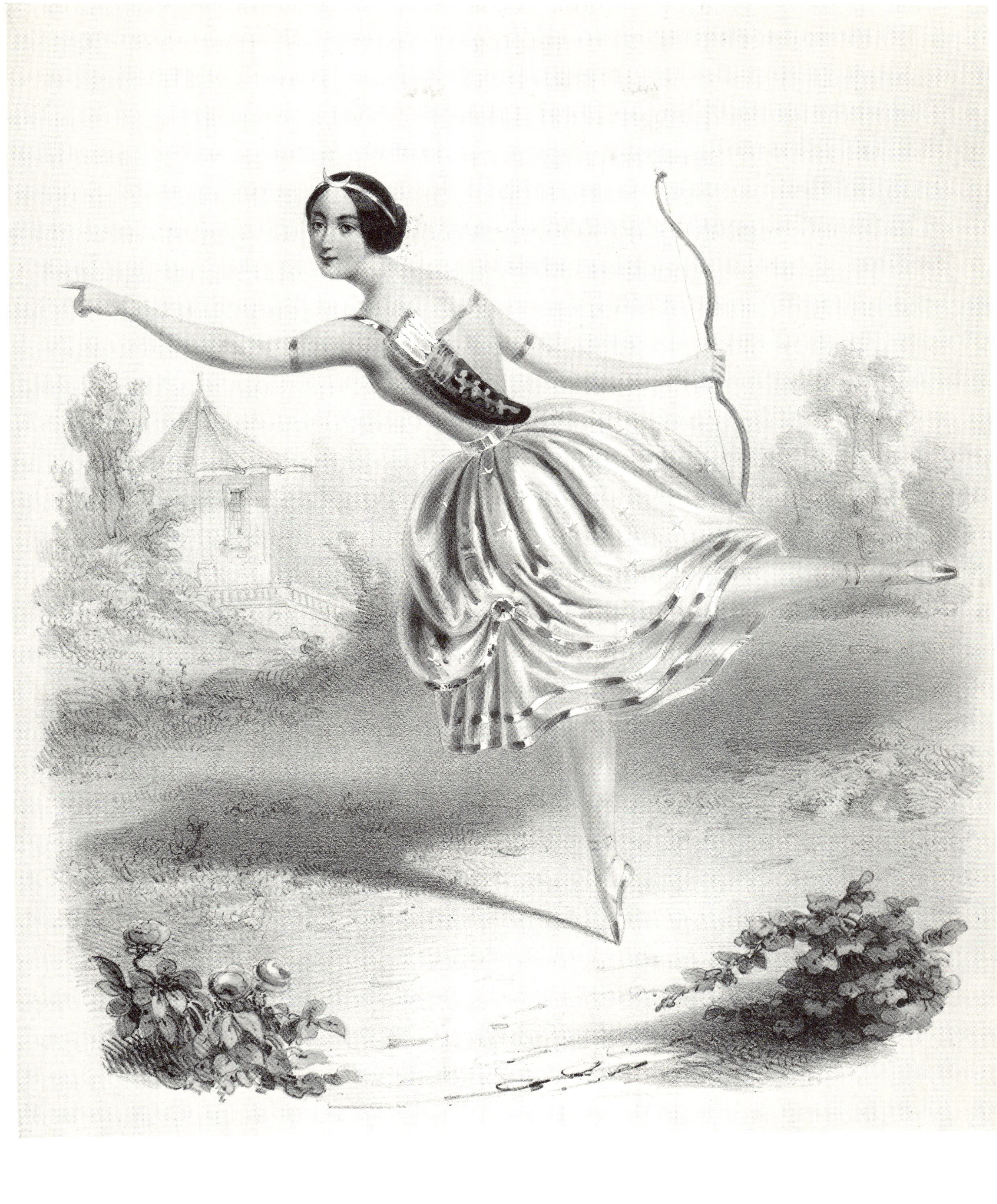

47. Louise Fleury in *The Beauty of Ghent* [La Jolie Fille de Gand] (Drury Lane Theatre, London, 1844).

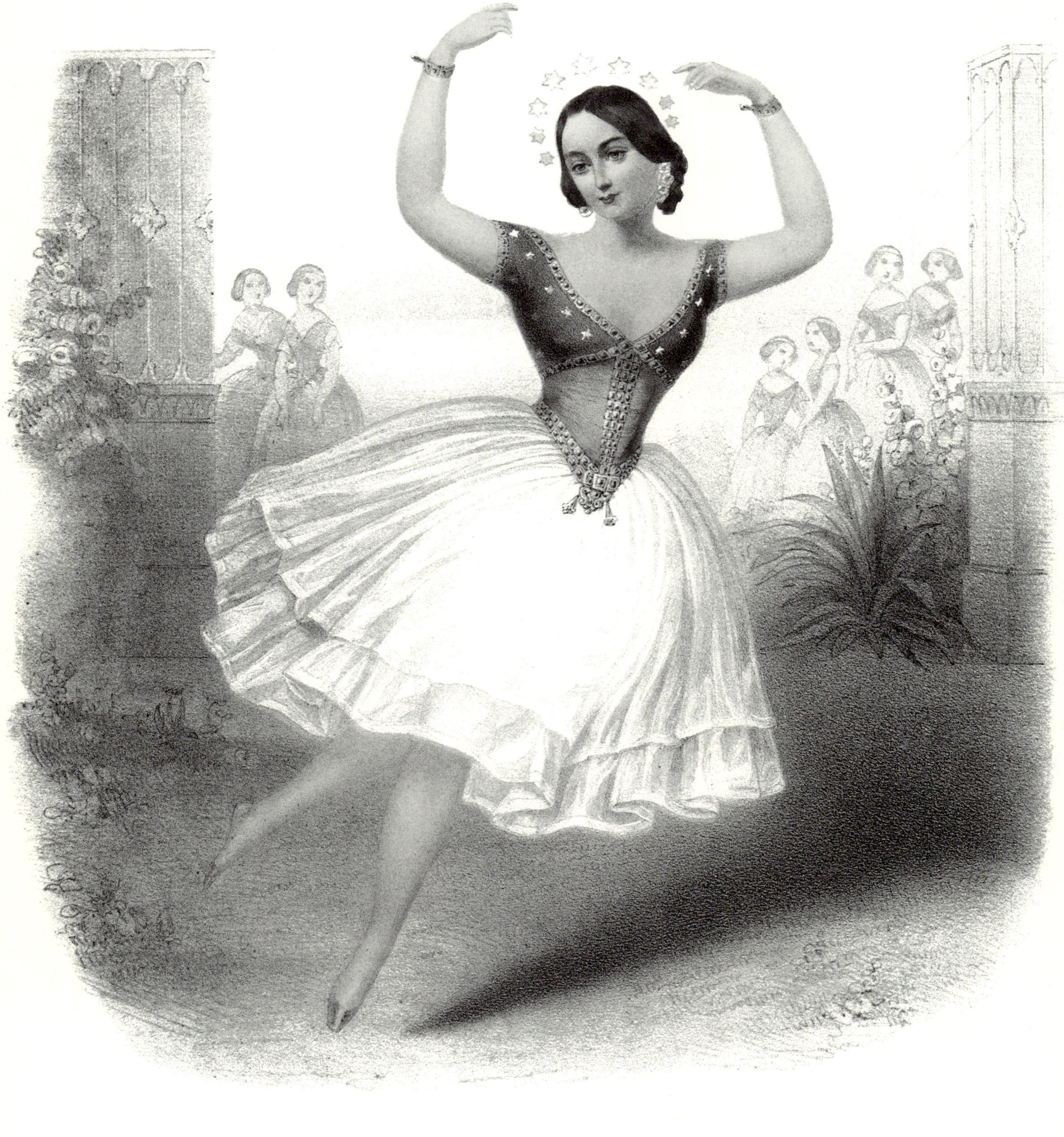

48. Carlotta Grisi in *La Péri* (Opéra, Paris, 1843).

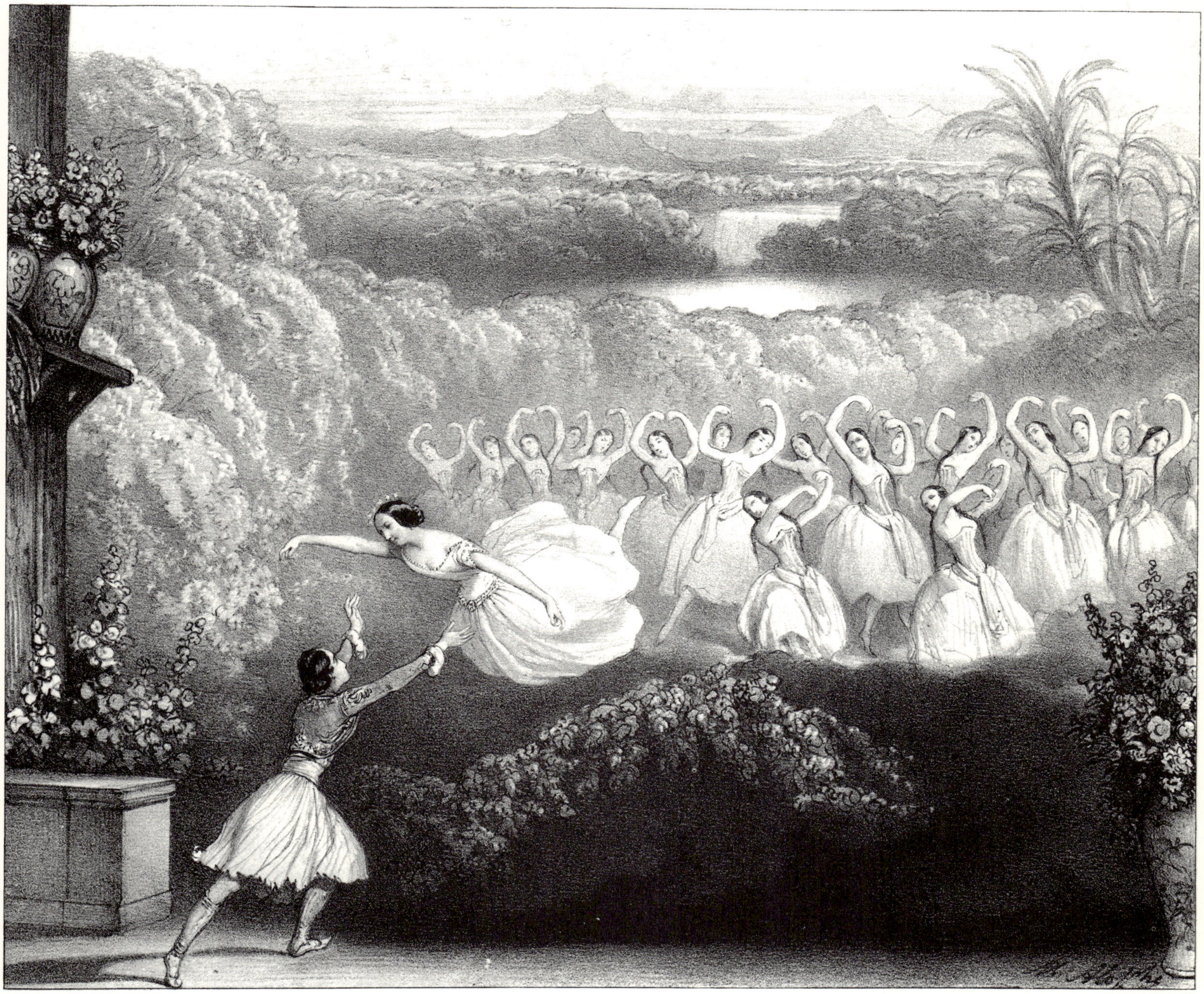

49. Carlotta Grisi and Lucien Petipa in the Leap from *La Péri* (Opéra, Paris, 1843).

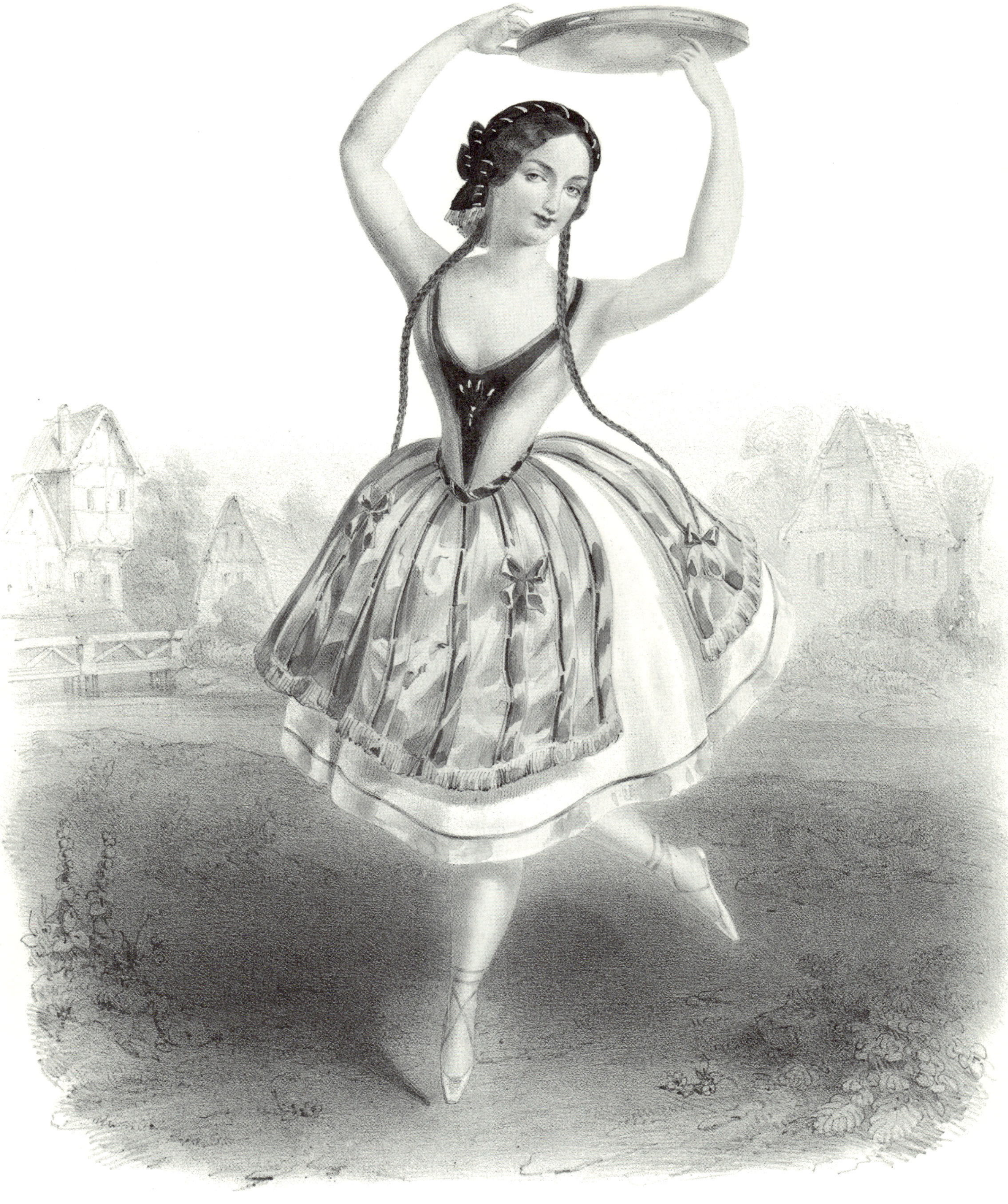

50. Fanny Cerrito in *Alma ou la fille du feu* (Her Majesty's Theatre, London, 1842).

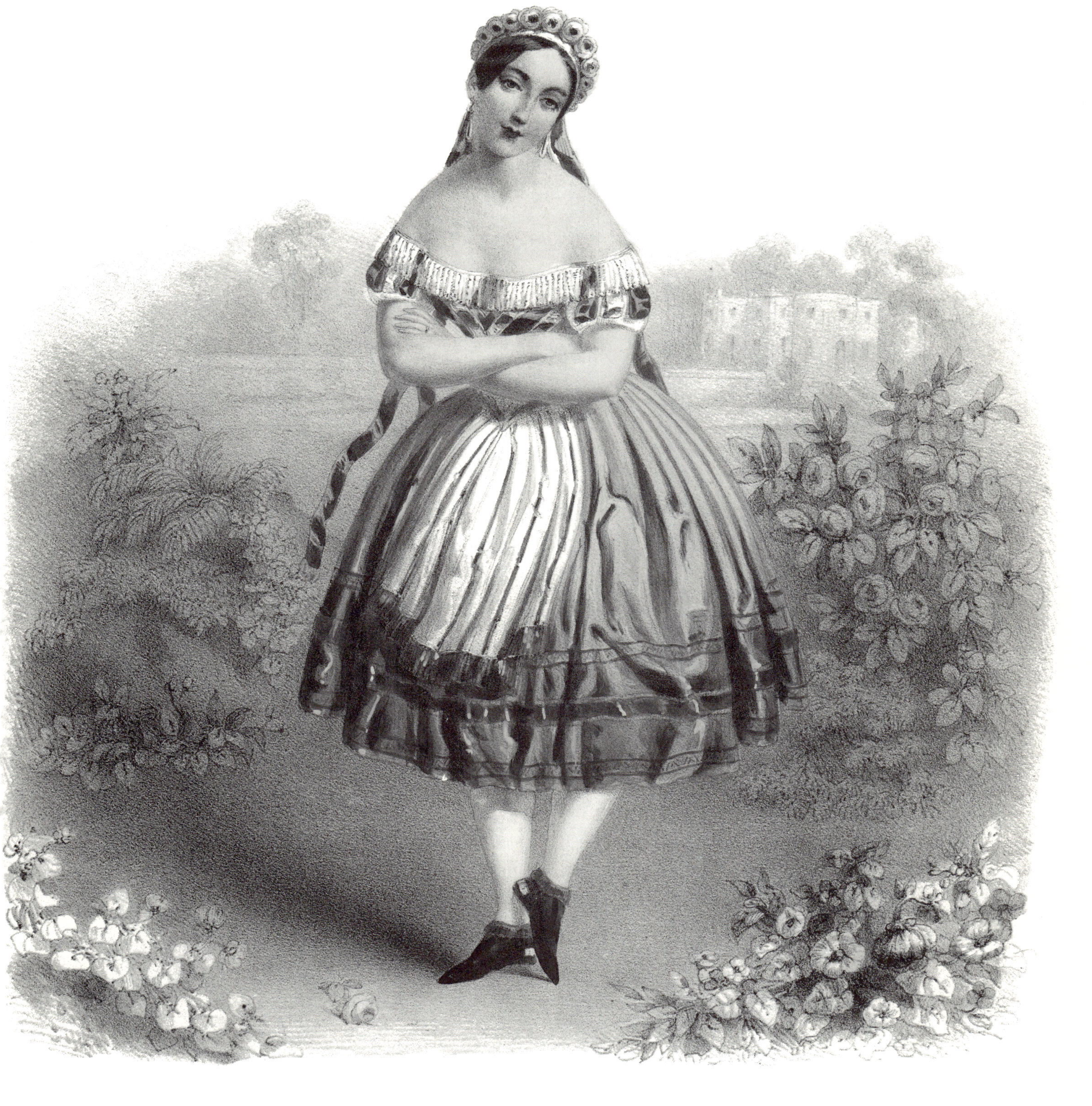

51. Marie Guy-Stéphan in the Cracovienne in *Une Soirée de carnaval* (Her Majesty's Theatre, London, 1842).

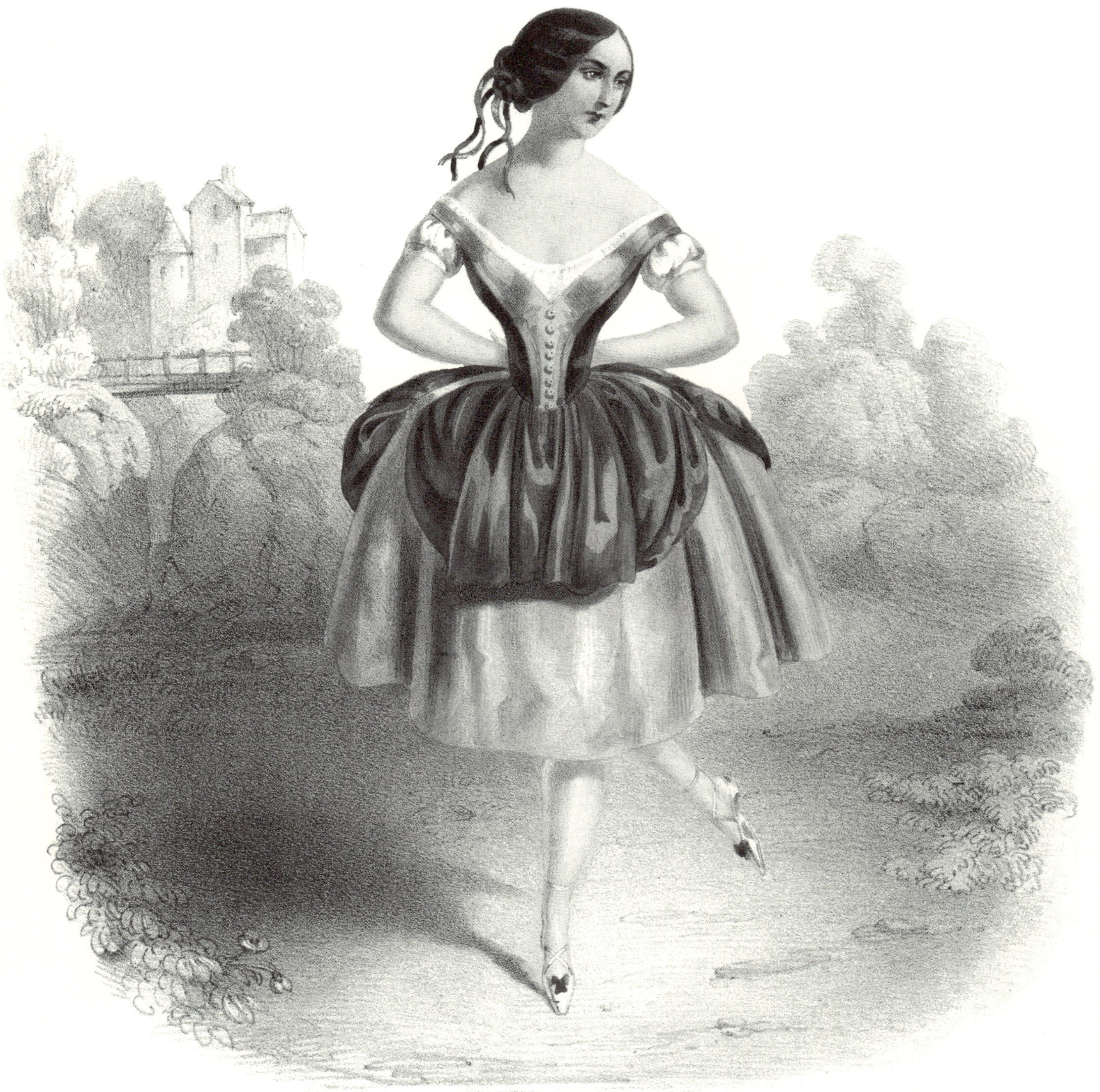

52. Fanny Cerrito in the Polka in *La Vivandière* (Her Majesty's Theatre, London, 1844).

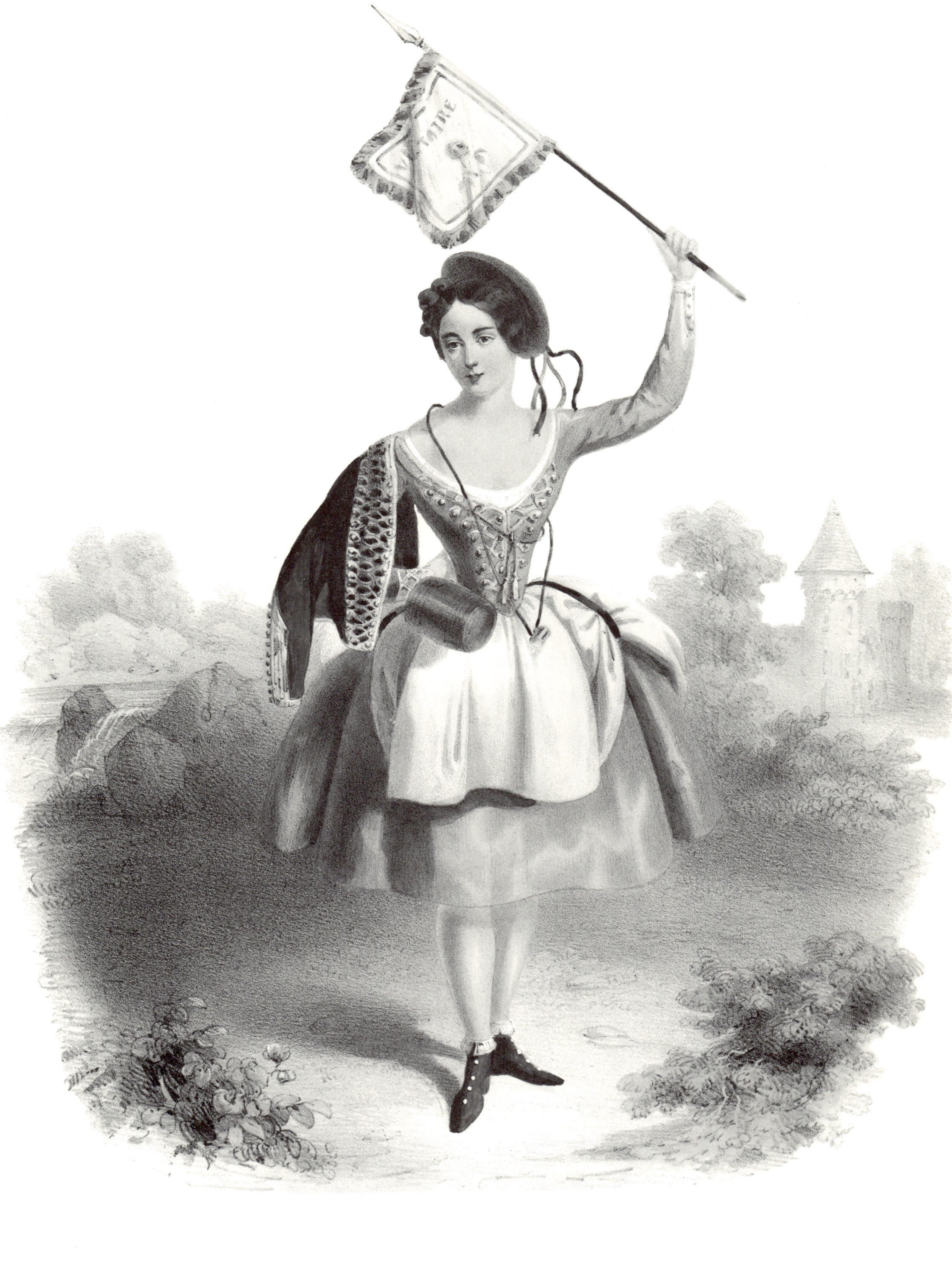

53. Fanny Cerrito in the Polka in *La Vivandière* (Her Majesty's Theatre, London, 1844).

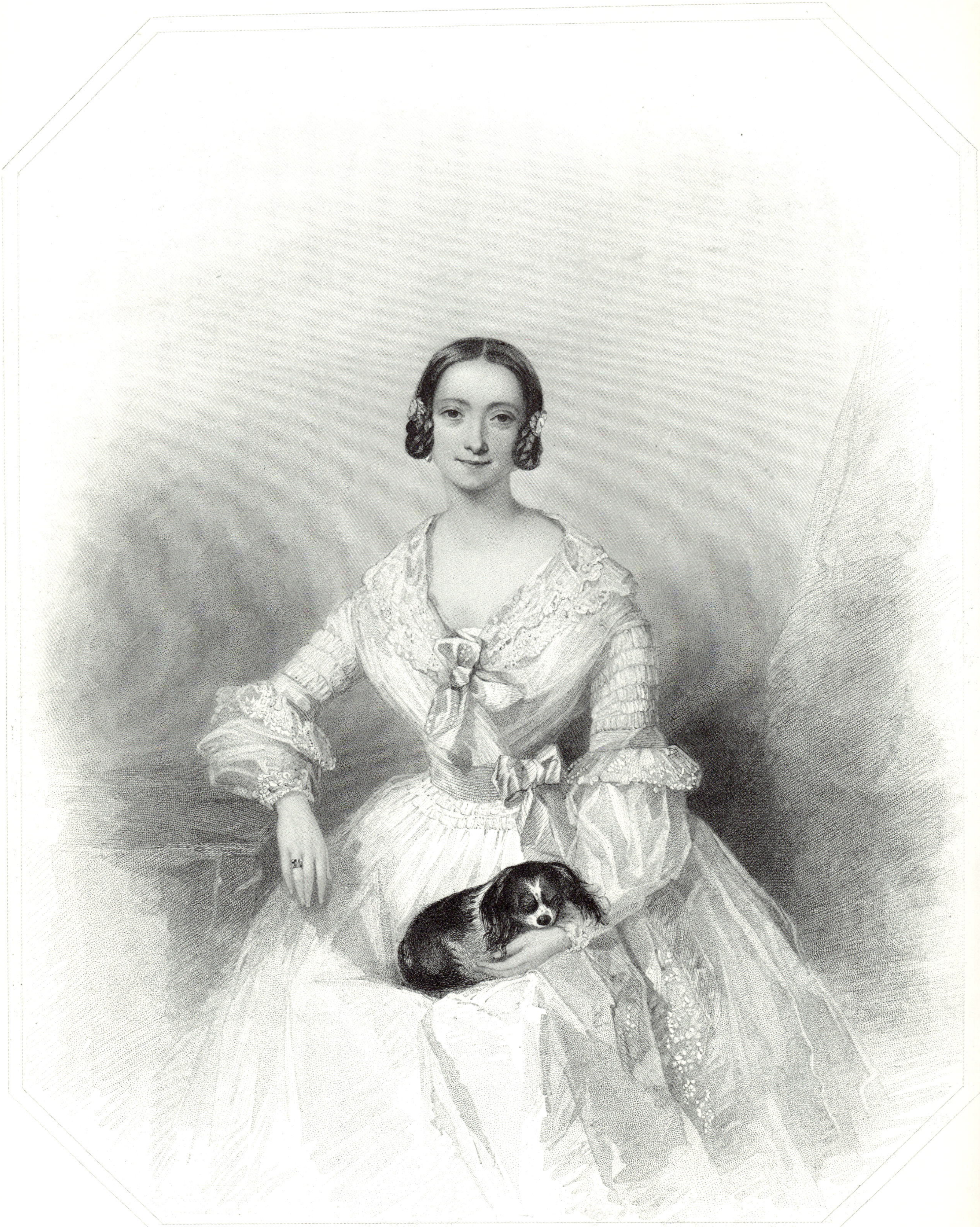

54. Marie Taglioni, portrait, London, 1842.

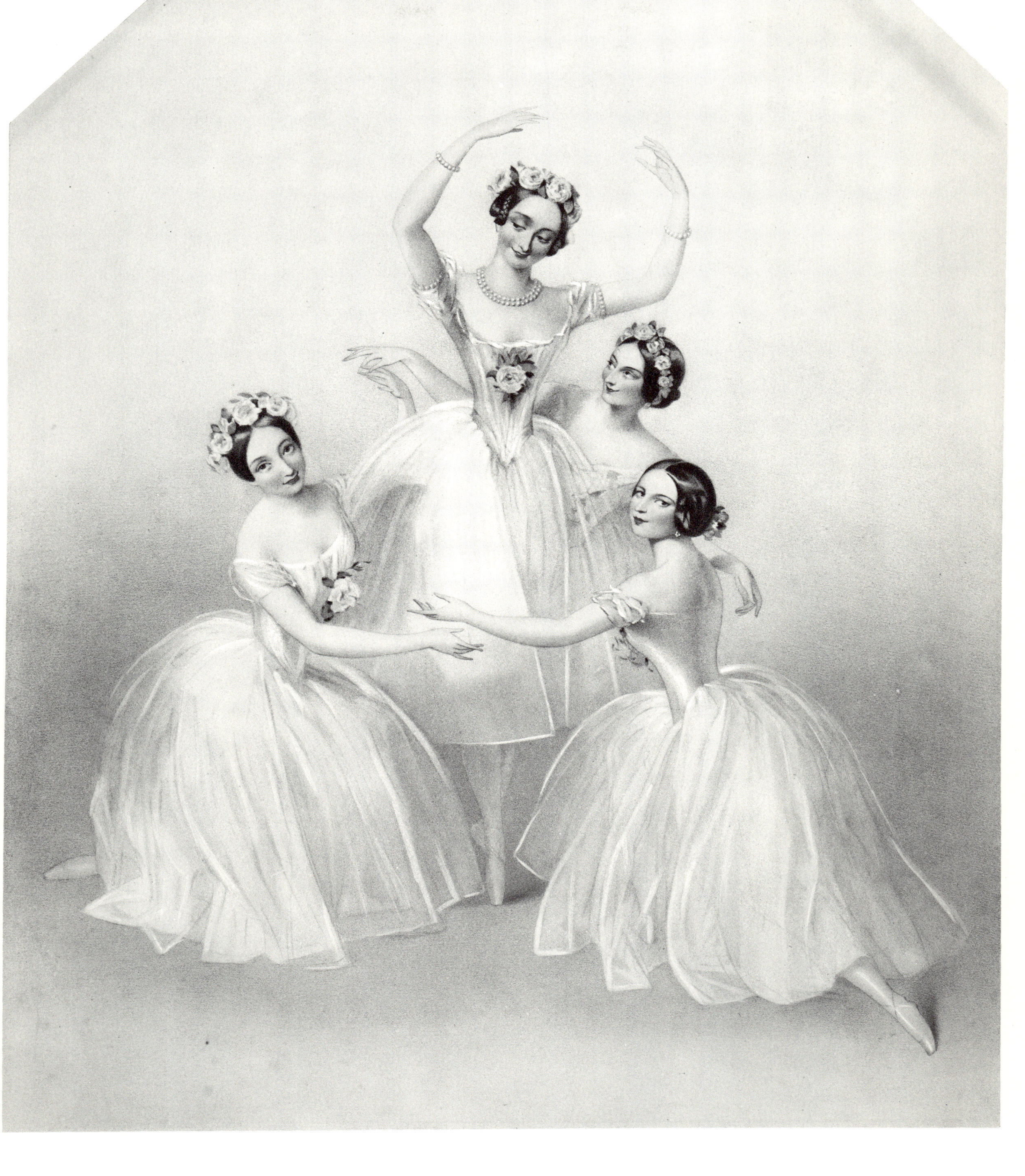

55. Grisi, Taglioni, Grahn and Cerrito in *Pas de Quatre* (Her Majesty's Theatre, London, 1845).

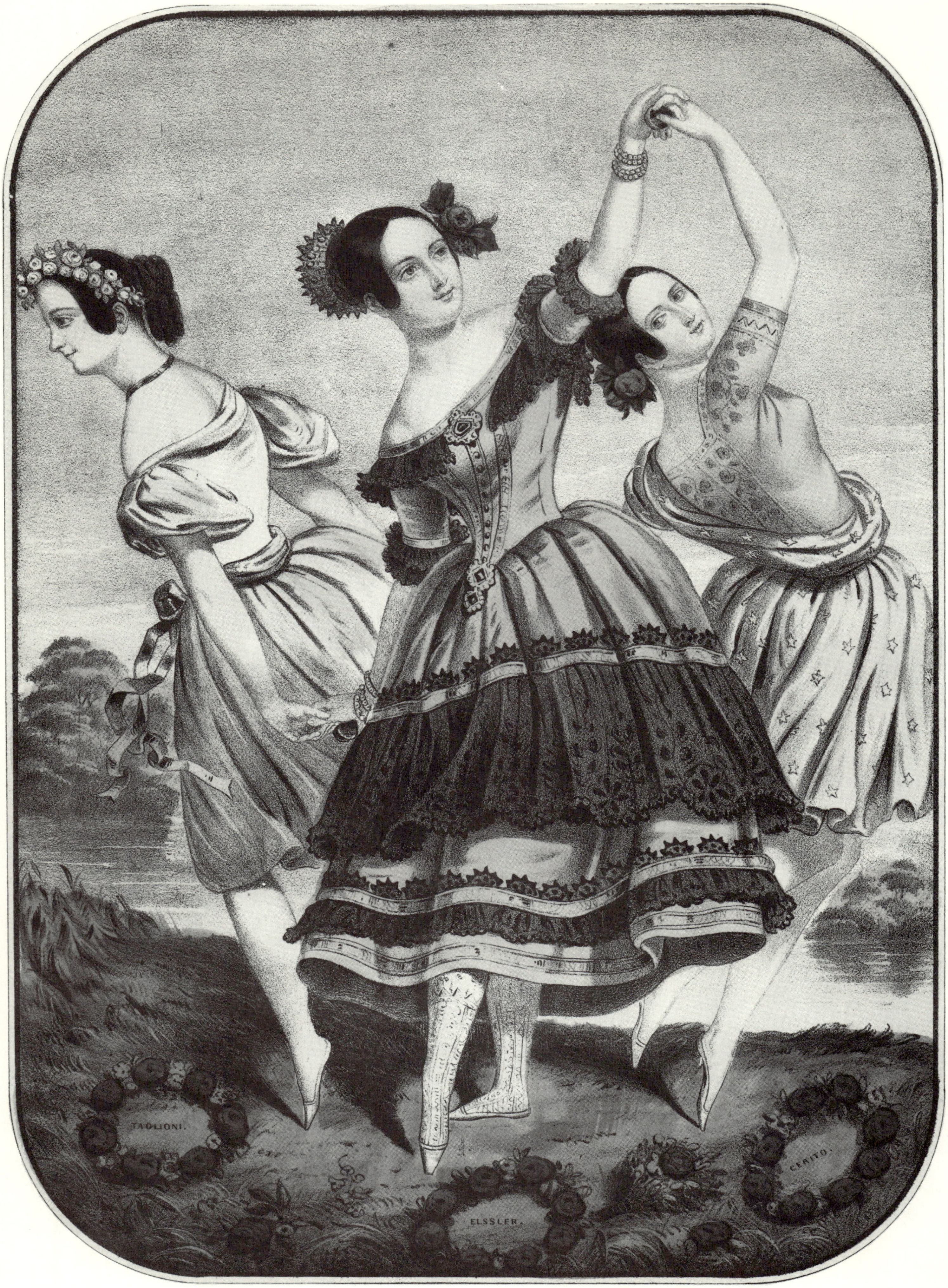

56. Taglioni, Elssler and Grisi (NOT Cerrito as on the print) as the Three Graces, 1845.

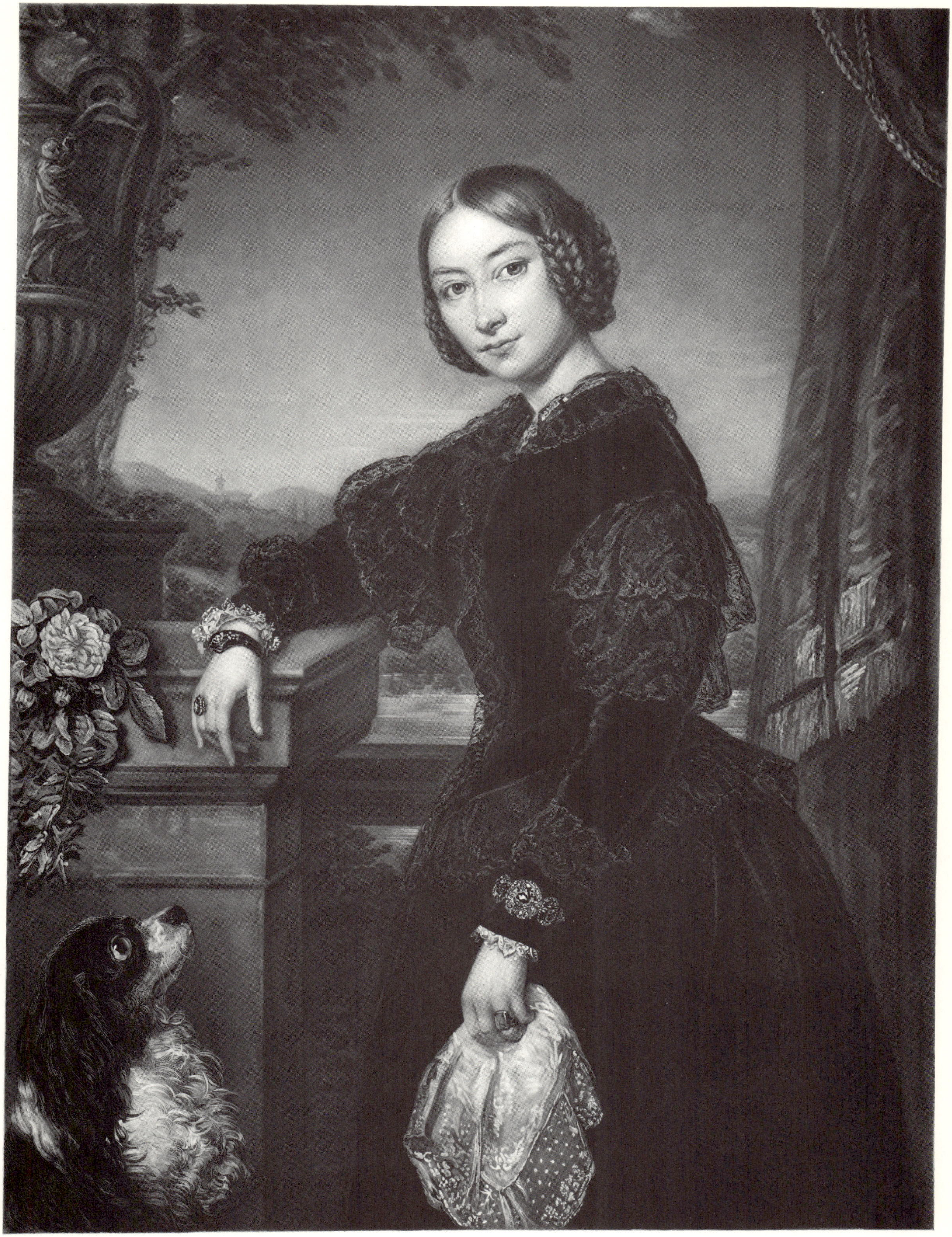

57. Lucile Grahn, portrait, London, 1847.

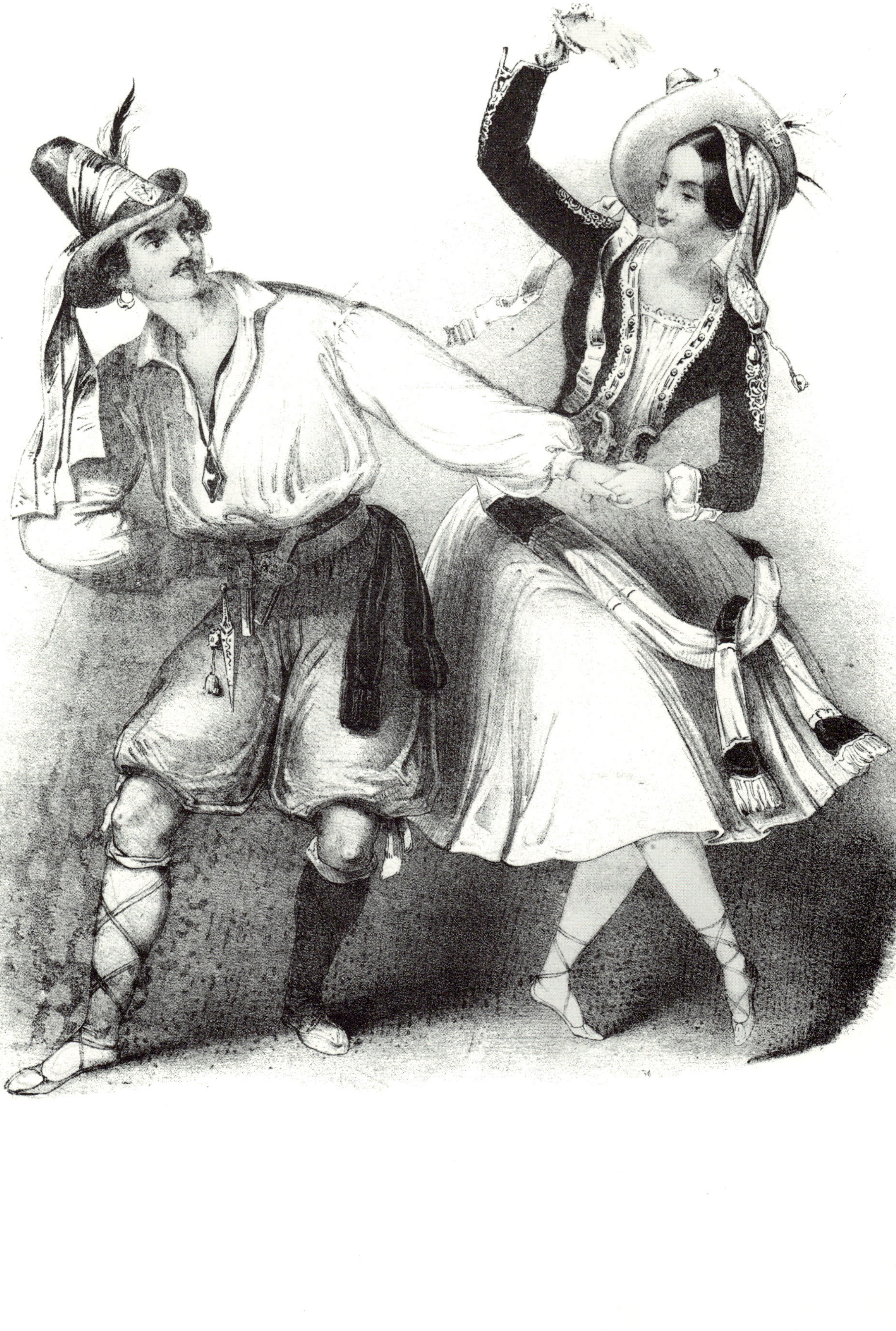

58. Jules Perrot and Lucile Grahn in the Brigand Polka in *Catarina, ou la Fille du bandit* (Her Majesty's Theatre, London, 1846).

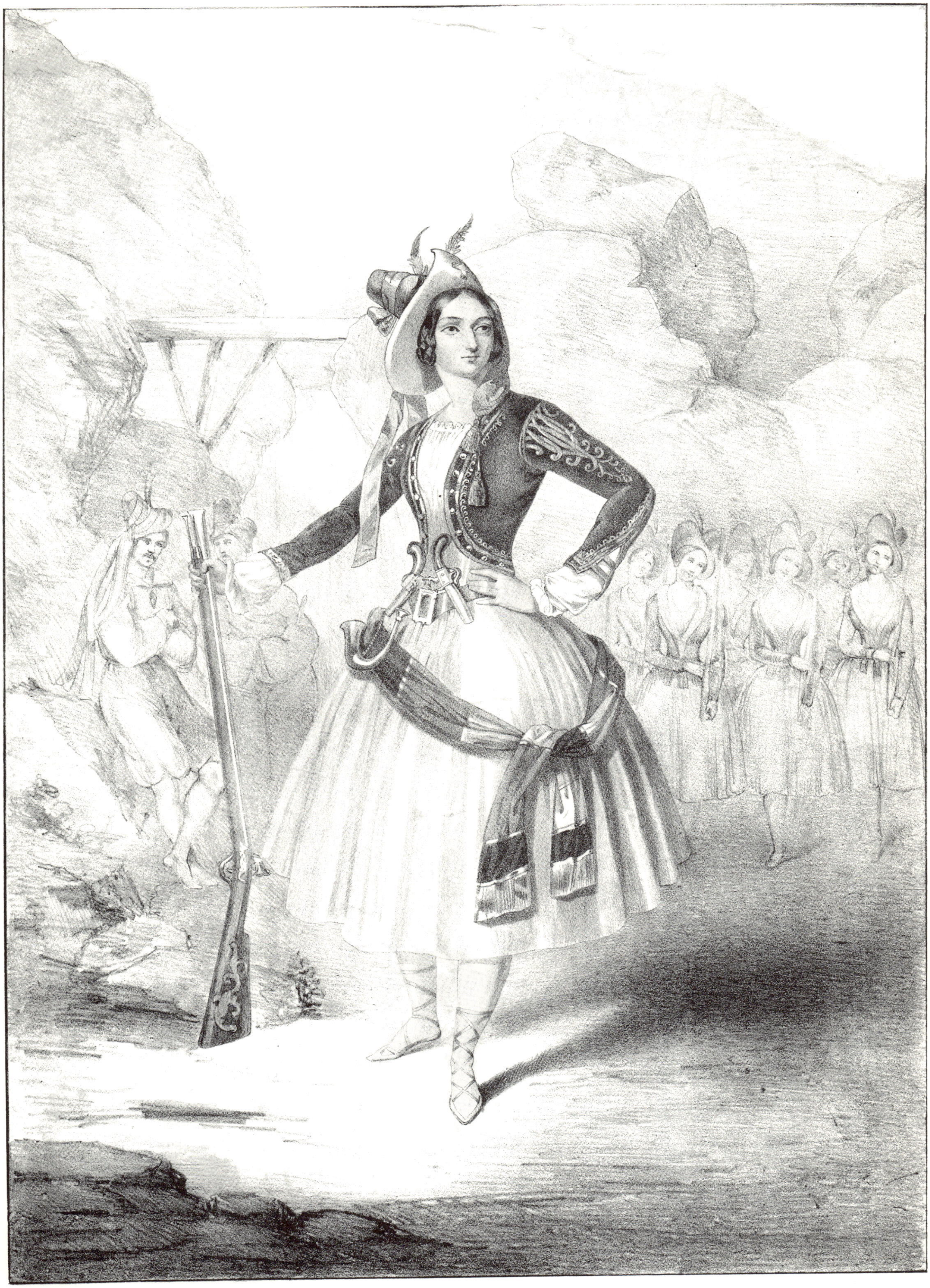

59. Lucile Grahn in the Pas Stratégique in *Catarina* (Her Majesty's Theatre, London, 1846).

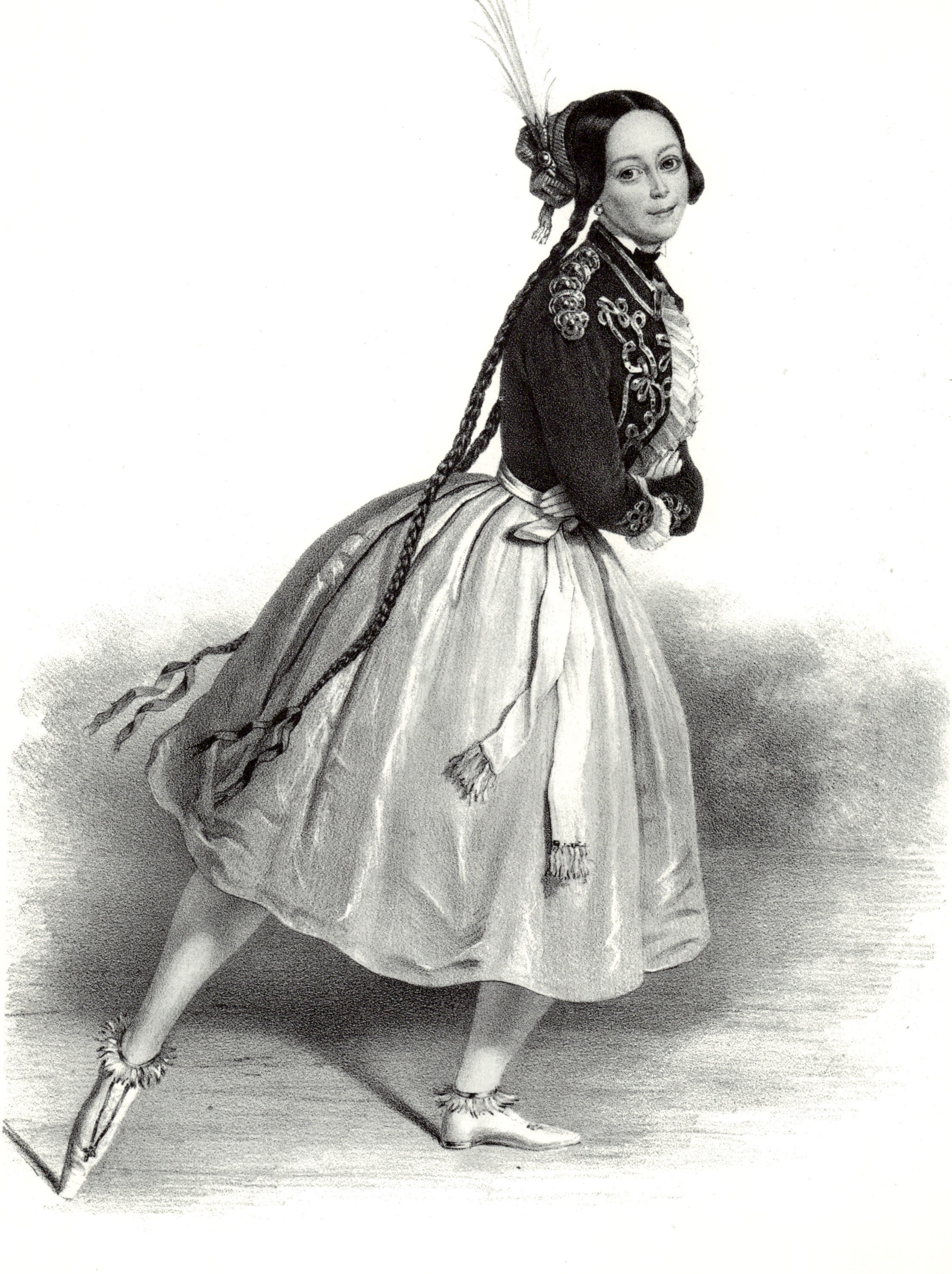

60. Augusta Nielsen in *La Lithuanienne* (Royal Theatre, Copenhagen, 1844).

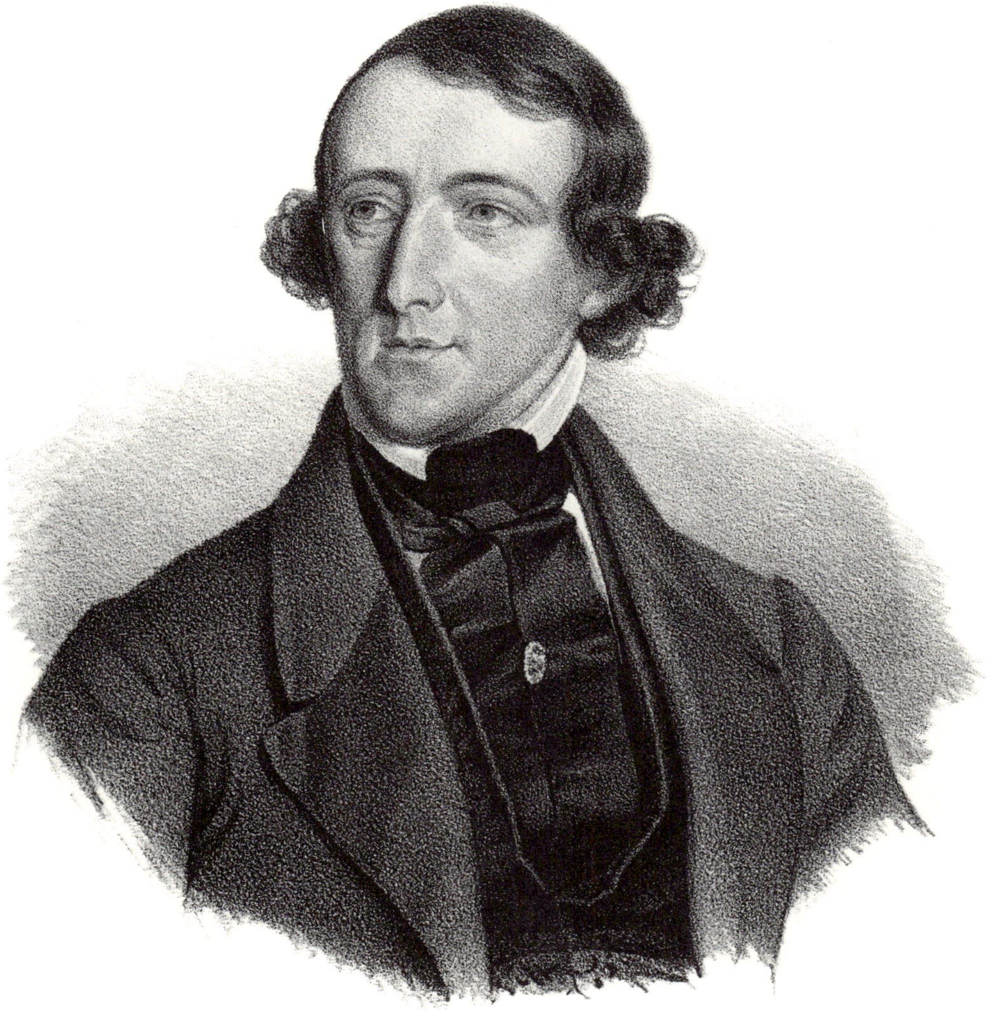

61. August Bournonville, portrait, Copenhagen, 1842.

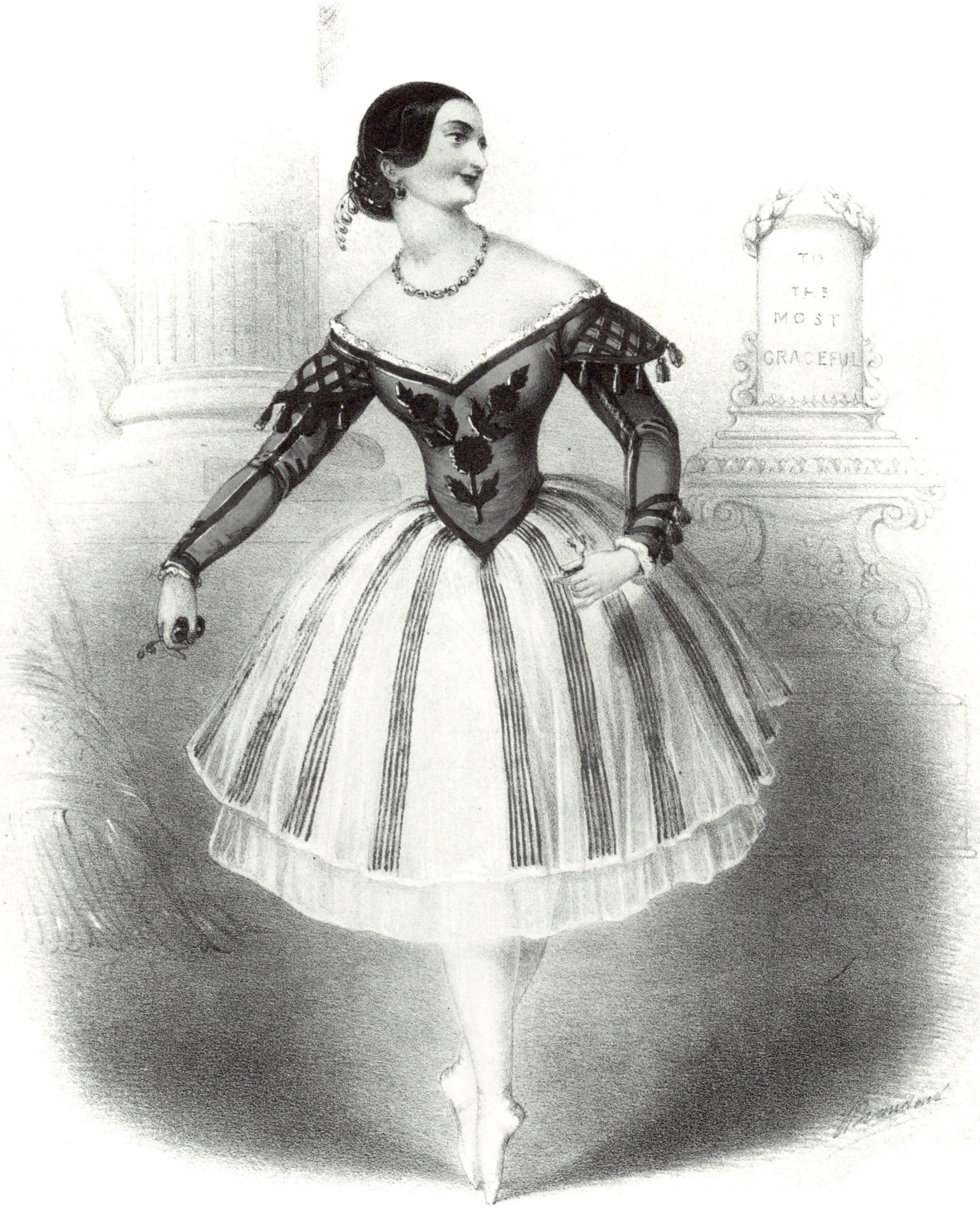

62. Flora Fabbri in the pas La Castigliana in *The Offspring of Flowers* (Drury Lane Theatre, London, 1846).

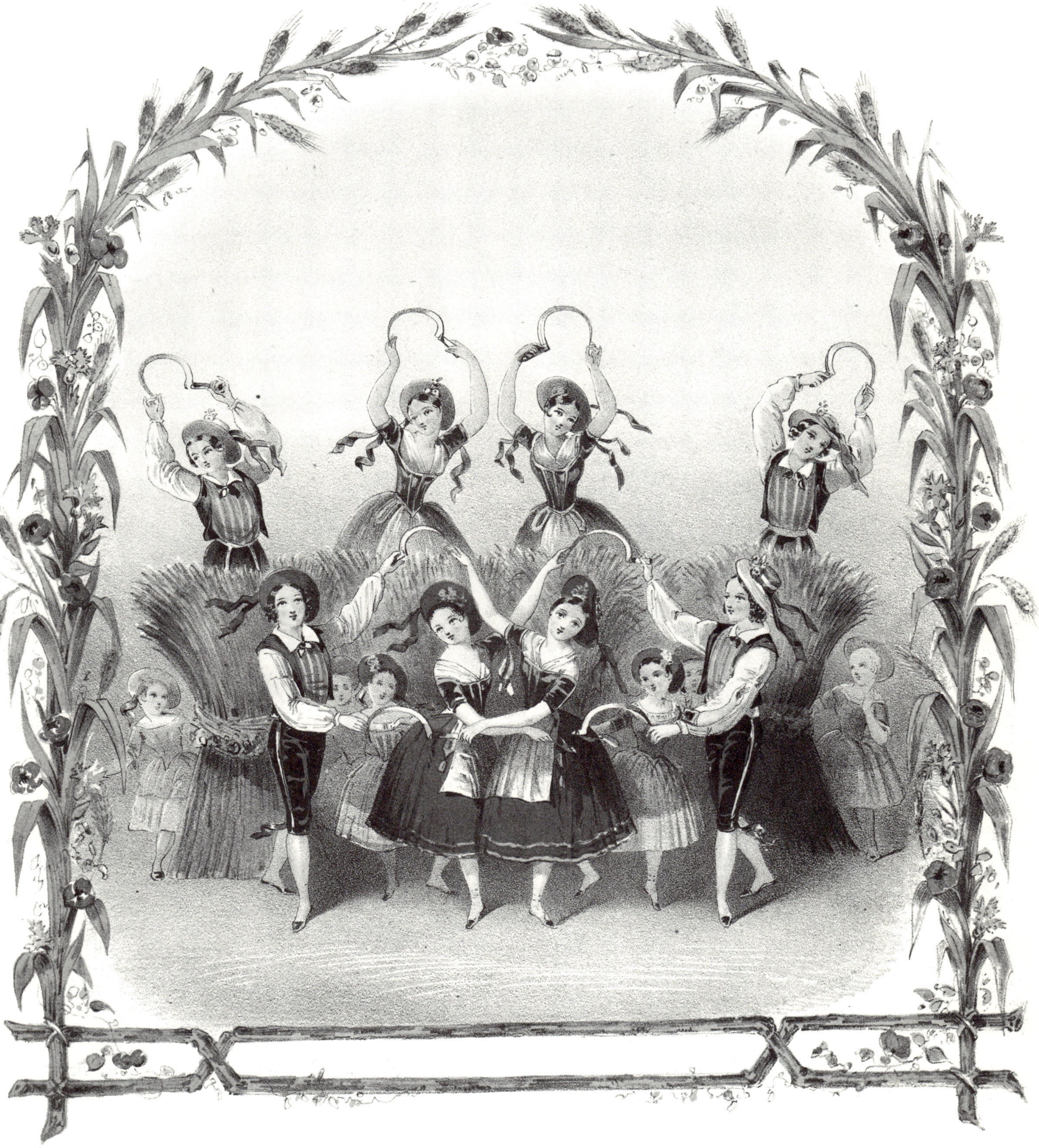

63. The Vienna Children in *The Harvest Dance*, ca. 1846.

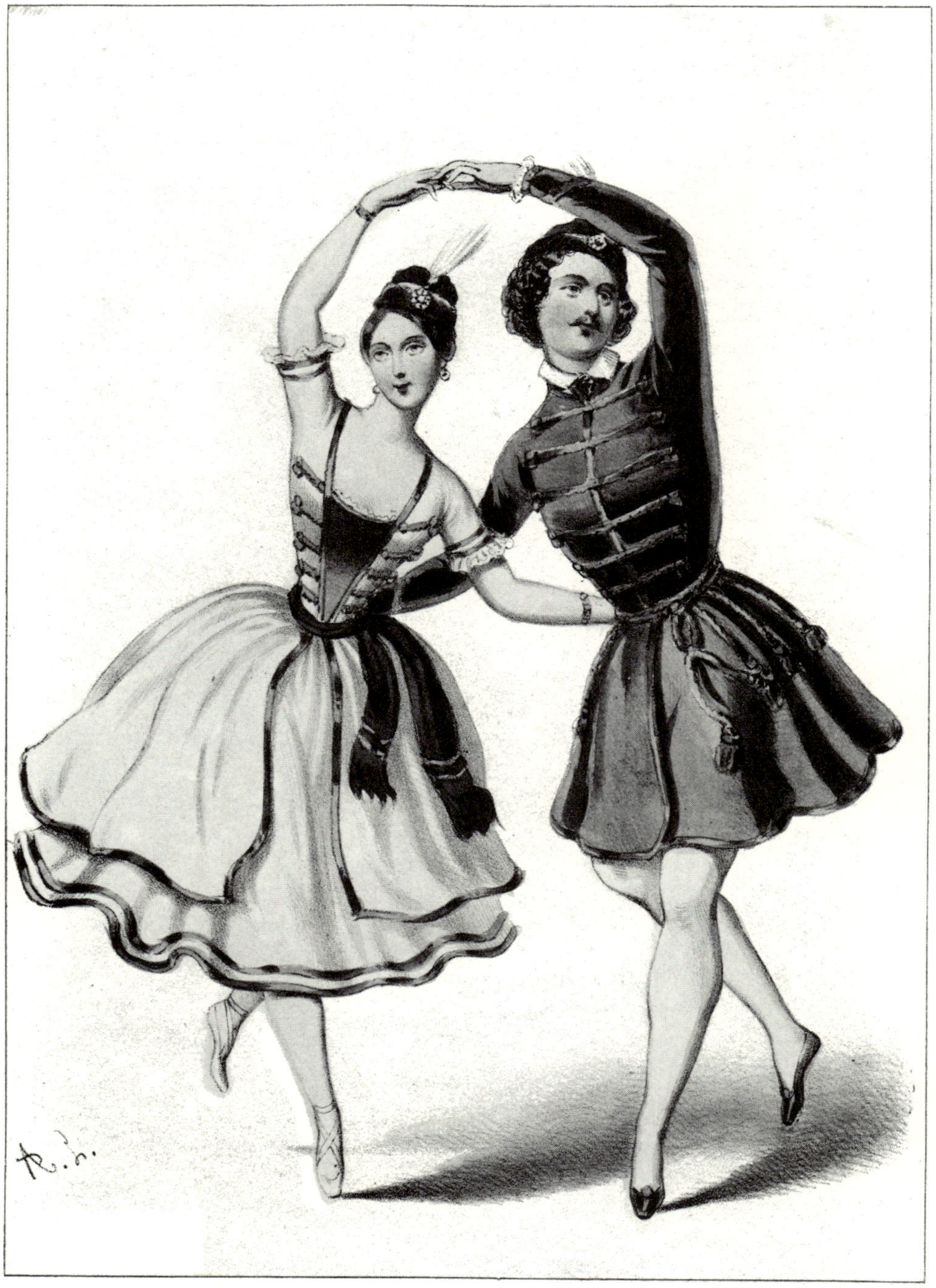

64. Sophie Dumilâtre and Michel-François Hoguet (Hoguet-Vestris) in *Le Diable à Quatre* (Opéra, Paris, 1845).

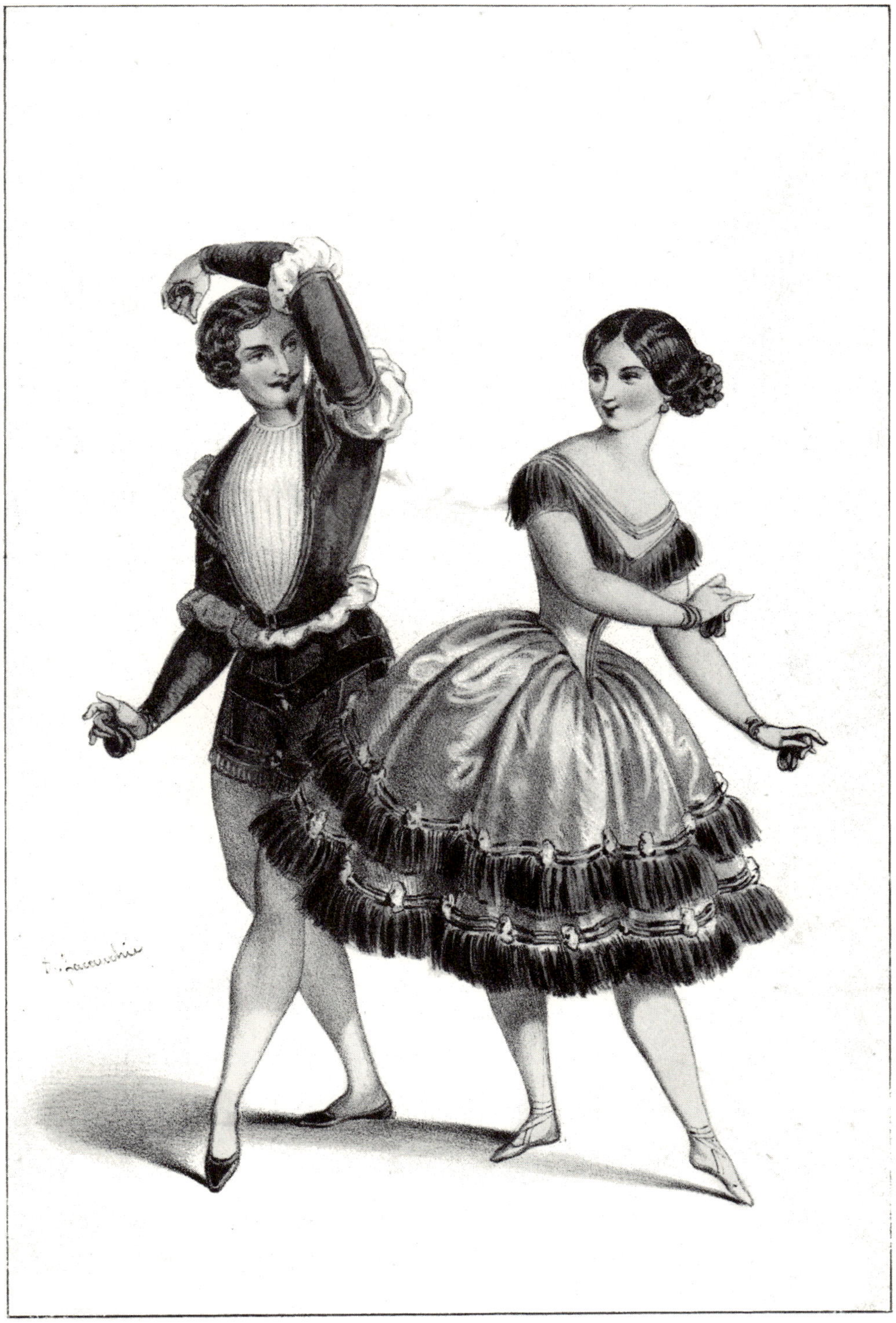

65. Arthur Saint-Léon and Fanny Cerrito in *La Fille de Marbre* (Opéra, Paris, 1847).

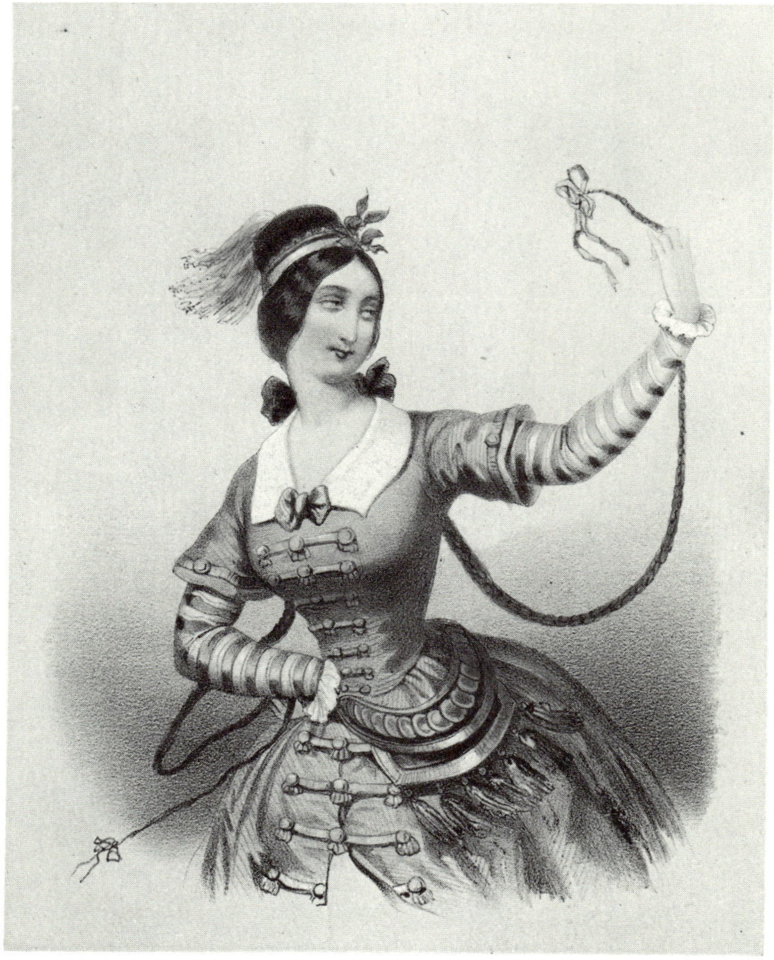

66. Adèle Dumilâtre in "La Polka" (Opéra, Paris, n.d.).

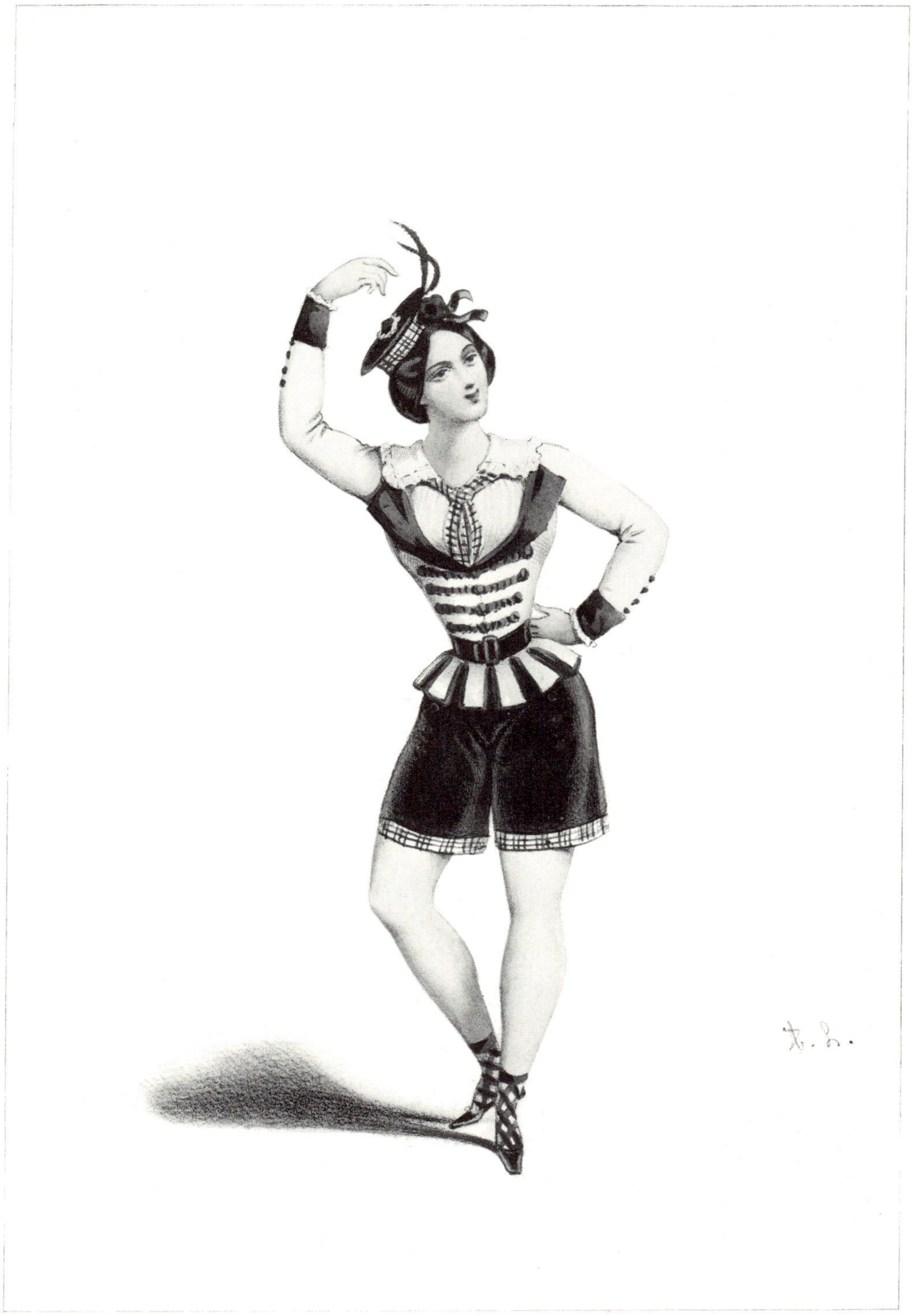

67. Zina Richard in *Trilby* (Théâtre de la Porte-Saint-Martin, Paris, 1846).

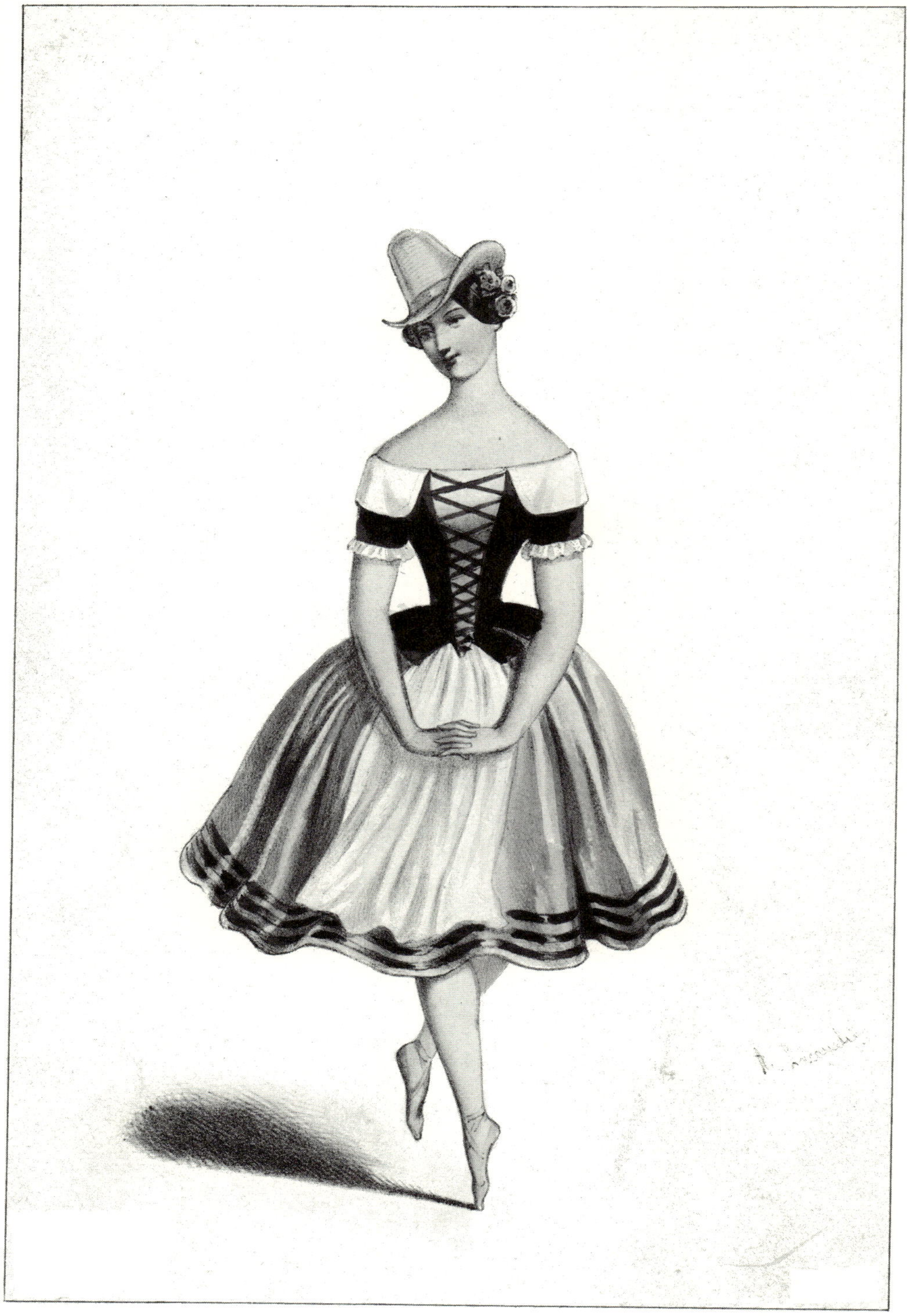

68. Sofia Fuoco in *Betty* (Opéra, Paris, 1846).

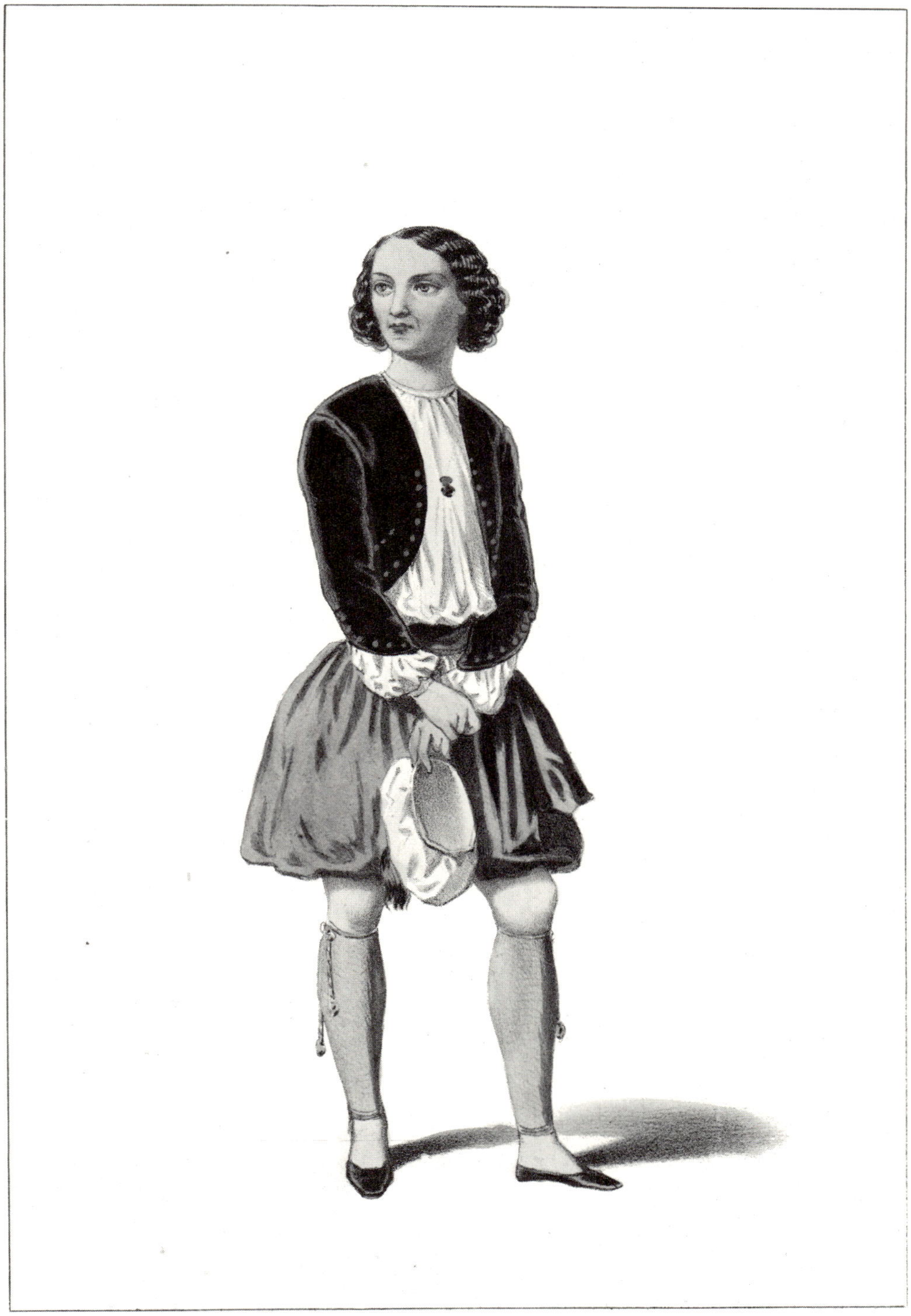

69. Jules Perrot in *La Filleule des fées* (Opéra, Paris, 1849).

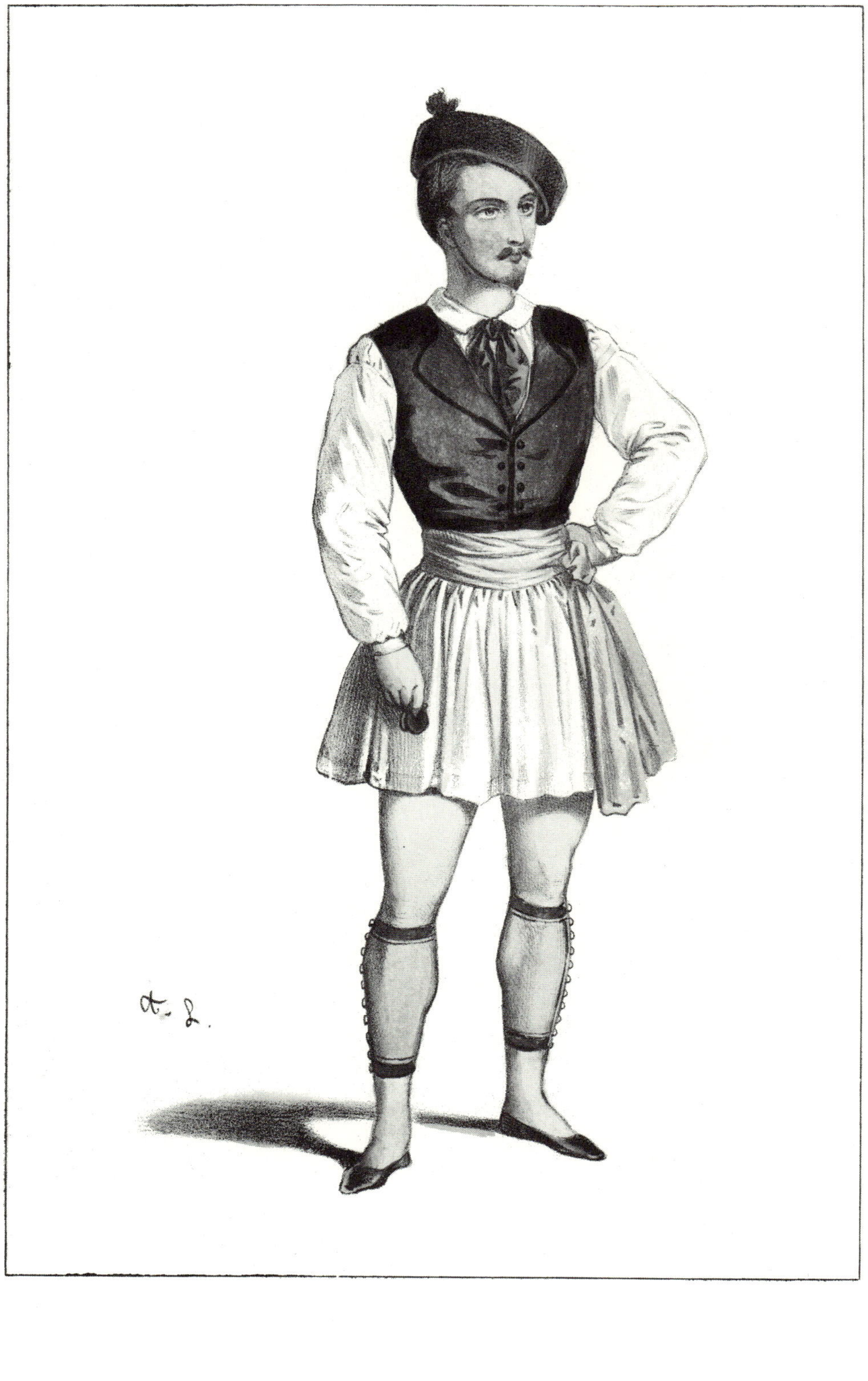

70. Arthur Saint-Léon in *Le Lutin de la vallée* (Théâtre Lyrique, Paris, 1853).

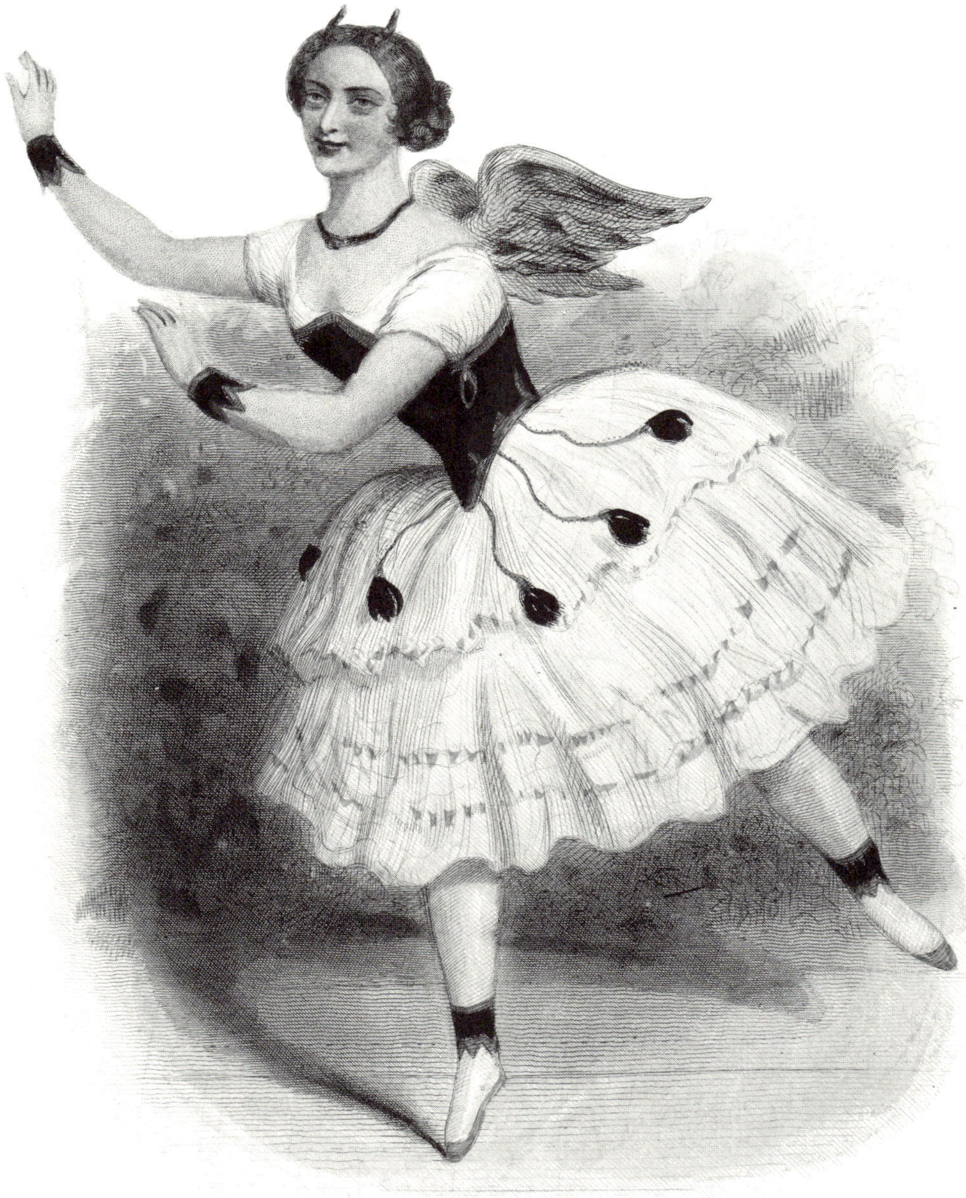

71. Fanny Cerrito in *Le Violon du Diable* (Opéra, Paris, 1849).

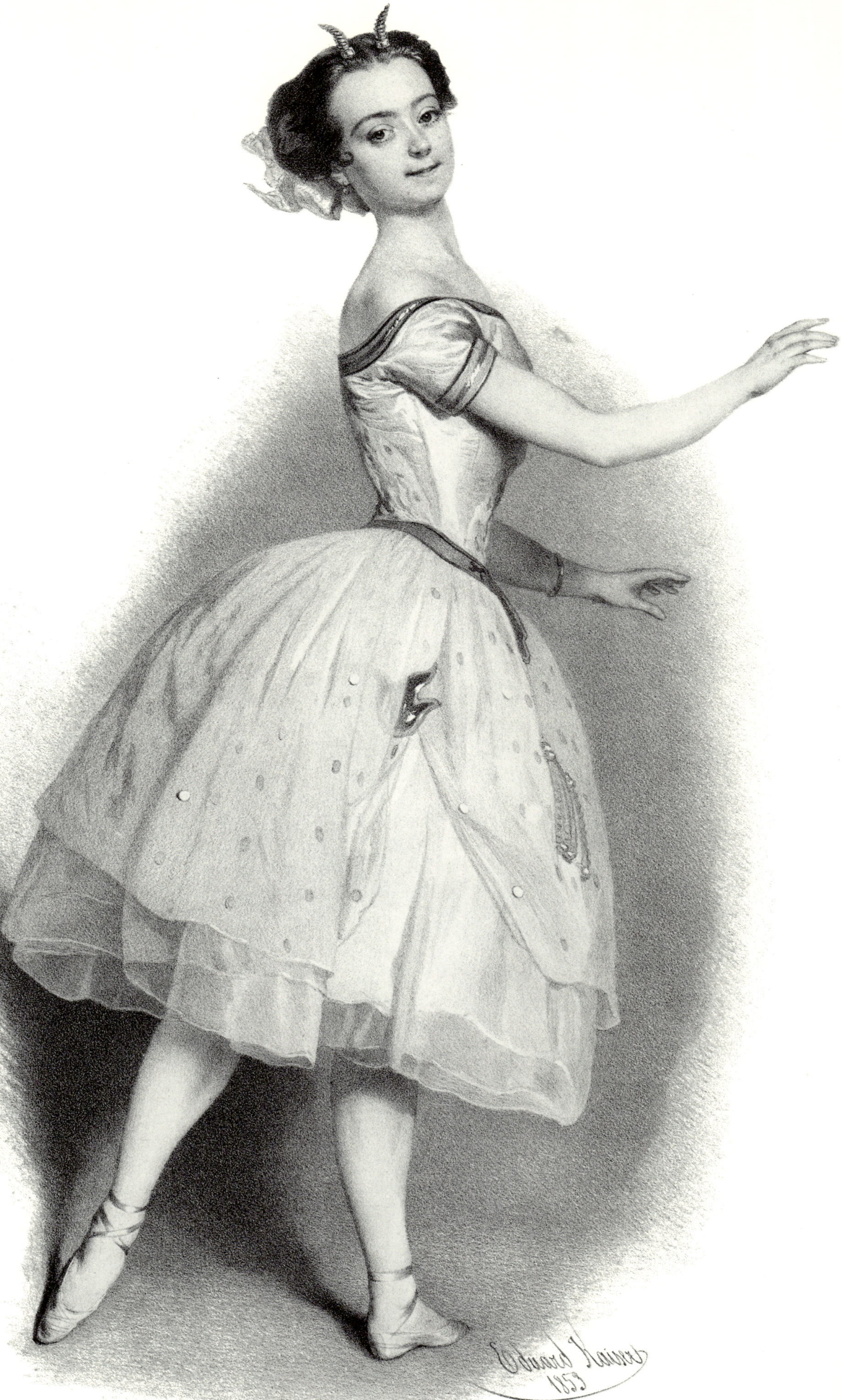

72. Marie Taglioni, the Younger, in *Satanella* (Opera House, Berlin, 1853).

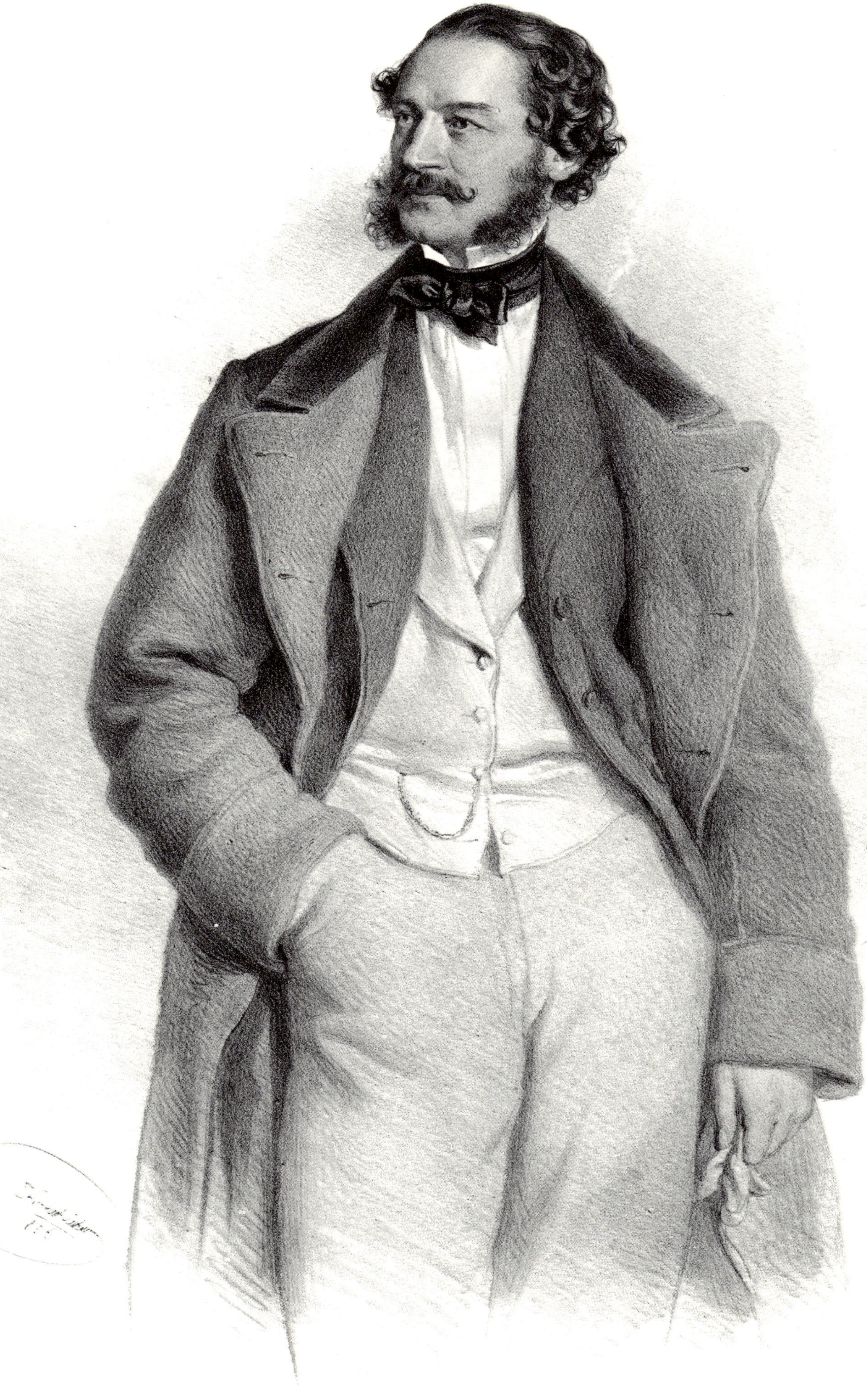

73. Paul Taglioni, portrait, Vienna, 1856.

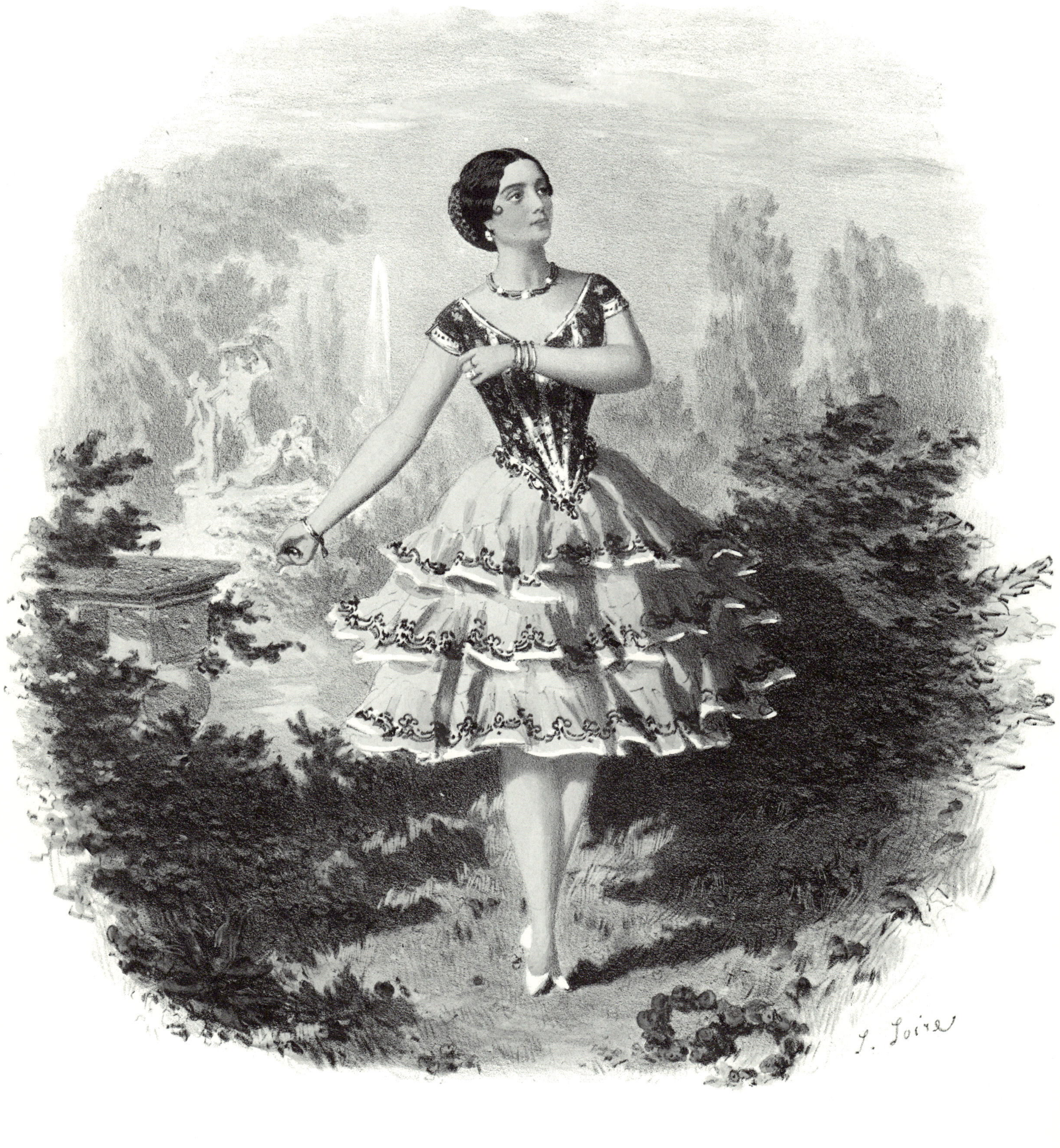

74. Pepita de Oliva, Paris, ca. 1855.

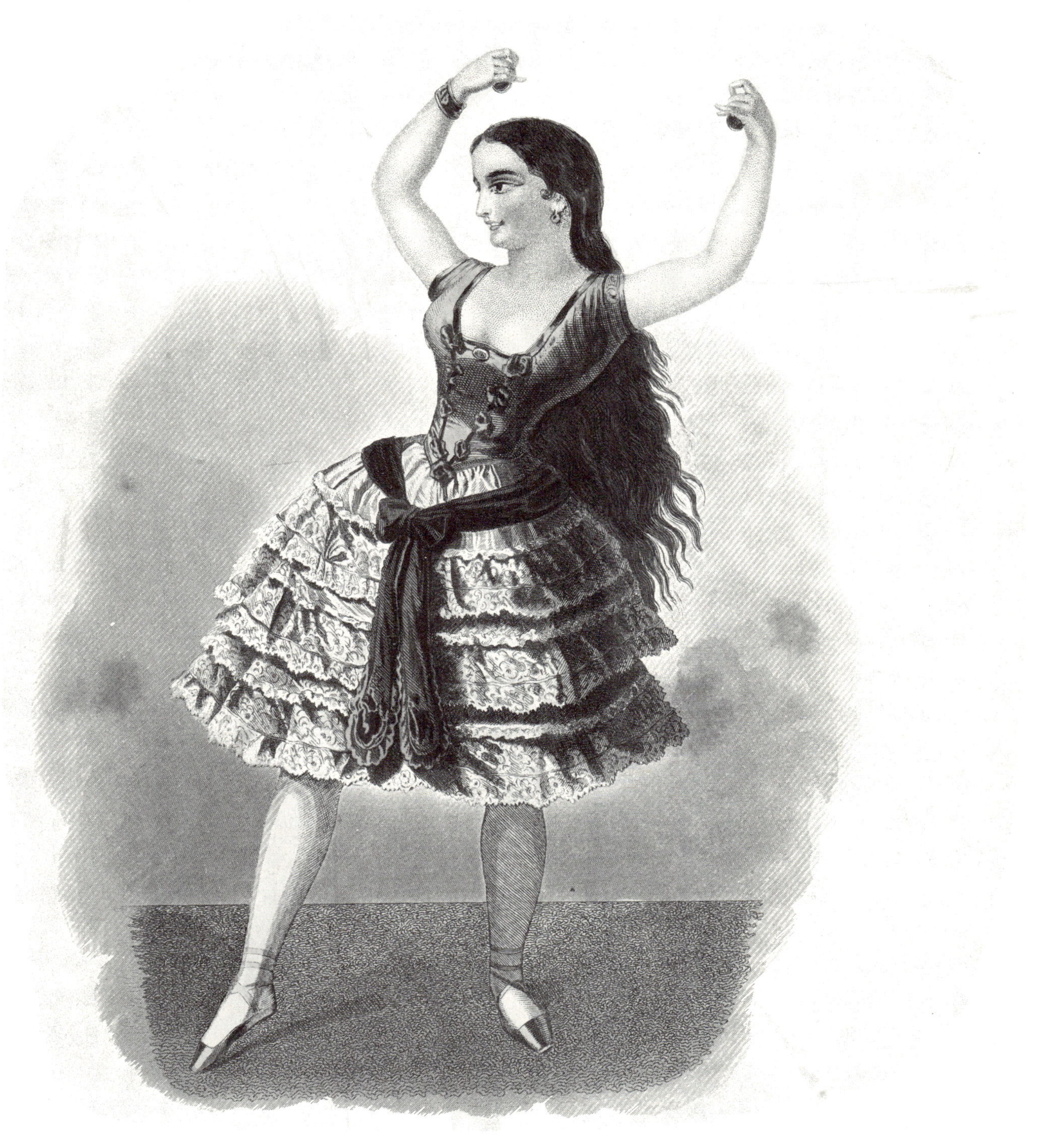

75. Pepita de Oliva, Vienna, 1851.

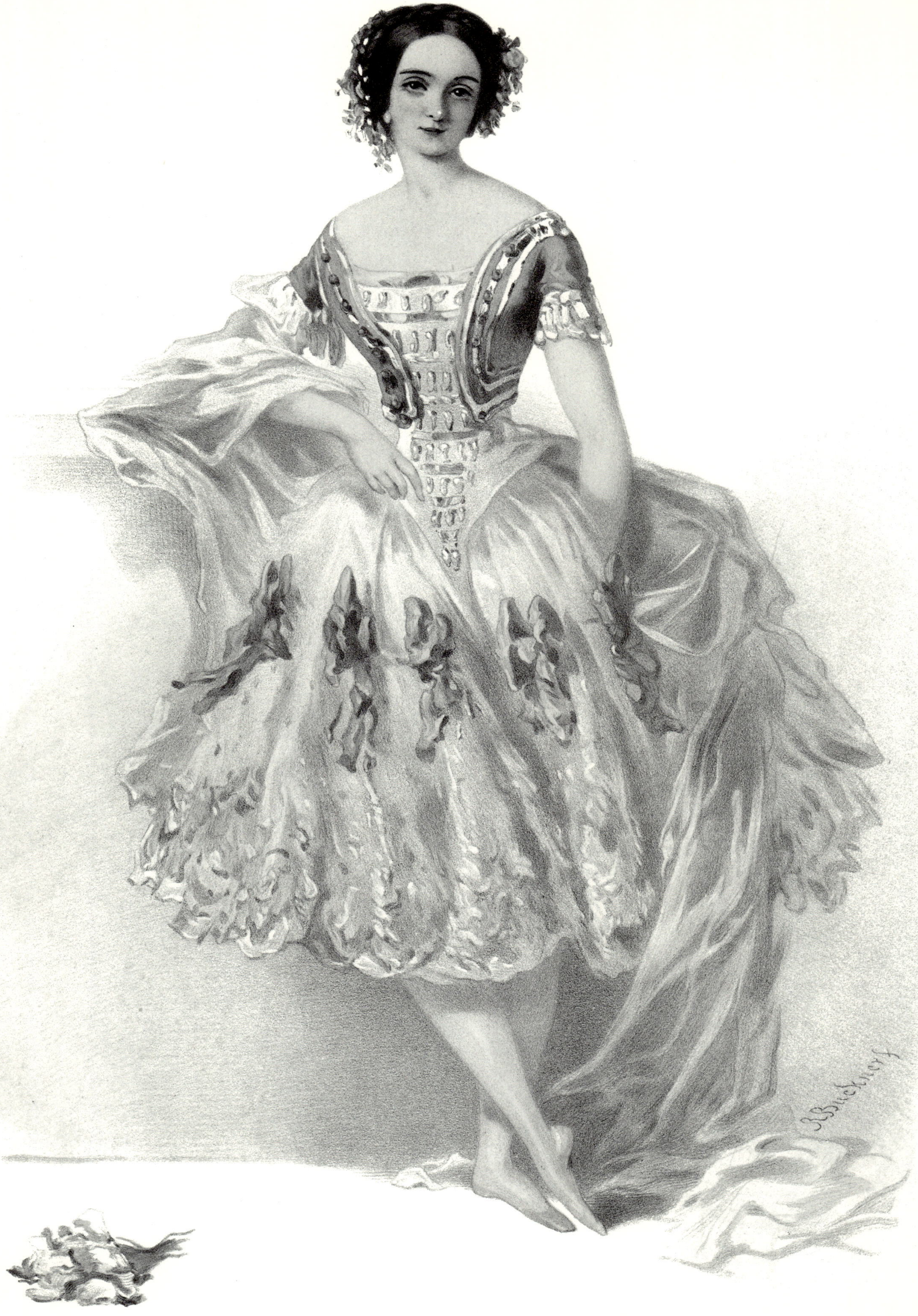

76. Adeline Plunkett, portrait, London 1854.

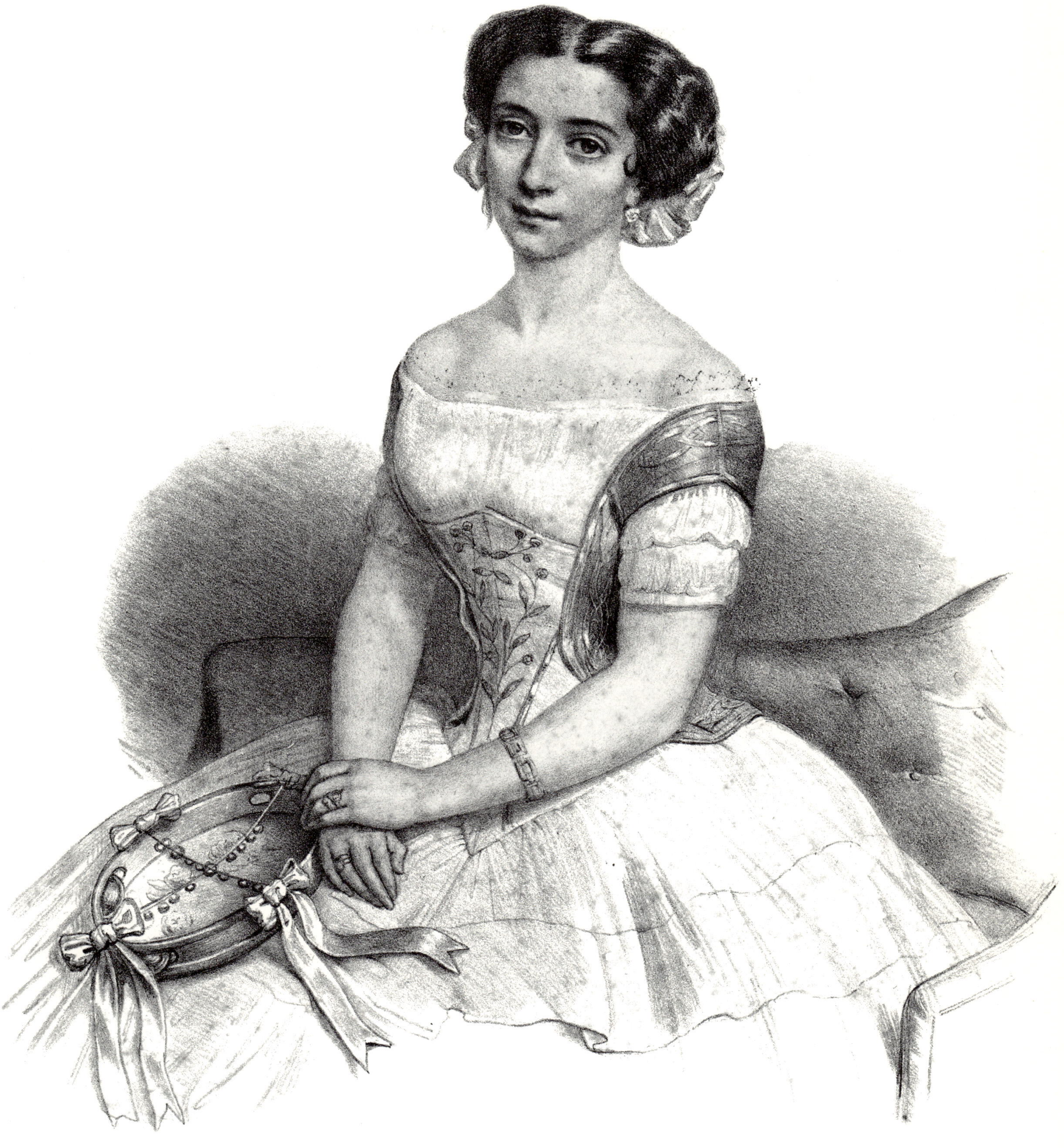

77. Amalia Ferraris, portrait, Rome, 1854.

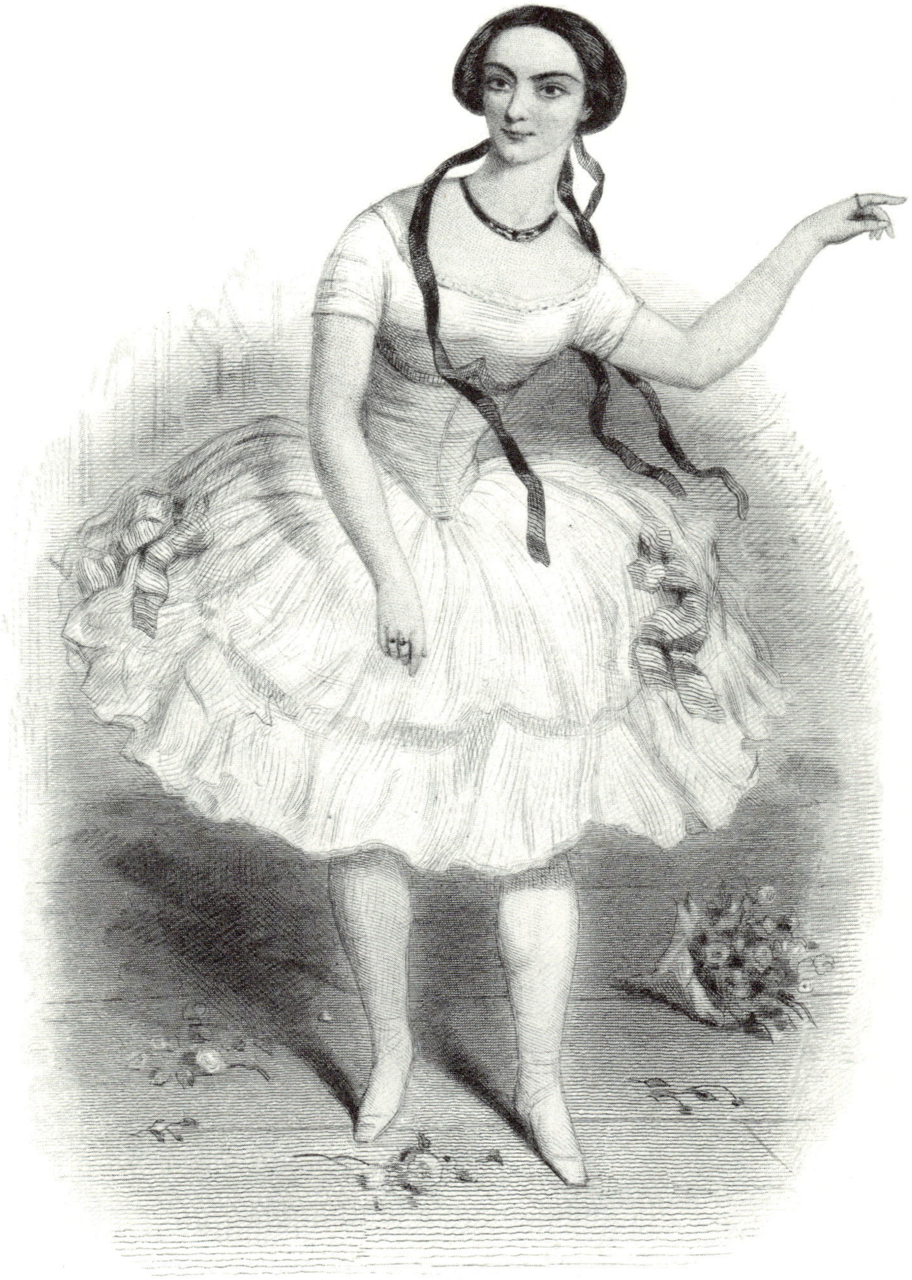

78. Carolina Rosati in *La Fonti* (Opéra, Paris, 1855).

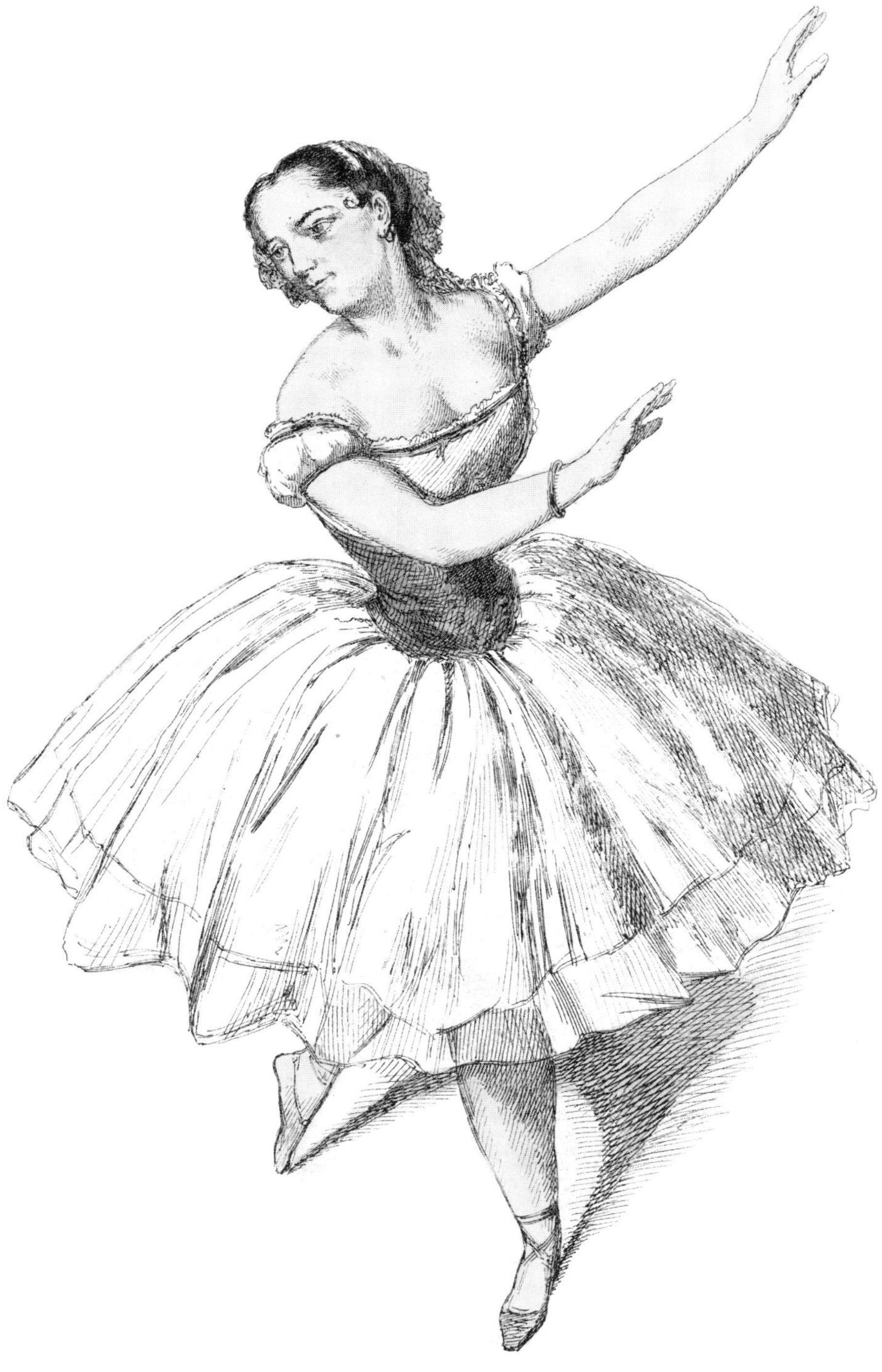

79. Catarina Beretta, portrait, 1855.

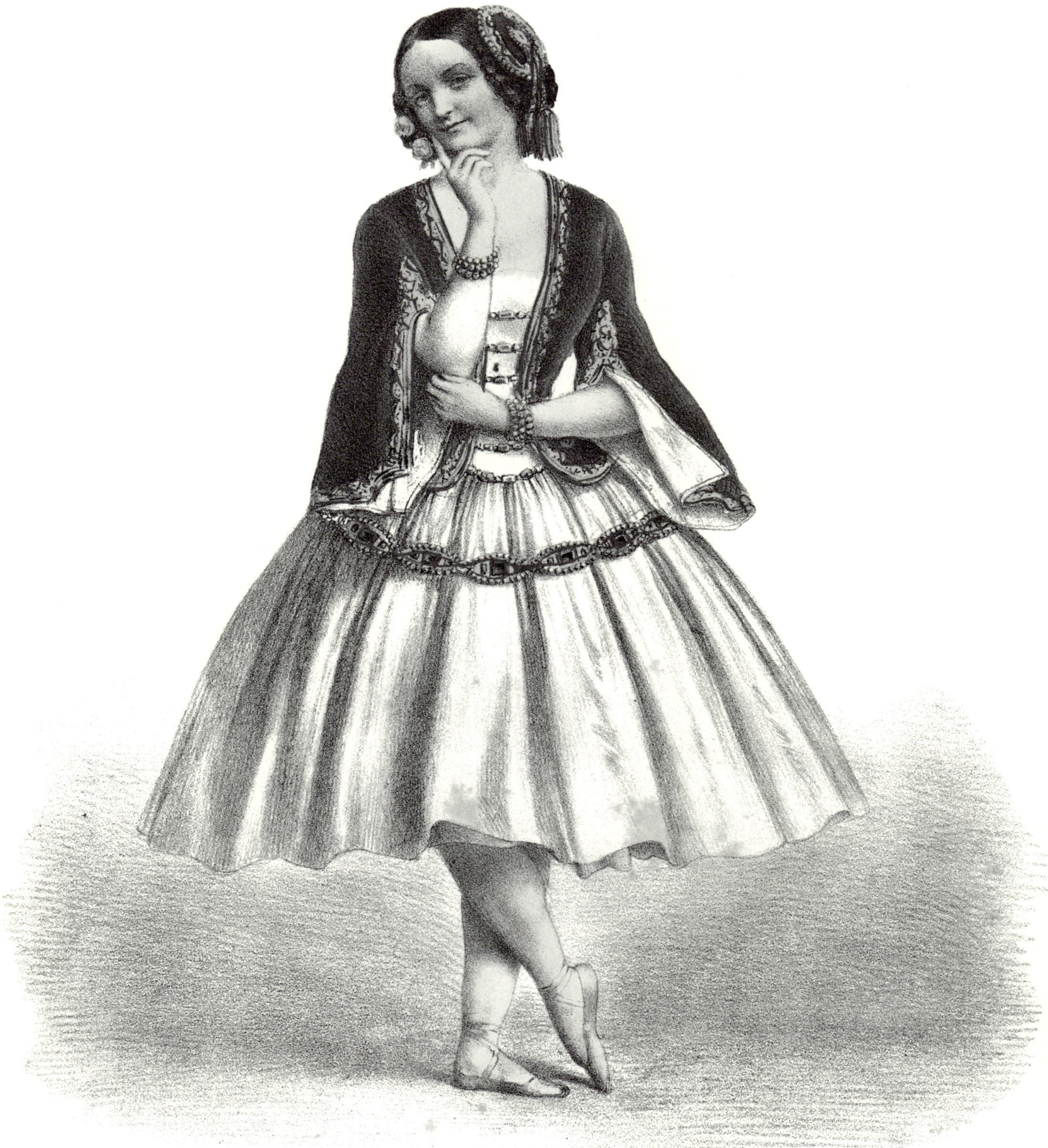

80. Carolina Rosati in *Le Corsaire* (Opéra, Paris, 1856).

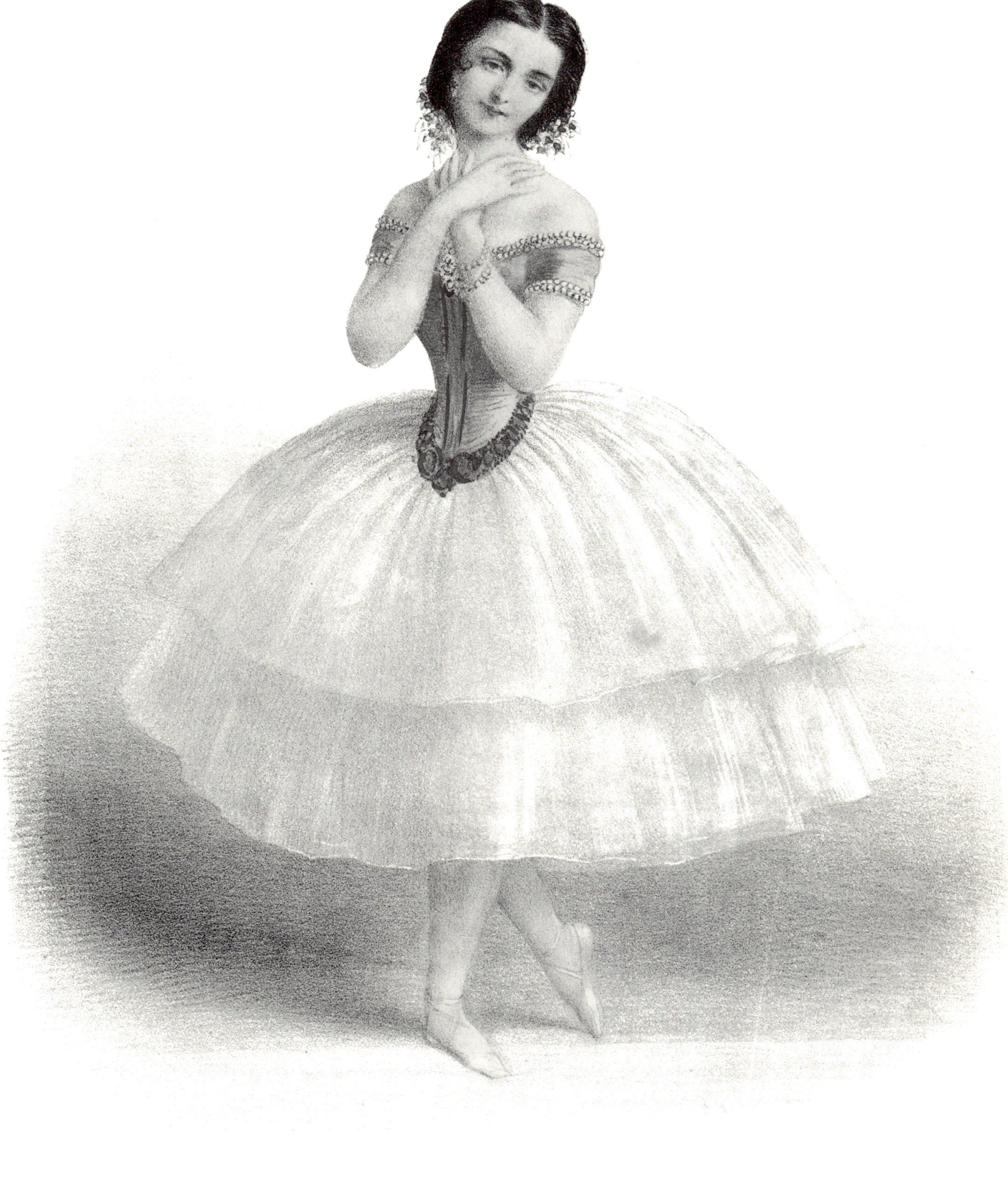

81. Amalia Ferraris in *Les Elfes* (Opéra, Paris, 1856).

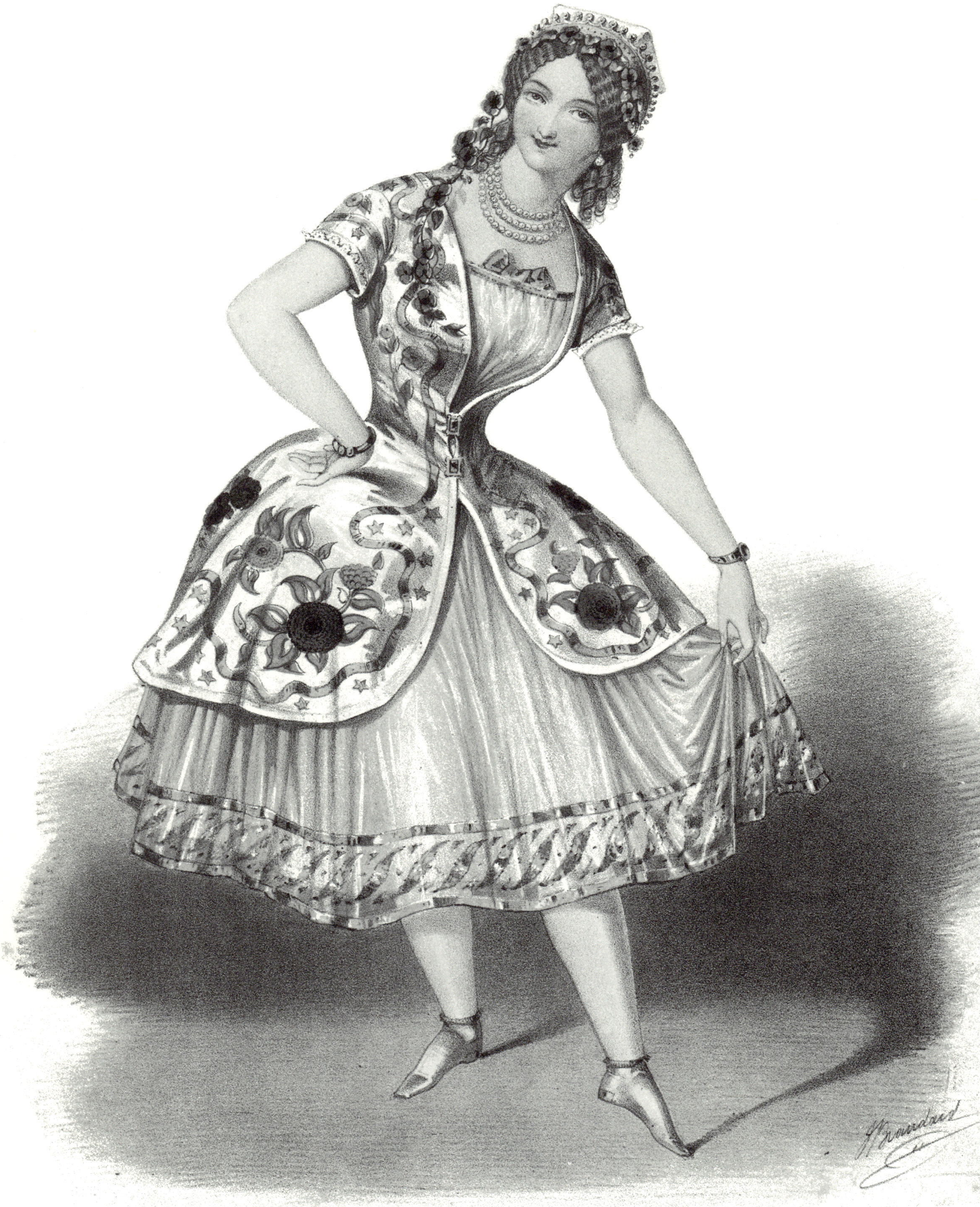

82. Elena Andreianova in *Pietro il Grande* (Covent Garden, London, 1852 revival).

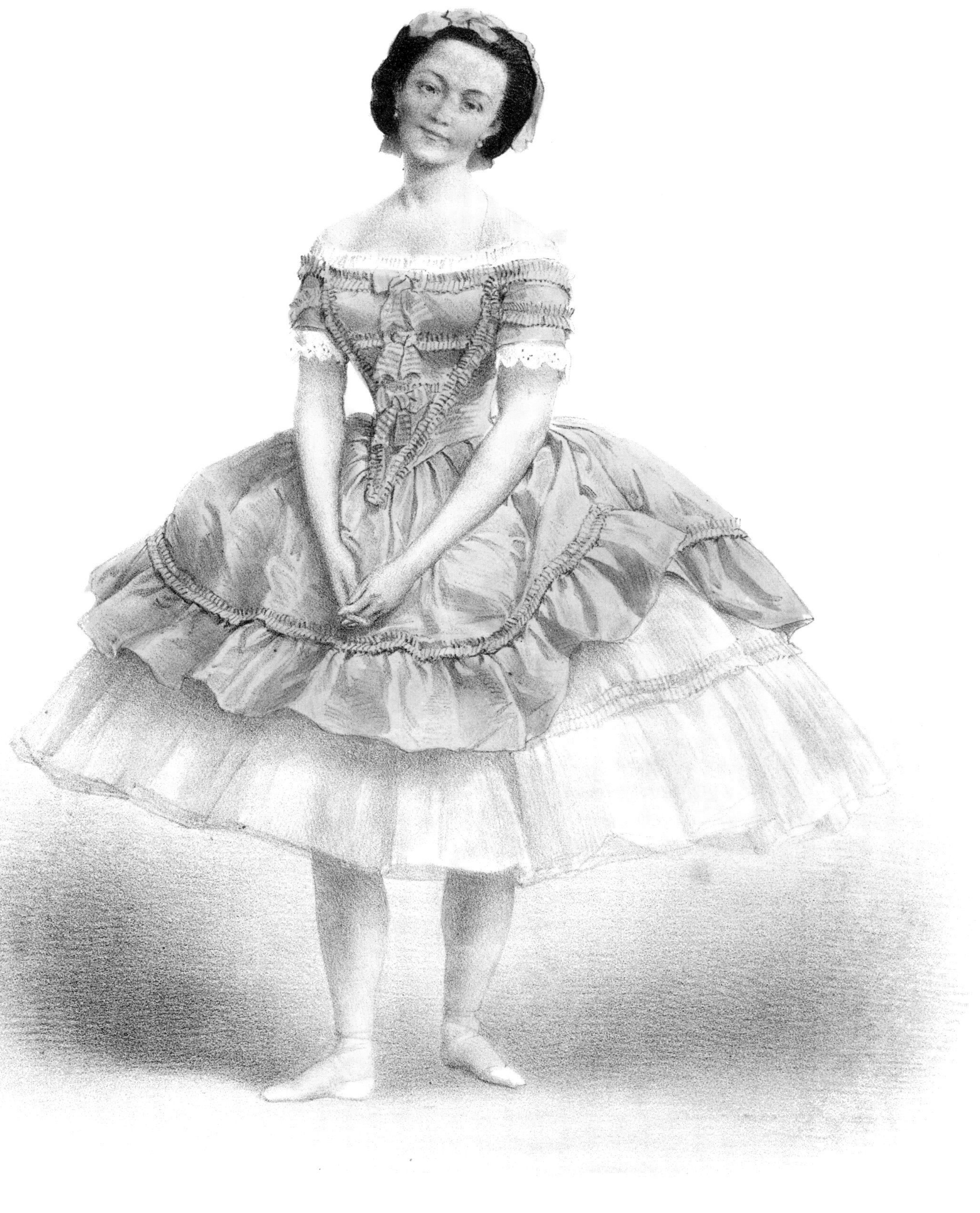

83. Zina Richard in *Marco Spada, ou la Fille du bandit* (Opéra, Paris, 1857).

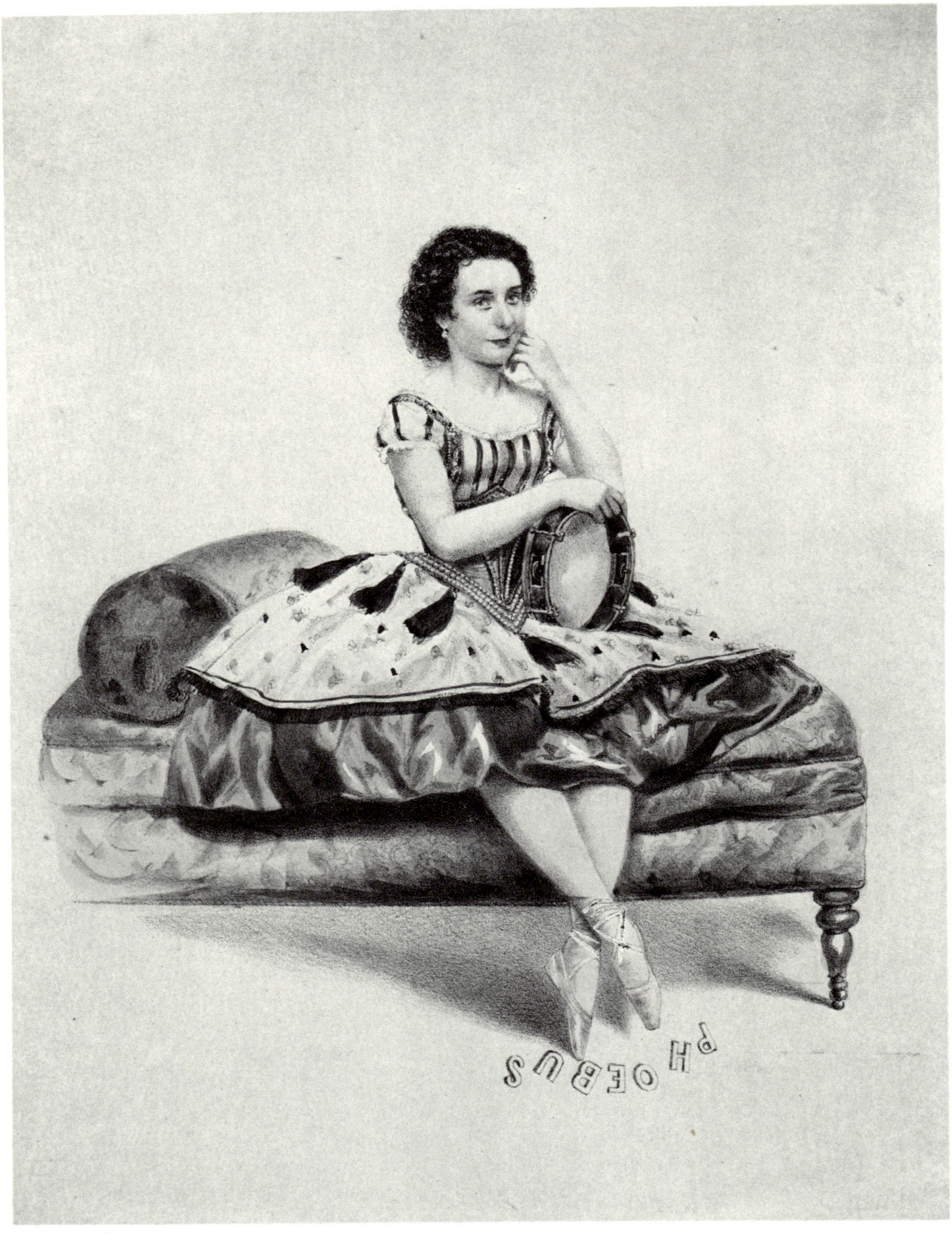

84. Nadezhda Bogdanova in *La Esmeralda* (Court Theatre, St. Petersburg, 1859 revival).

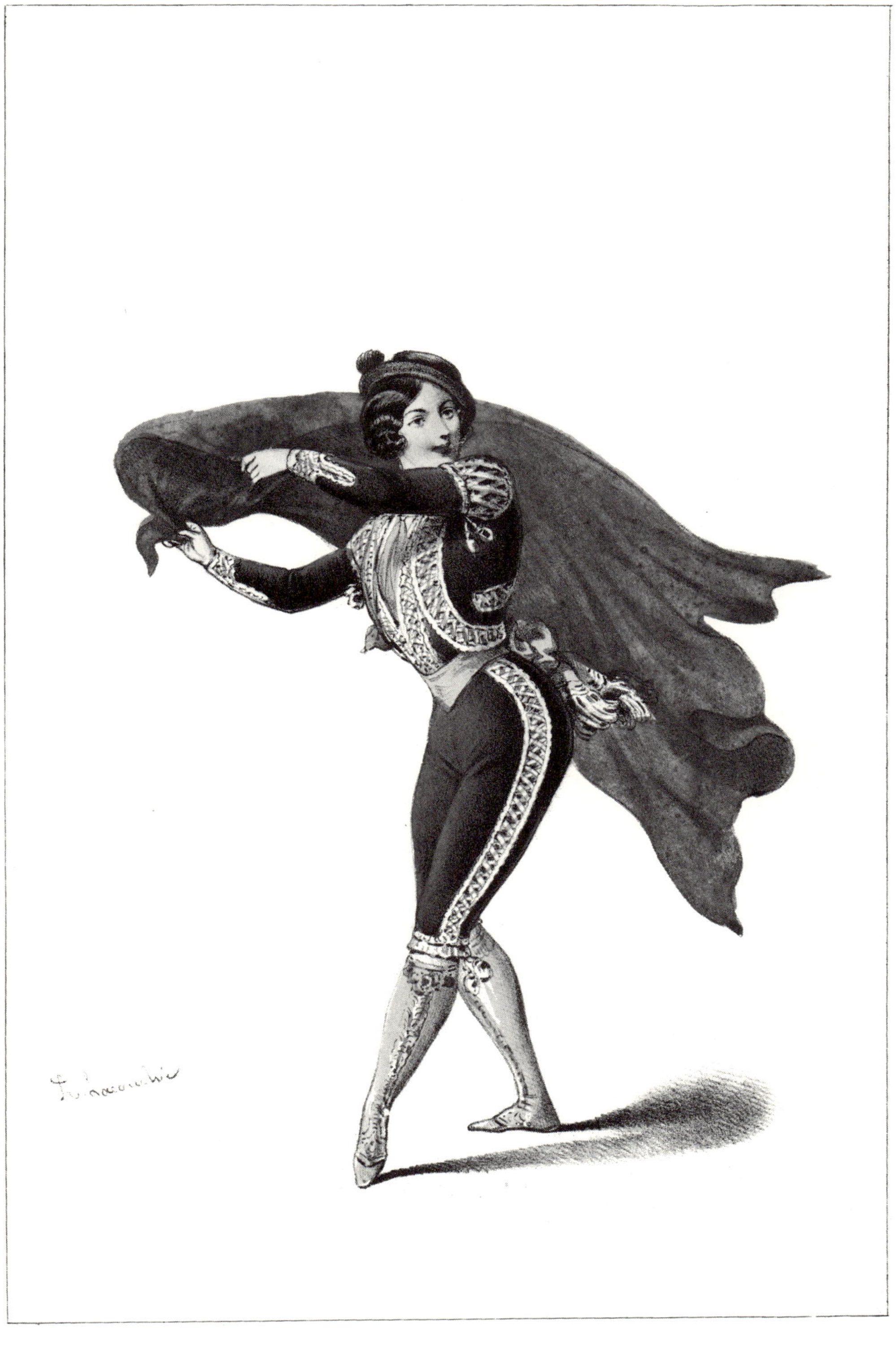

85. Caroline Lassiat (later Mme Dominique) in *Paquita* (Opéra, Paris, 1846).

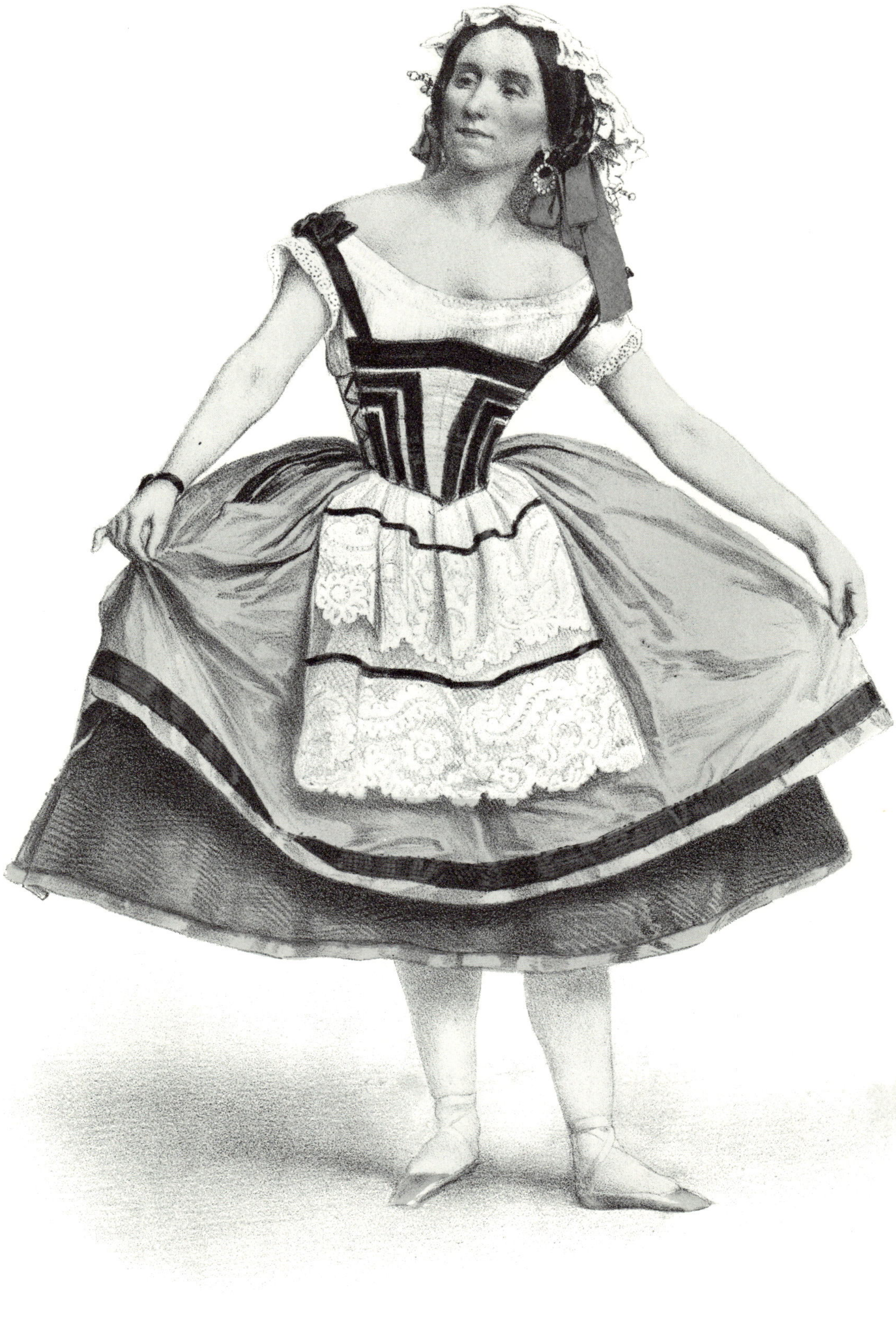

86. Célestine Emarot in *Guillaume Tell* (revival, Opéra, Paris, n.d.).

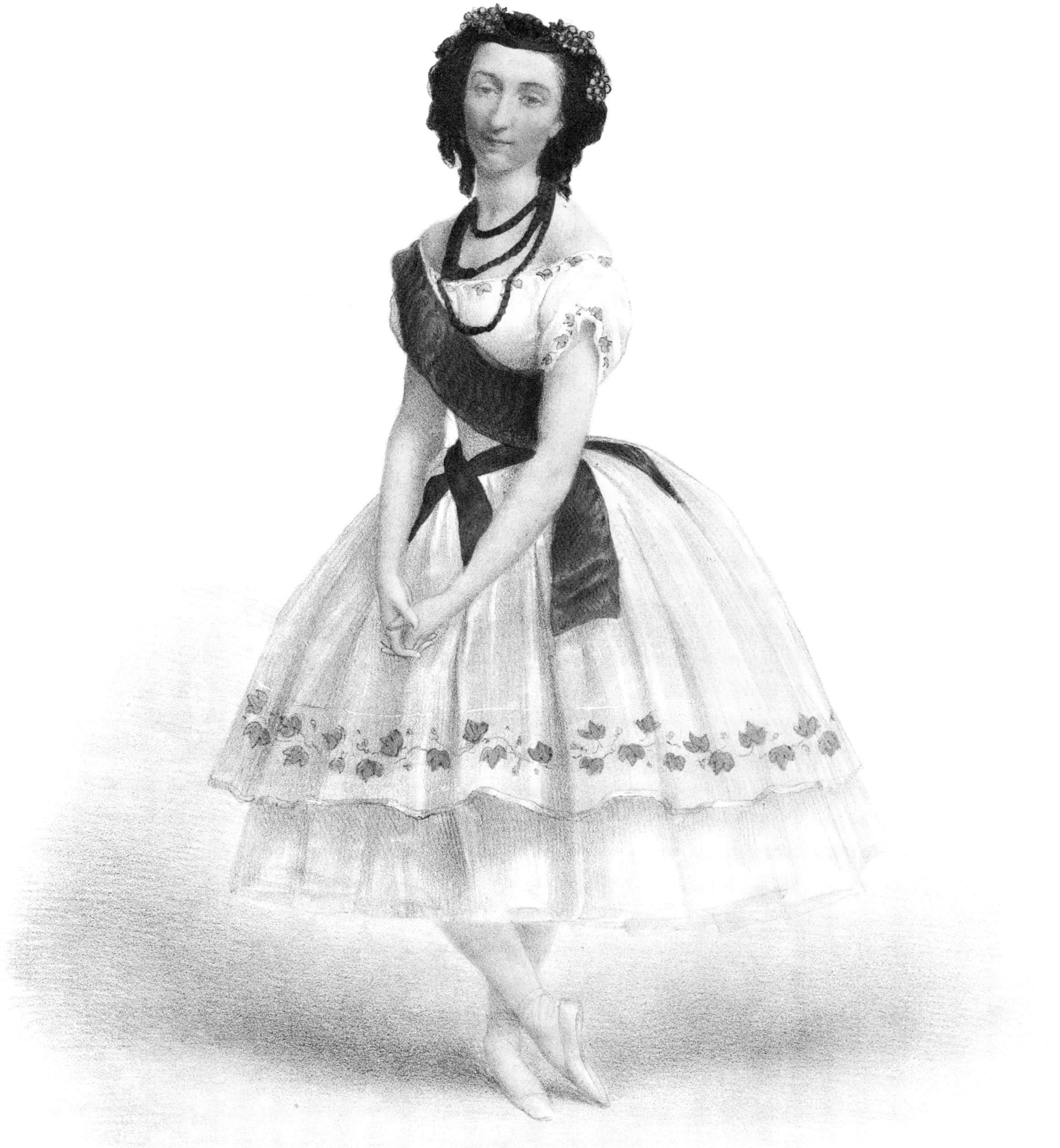

87. Emma Livry in *Herculanum* (Opéra, Paris, 1859).

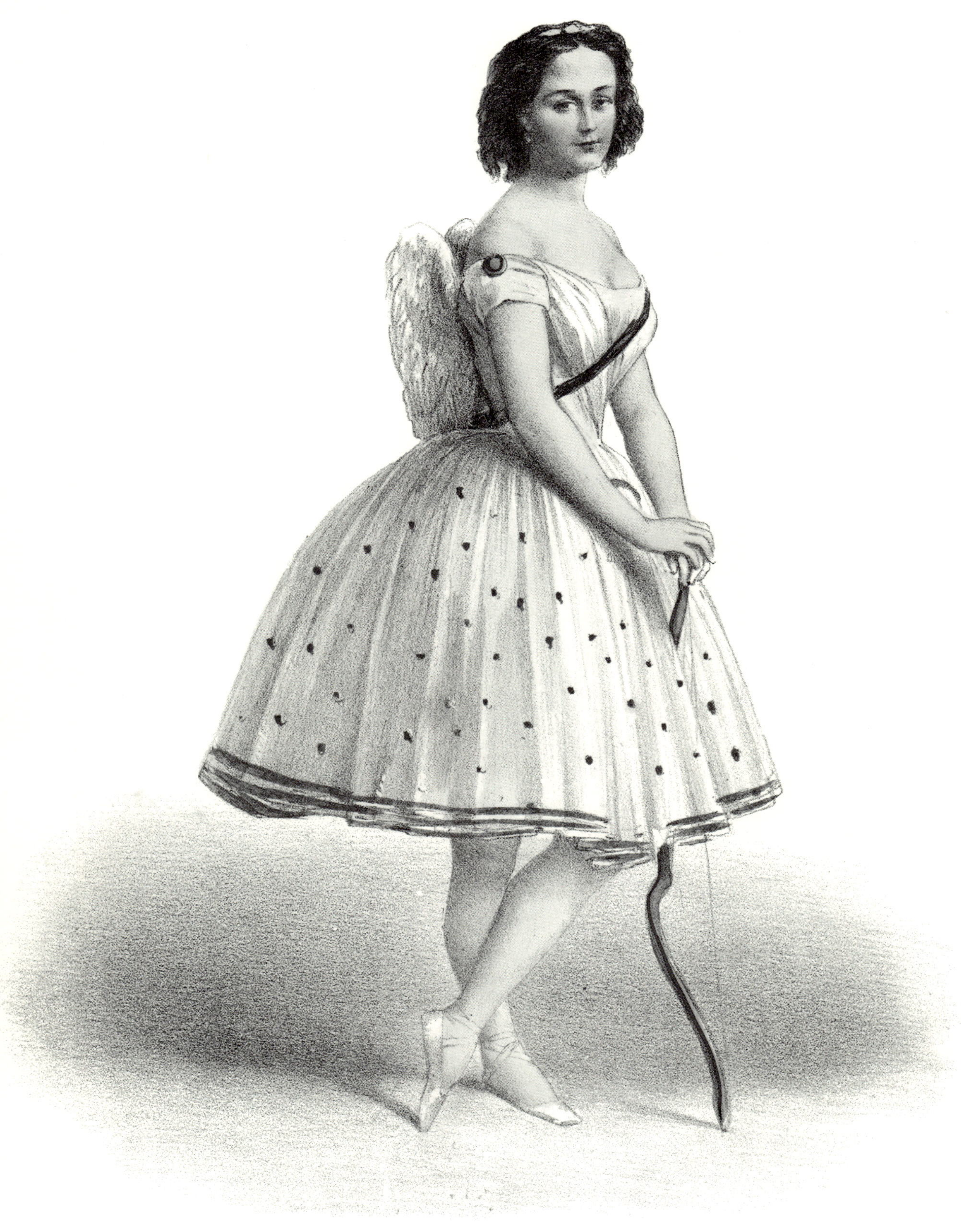

88. Eugénie Fiocre in *Pierre de Médicis* (Opéra, Paris, 1860).

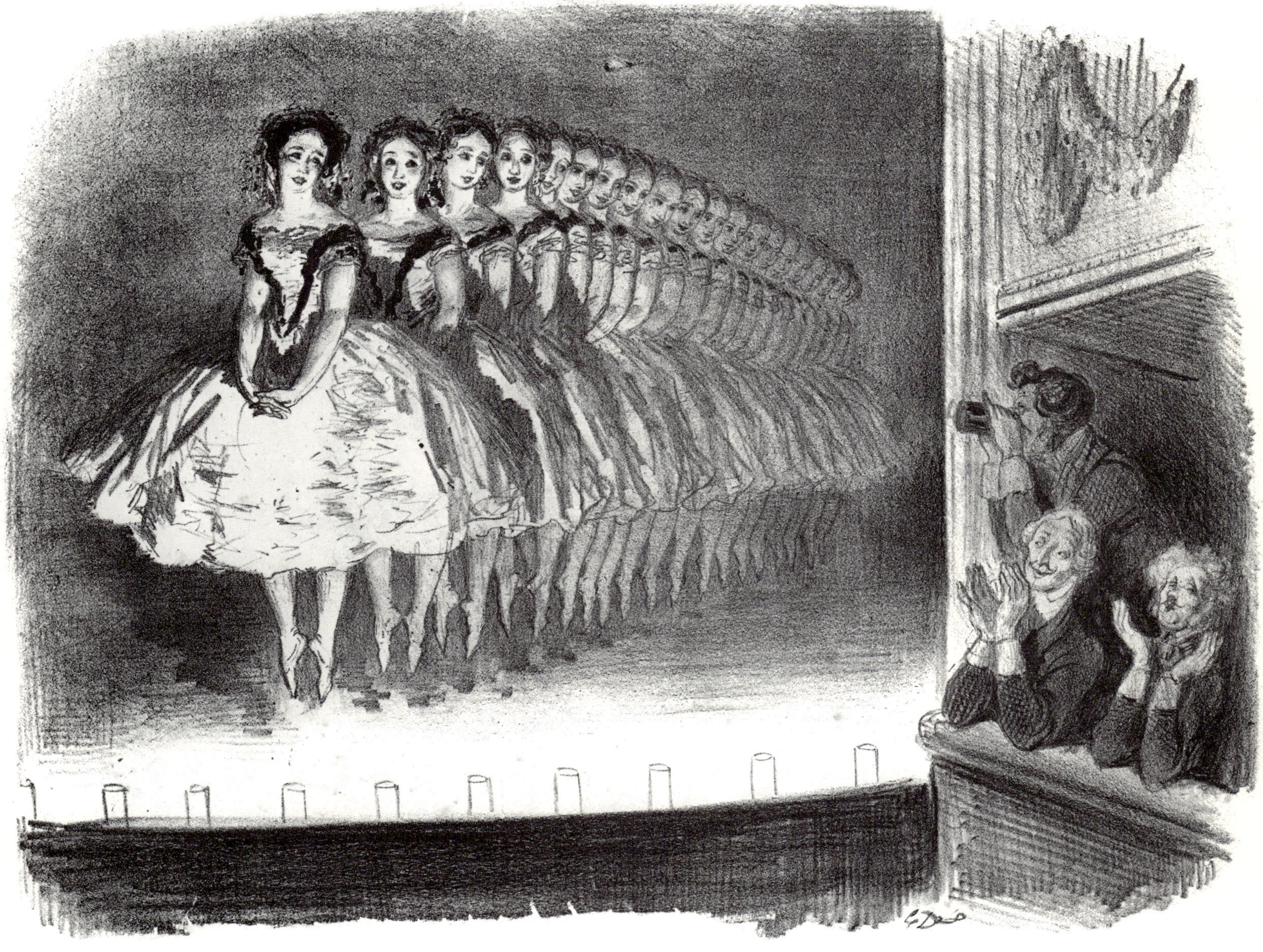

89. "Rats d'opéra," Paris, 1854.

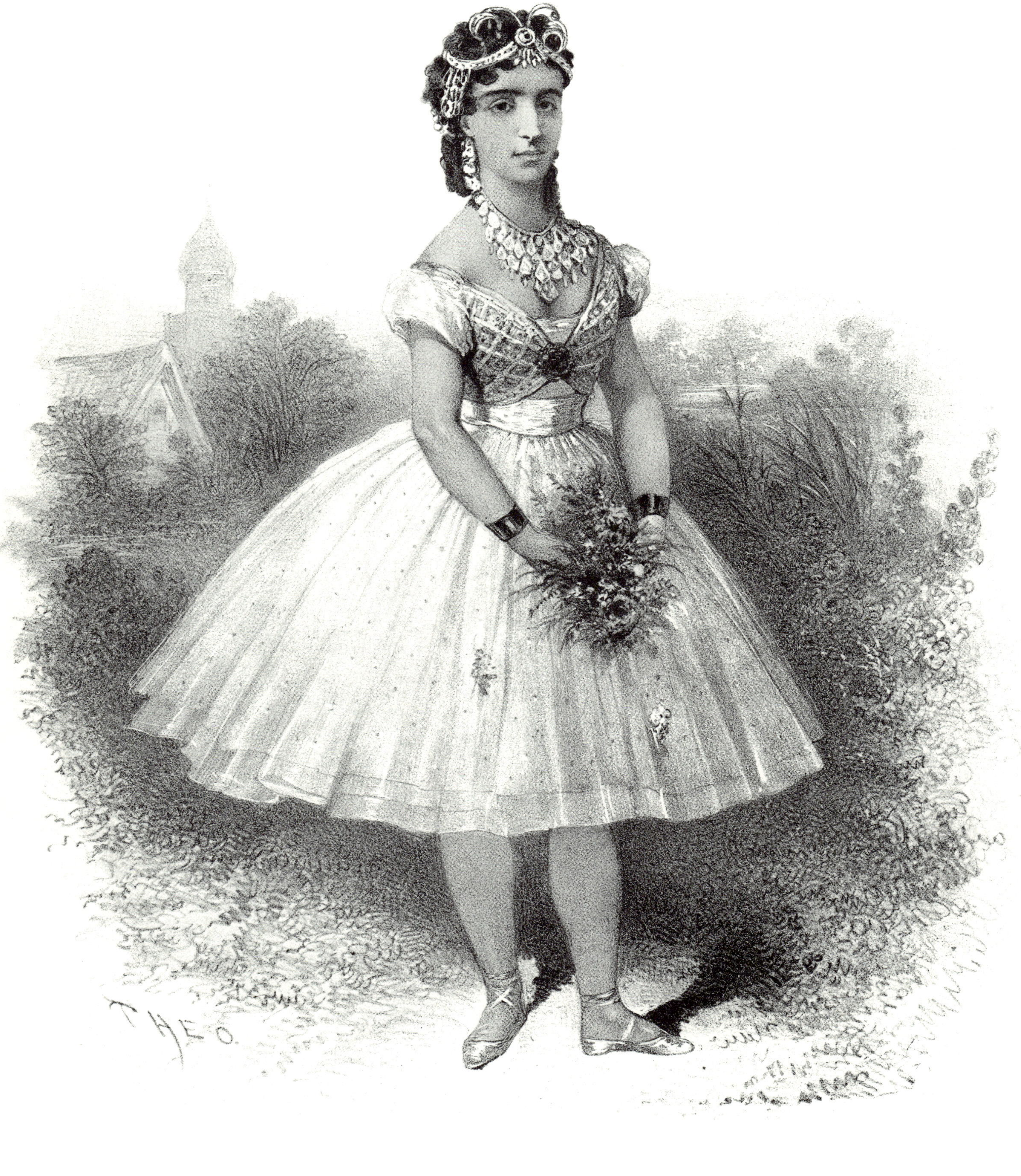

90. Giuseppina Bozzacchi in *Coppélia* (Opéra, Paris, 1870).

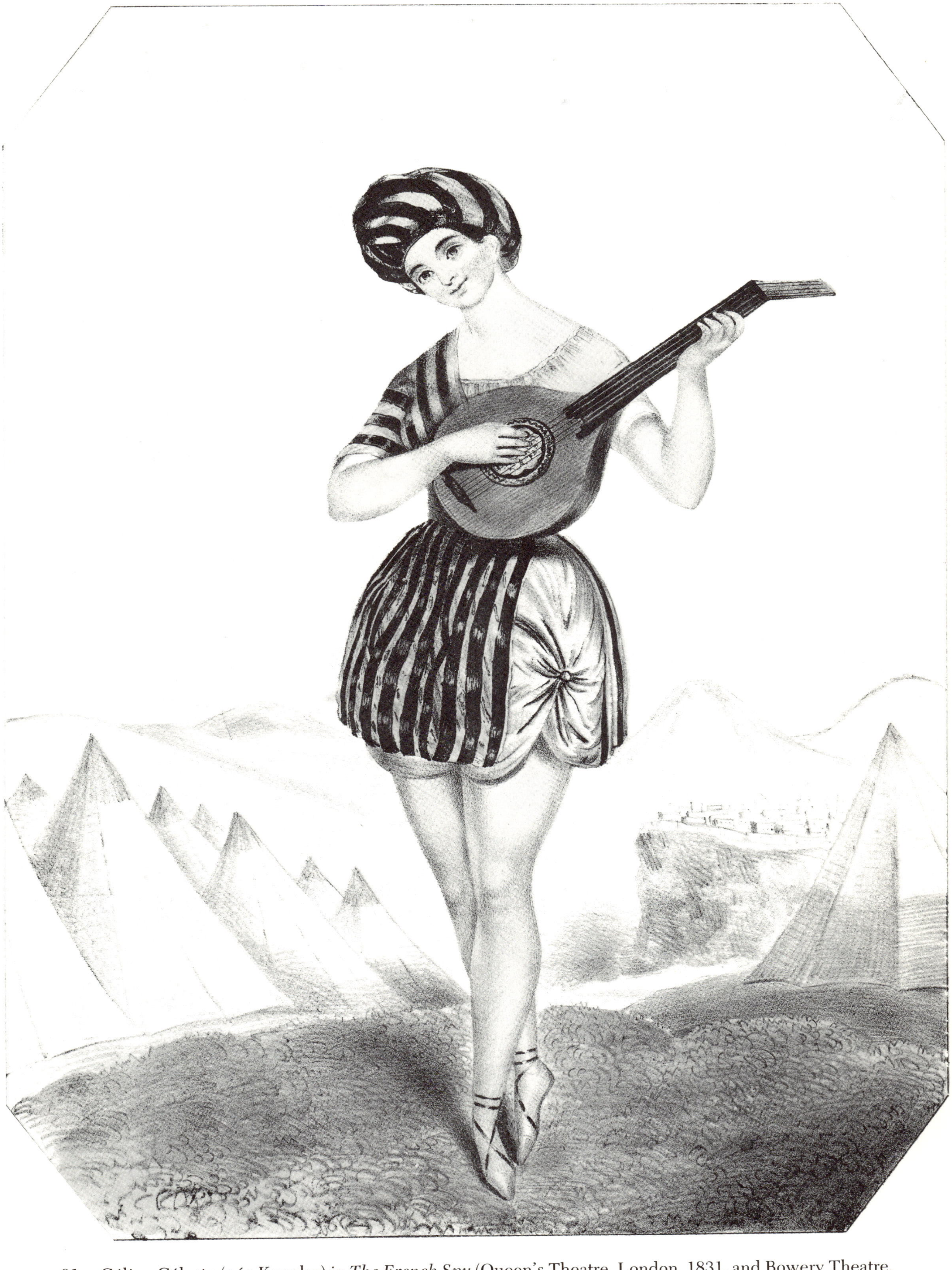

91. Céline Céleste (née Keppler) in *The French Spy* (Queen's Theatre, London, 1831, and Bowery Theatre, N.Y., 1834).

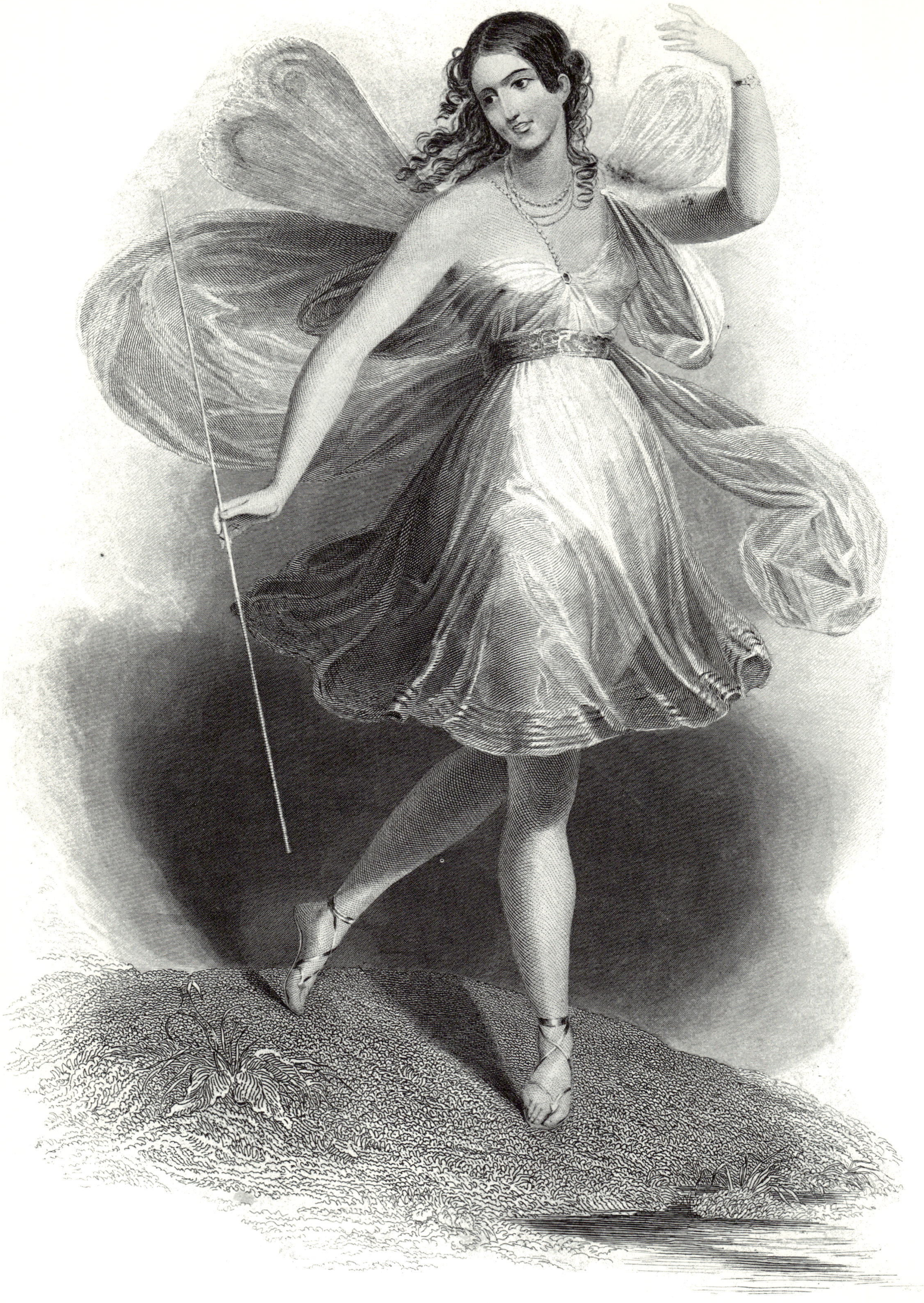

92. Mlle Augusta (née Fuchs) in *La Sylphide* (Park Theatre, N.Y., 1838).

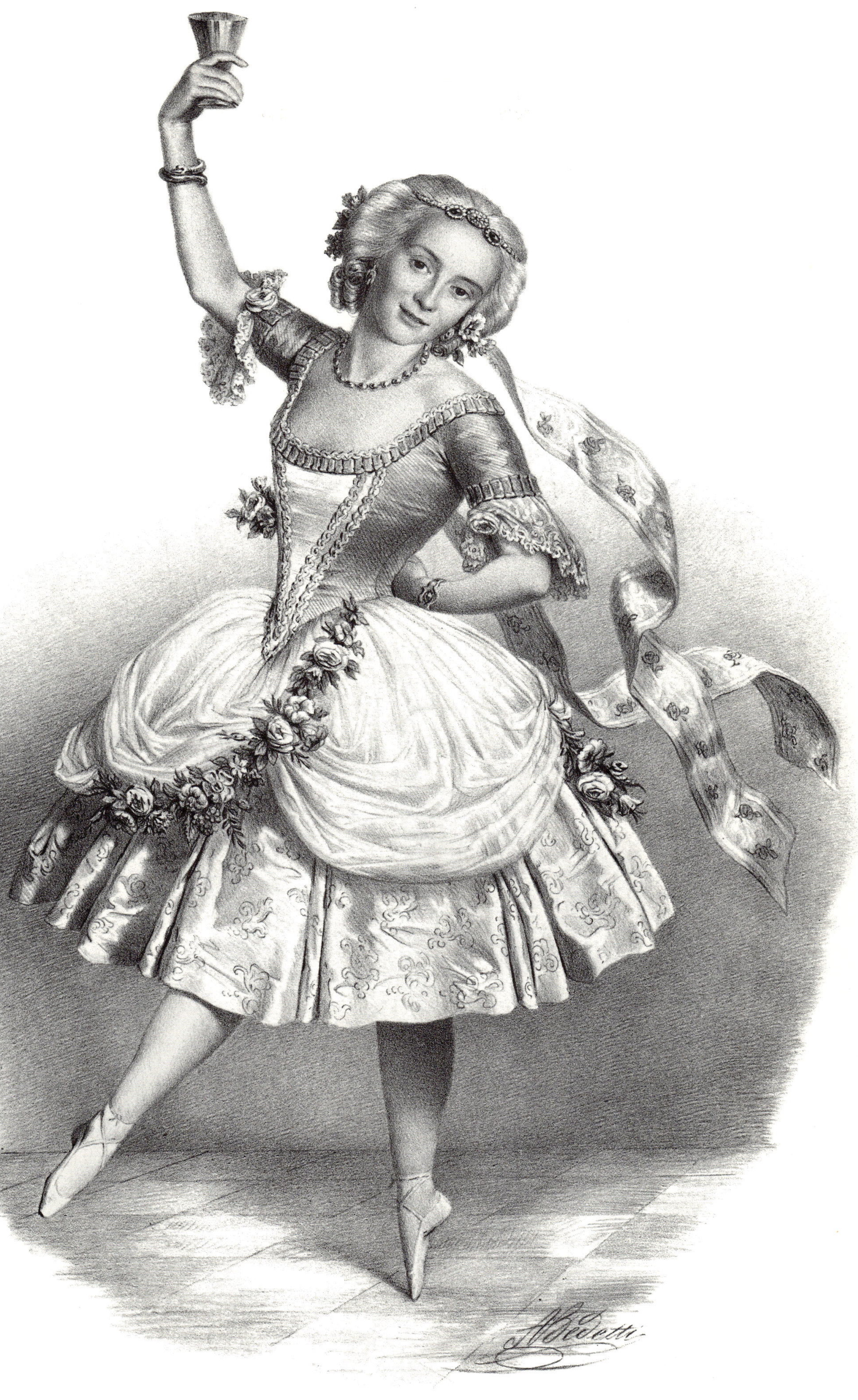

93. Augusta Maywood in *Rita Gauthier* (Ancona, 1856).

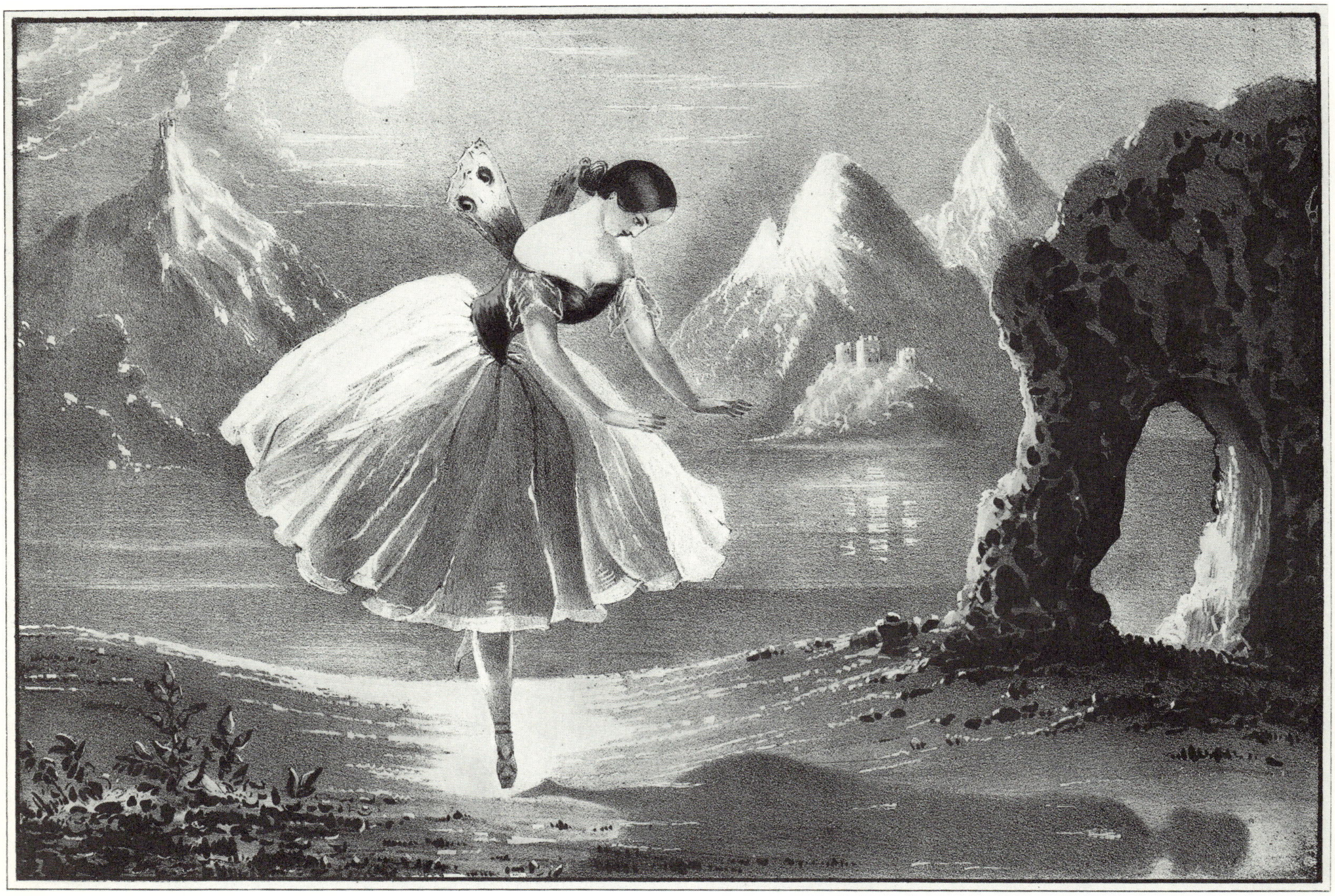

94. Fanny Elssler in the Shadow Dance in *Ondine*.

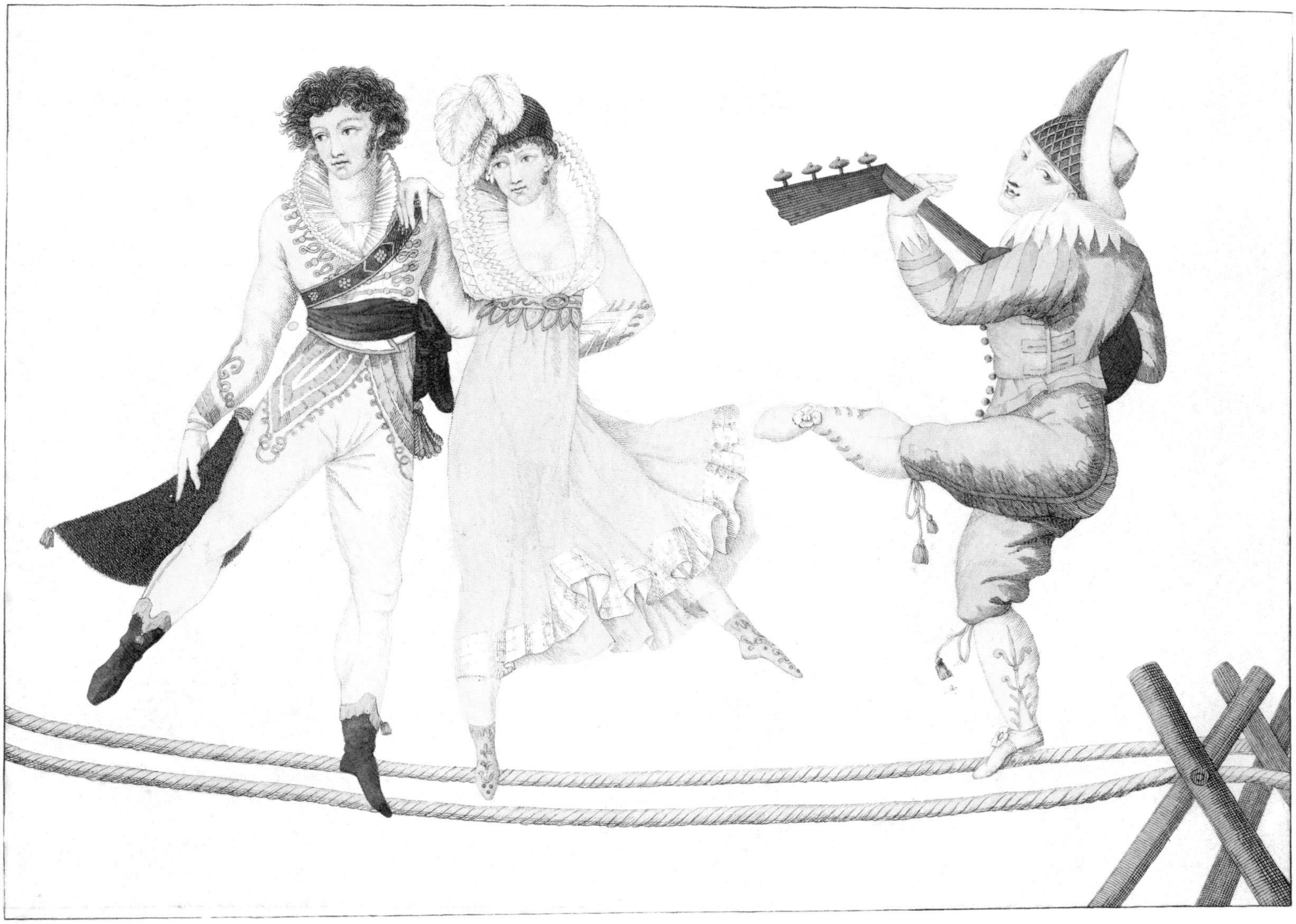

95. Gabriel Ravel and his troupe in their early days in Paris (in U.S.A. 1830s to 1860s).

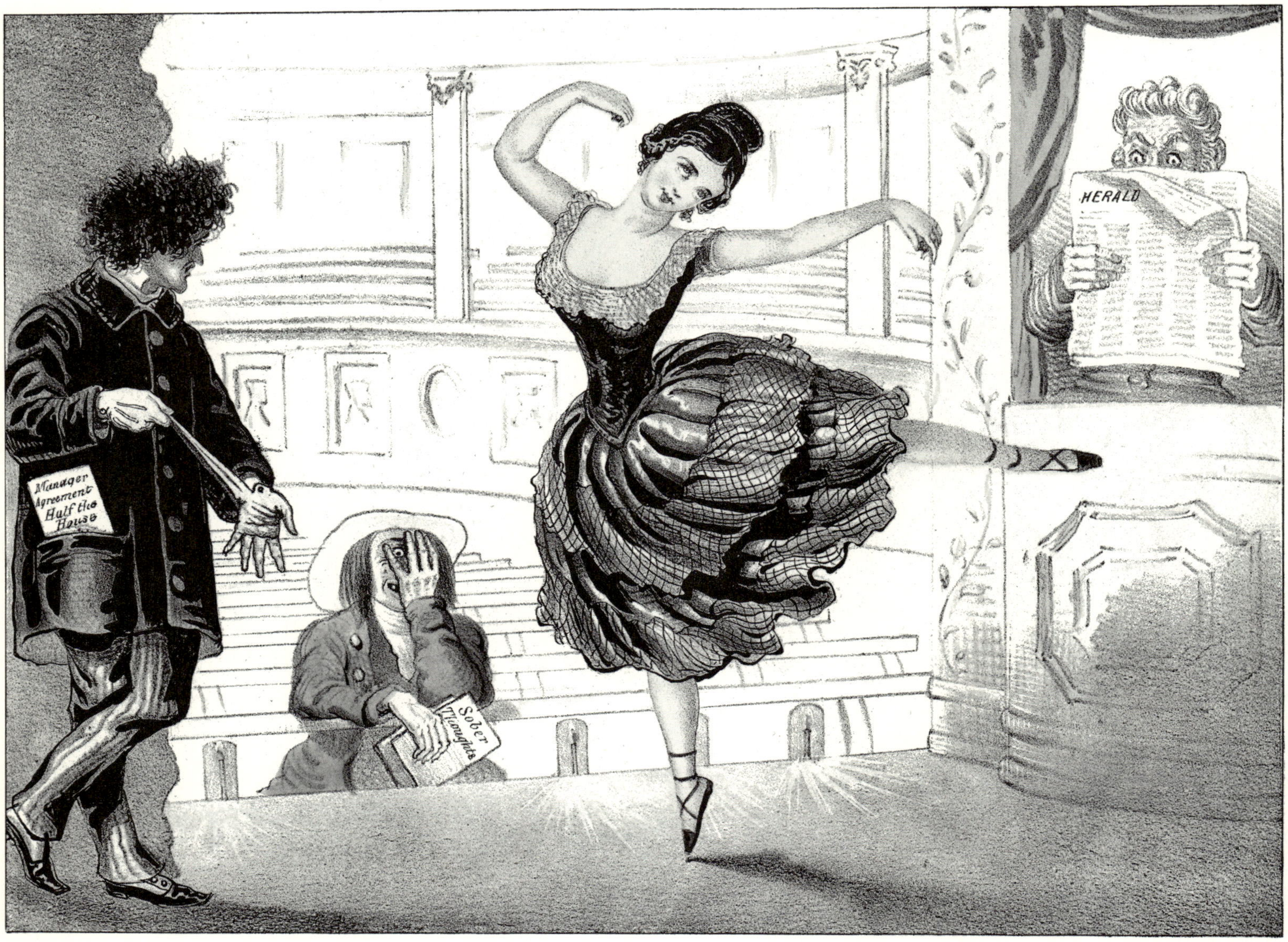

96. Lola Montez at the Park Theatre, N.Y., 1851.

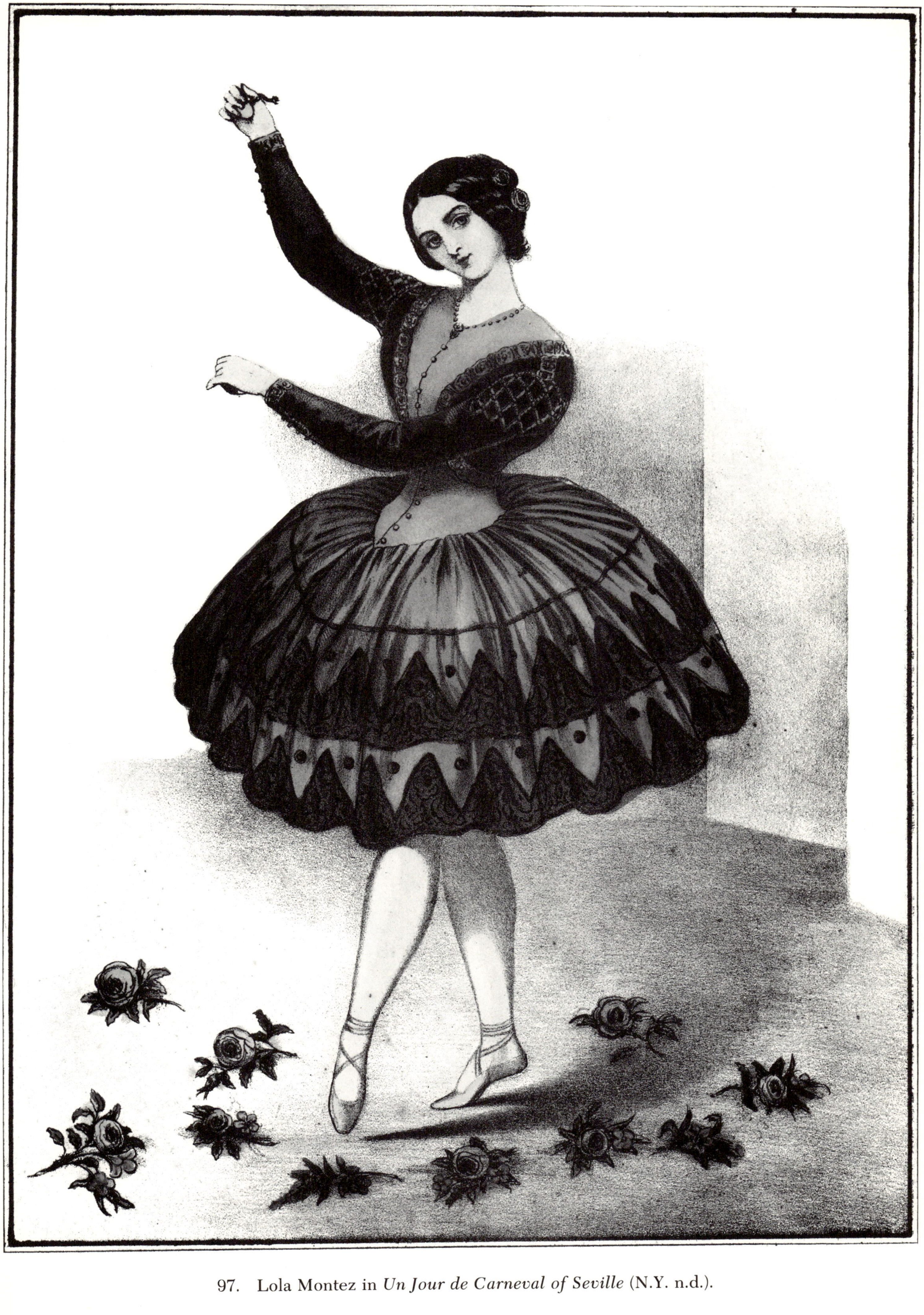

97. Lola Montez in *Un Jour de Carneval of Seville* (N.Y. n.d.).

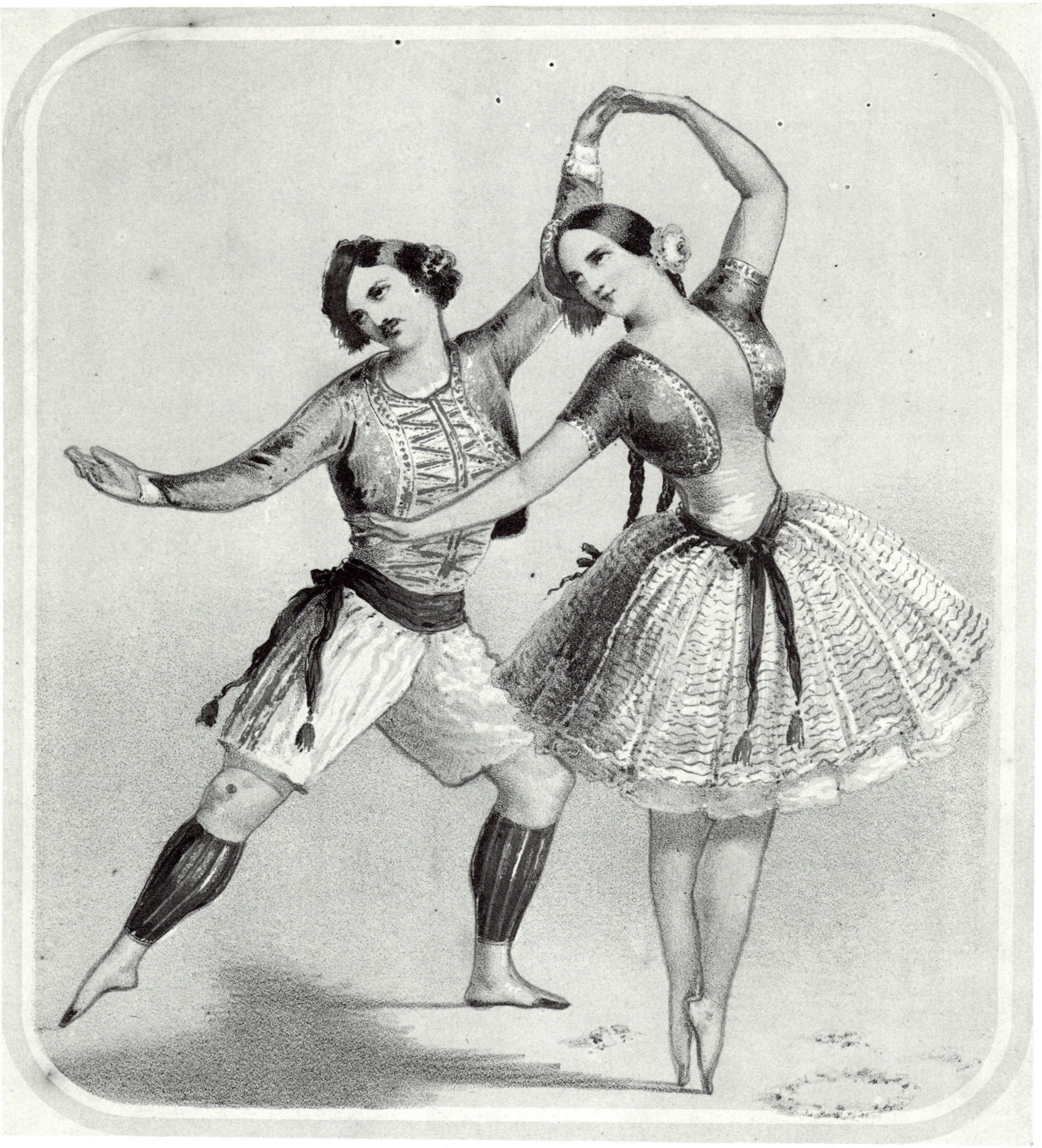

98. Hippolyte and Adèle Monplaisir (Georges Sornier and Adèle Bartholomin) in *L'Almée* (Broadway Theatre, N.Y., 1847).

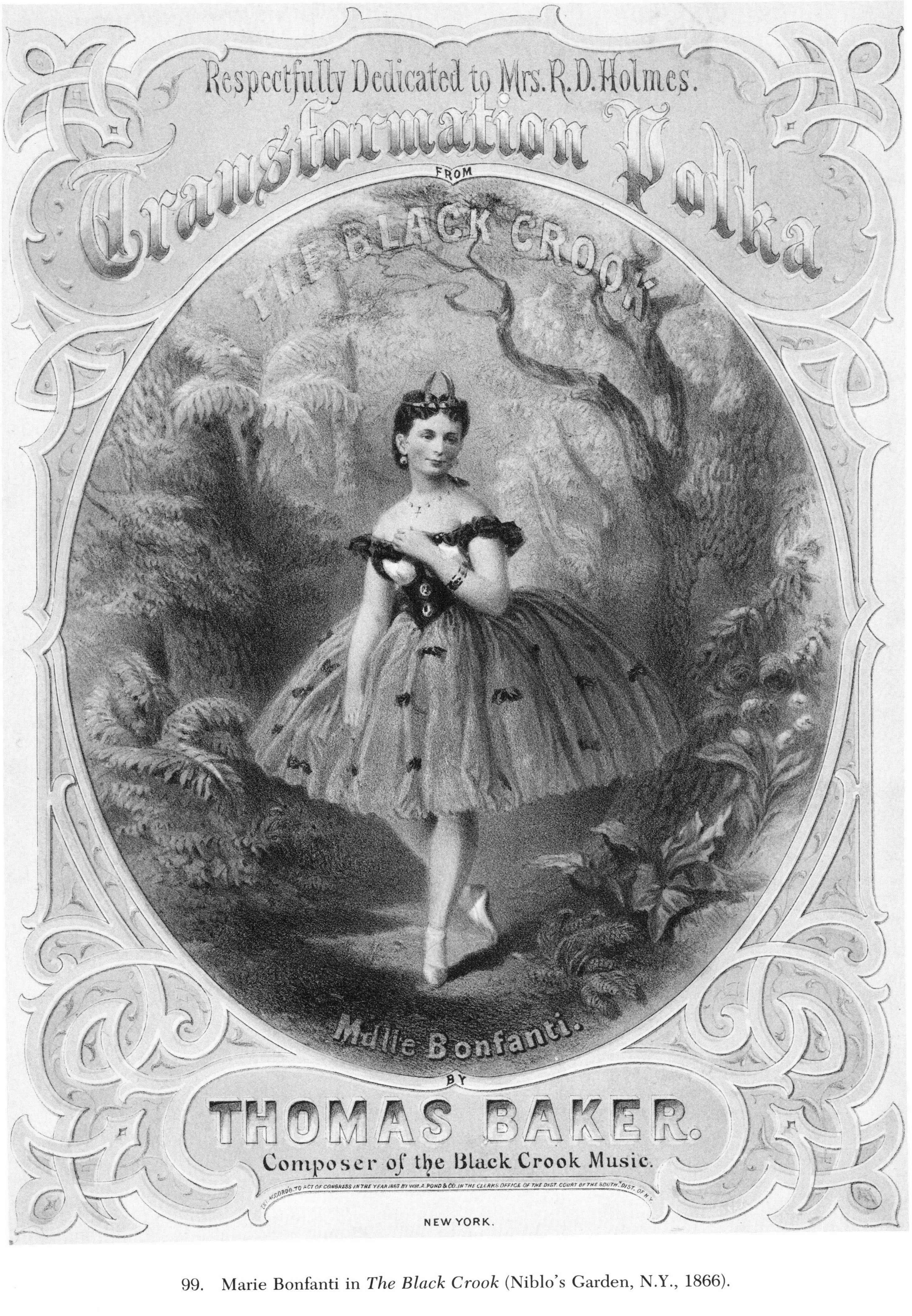

99. Marie Bonfanti in *The Black Crook* (Niblo's Garden, N.Y., 1866).

A Postscript

IN THIS BOOK there are several illustrations which, at first glance, may seem to have little or nothing to do with classical ballet. However, all of them have been included because they represent important aspects of the Romantic era and their ballet association soon becomes apparent.

Plate 17 depicts Madame Vestris, *en travesti*, as Orpheus, in a very brief costume (quite shocking in those days), swimming across the River Styx in search of "Euridice! Euridice! Euridice!" The year was 1832 and "Madame" was not only the star performer of the comic extravaganza *Olympic Devils*, but also the very successful manager of the Olympic Theatre. Born Eliza Bartolozzi, granddaughter of one of the most celebrated London engravers, she left home to study ballet with the *premier danseur* of the King's Theatre, Armand Vestris, whom she married in 1813, when she was not yet seventeen. In 1814, Armand was appointed ballet master and he was also a busy choreographer, while his wife appeared with modest success in dancing and singing roles, but after two years the marriage broke up and Armand departed for Italy and eventually Vienna, where he died prematurely in 1825. Left to her own devices, "Madame" forged a brilliant if stormy career for herself as actress, singer and theater manager, specializing in remarkably well-staged musical burlesques, not to mention the melodramas connected with her private life and legion lovers. William W. Appleton, in his delightful biography *Madame Vestris and the London Stage* (Columbia University Press, 1974), quotes Leigh Hunt as saying of "Madame": "She is a true singer, a pleasing actress, and a handsome woman, three graces not very frequently united in the same woman," and Appleton adds that for twenty years she "was to exercise an extraordinary influence on both production and acting styles." In 1838, aged forty-two, she married the actor Charles James Mathews, who remained touchingly devoted to her until her death in 1856.

Of special interest is Madame Vestris' first husband, Armand, the grandson and son of France's two most famous dancers, Gaëtan and Auguste Vestris, for was it not Armand from whom Brugnoli learned to perform "upon the extreme point of the toe"? Where and how had Armand originally acquired this knowledge? He was at the Paris Opéra at the time when Geneviève Gosselin was making her first tentative efforts to rise on *pointe;* did he try to teach her before he ever knew Brugnoli? Or was it Mlle Gosselin who gave him the idea?

Ravishing, raven-haired, blue-eyed, Irish Eliza Gilbert contrived a career and international notoriety as Lola Montez, less because of her abilities as a Spanish dancer (she had acquired a smattering during a brief visit in Spain) than because of her penchant for scandal. Among the many celebrities she accumulated as lovers was King Ludwig I of Bavaria, who gave her the title of Countess of Landsfeld and a palace and allowed her to meddle in politics until she brought about a government crisis that obliged the King to abdicate. Her travels had taken her to London, Paris and Poland, and after the Munich affair she went to the United States, where reports of her outrageous doings had preceded her (Plate 96). For another decade, she continued to perform in public, making long tours in America and Australia and adding to her collection of husbands and lovers along the way. Nevertheless, she should not be thought of, as she too often is, as merely an adventuress—like Casanova, who has come down in history as the great seducer rather than the keen and witty observer that he was of eighteenth-century mores and scenes. Lola introduced ballet and Spanish dancing (Plate 97) in Far Western mining towns and other places where nothing of the sort had ever been seen; she was the author of several books and was able to address a Boston lecture audience in Latin; and she should also be remembered for teaching and inspiring Lotta Crabtree, one of America's most important actresses of the post-Civil War era.

Friedrich Horschfelt, ballet master at the Theater an der Wien, 1815–1821, established a school and performing company of children there, the Kinderballett. For several years he trained such future outstanding dancers as Anton Stuhlmüller, Therese Heberle and Fanny Elssler, though Mlle Elssler later denied the connection, no doubt because the school had acquired a bad reputation. Suspected of purveying young girls to jaded aristocrats, Horschfelt was forced to close the school by a decree of the Emperor. Far more successful was the ballet school for girls founded afterwards by Frau Josephine Weiss. In 1845, a time when travel was far from simple, this extraordinary woman piloted her troupe to Paris, where the thirty-six *petites danseuses* (and one little boy), five to twelve years old, performed at the Opéra with such ease, charm and precision that the critics held them up as models for the often careless and self-indulgent Opéra *corps de ballet*. The Danseuses Viennoises went on to great acclaim, appearing in fourteen different ballets and *pas* at Her Majesty's

Theatre, London, and in Canada and the United States (Plate 63).

And then there was the Spanish Gypsy, Pepita de Oliva, whose life story was more romantic than the plot of any ballet such as *La Gipsy* or *La Gitana*. She grew up in a miserable basement with her widowed mother, who peddled old clothes to eke out a living, but who fully understood the inborn talent and possibilities of her beautiful daughter. She took Pepita to the director of the main theater of Madrid, persuaded him to arrange for dancing lessons and, in no time at all, the young girl had become a star performer and, in fact, was advertised and known all over Europe as "the Star of Andalusia." It would seem that only prudish Bournonville did not appreciate her. After attending her Copenhagen debut, he spoke of "the enthusiasm for her [that] amounted to madness," adding: "I wept over the desecration of my lovely Muse"—much as he did in Russia when he tried to commiserate with Marius Petipa over "the excessively short skirts" and "the obvious lascivious tendency that pervades the whole choreographic movement." In 1851, Pepita contracted a loveless and unfortunate marriage with the dancer Juan de Oliva—unfortunate because only a year later she met the English diplomat Lionel Sackville-West and from the first moment they were madly and eternally in love. For Catholic Pepita a divorce was out of the question and it was equally impossible for Sackville-West to share his public life with her without jeopardizing his career. However, he settled her in a house in France, stayed there with her whenever his duties permitted and was heartbroken when she died in 1872, giving birth to their fifth child. In the meanwhile, her triumphant progress as a dancer (Plates 74 & 75) had only increased until she retired in 1866. After her death, her faithful Sackville-West became Lord Sackville and inherited Knole, one of the most spectacular castles in England. Amid that splendor (what a contrast with the dancer's sordid childhood!) Pepita's eldest daughter grew up, eventually becoming the Dowager Lady Sackville, whose daughter in turn became the celebrated author Vita Sackville-West.

Pepita is memorable for having carried forward the noble tradition of Spanish dancing, which was first absorbed into the classical ballet by Fanny Elssler and which, in our century, was to find expression through Picasso, Manuel de Falla and Massine in Diaghilev's production of *Le Tricorne*.

Plate 44 shows the cancan in full swing at the Bal Mabille, the most elaborate, attractive and famous of the many public balls which flourished in Paris during the mid-nineteenth century. Its founder, Jacques Mabille, for many years had run a fashionable dancing school in the Rue Saint-Honoré for professionals as well as members of the aristocracy and two of his three sons became well-known dancers at the Opéra, Auguste and Charles, who married the American ballerina Augusta Maywood.

In 1840, Mabille bought a large tract of woods along the Allée des Veuves (today Avenue Montaigne, site of the Théâtre des Champs-Elysées) where he set up a modest place for public dancing and refreshments. The success of this venture was such that his eldest son, Victor, abandoned his career as a lawyer in order to supervise the landscaping and development of the locale, which was soon to be described as magical, a fairyland of lights and flowers. Huge wrought-iron gates were erected which opened into an avenue of poplar trees, beyond which lay a vast semicircle of columns topped by flower-filled urns and gas lights. In the center stood a Chinese pavilion for the musicians, flanked by lampposts and tall palm trees made of painted tole, surrounded on all sides by flower beds, dance floors and bars, festooned everywhere with garlands of lights. Before long it was a mecca for performers from all the theaters of Paris, who demonstrated the newest dance crazes, such as the polka and cancan; it was also the preferred rendezvous for men-about-town and women of easy virtue and a sine qua non for tourists.

In the summer of 1853, the author of *Uncle Tom's Cabin*, Harriet Beecher Stowe, wrote an ecstatic description of the place in her travel book *Sunny Memories of Foreign Lands*, London, 1854, p. 242; the Bal Mabille was also immortalized in hundreds of prints and caricatures and was even denounced from the pulpit.

Our print is one of a pair, the other of which depicts the polka.

Some Notes on the Printmakers

THE MOST sought-after nineteenth-century ballet prints are those based on drawings and paintings by Alfred Edward Chalon, who was born in Geneva but settled in London while still young and devoted a good part of his life to portraits of actresses and dancers. Greatly influenced by English eighteenth-century painters, Chalon was much inclined to prettify his sitters, no doubt a main reason for the wide appeal of his work. It should be noted that he seldom made his own prints, relying instead on the lithographers Richard James Lane, John S. Templeton and Thomas Herbert Maguire. He is well represented among the fine illustrations of Beaumont and Sitwell's *The Romantic Ballet in Lithographs of the Time*, London, 1938, itself now a collector's item, but a book which, alas, teems with preposterous statements by Sacheverell Sitwell. For instance, he attributes "The Three Graces" to Chalon, whereas documents in the Bibliothèque de l'Opéra prove not only that it was the work of a French artist, Eugène Lejeune, 1844, but that the names in the wreaths at the feet of the three ballerinas (added later by another hand) should read Taglioni, Elssler and Grisi (not Cerrito). One of the most delightful in the whole gallery of prints, "The Three Graces" was quickly pirated by American lithographers (Currier; Sarony & Major) and it is amusing to observe that, to avoid offending the puritanical morals of the American public, the bare feet of all three dancers were tricked out with slippers and Grisi's nude bosom was concealed by an embroidered bodice. Taglioni also lost her sylphide wings; perhaps they too might have been considered wanton and ungodly (Plate 56).

Sitwell also affirms, in reference to his Battistelli lithograph of Amalia Ferraris, that this print "has a distinction all its own, as being nearly the only Italian print of the Romantic Ballet." Interested readers should know that Edwin Binney III's catalogue of Italian prints, 1815–1875 (in *Dance Perspectives*, No. 53), lists no less than 467, three of which are reproduced in the present volume. Neither does Sitwell scruple to say that he has omitted Madame Céleste (Keppler) because she was not a professional dancer, but one of "the popular beauties of the day, for whom the stage was but the frame in which they presented themselves to their admirers." On the contrary, by the time she was twenty-three, Céleste, one of the most valiant troupers of her era, had danced in Liverpool, Dublin and London (with Pauline Leroux at Covent Garden, 1834) and as the most beloved performer ever to tour the United States, she was famous as the Maid of Cashmere, was reported to have amassed $100,000, a staggering sum in those days, and had the distinction of being America's first Sylphide (Color Plate F, Plate 91).

Besides Chalon, other distinguished English portraitists of ballerinas include Joseph Bouvier, James Henry Lynch, Templeton and Maguire, all of whom produced their own prints, as did John Brandard, who practically made a career of lithographs for music covers. Perhaps the most unusual and precociously gifted was Madame Soyer (née Elizabeth Emma Jones), who first exhibited at the Royal Academy at the age of ten and, by the time she was twelve, had completed two hundred portraits (Plate 34).

Among Parisians, the most celebrated were Eugène-Louis Lami, who designed the costumes (but not Taglioni's tutu) for *La Sylphide*, whose painting *Le Foyer de la Danse* has been continually reengraved and published everywhere (Plate 37), and who illustrated many books; Achille Devéria, one of two famous brothers (Plate 12), and Pierre-Louis Grévedon, author of the loveliest portrait of Elssler (Plate 26). Marie-Alexandre Alophe is best known for his set of fourteen ballerinas which includes a print of Taglioni filched from Chalon's *Flore et Zéphire* (Plates 80, 81, 83, 86, 87, 88). The firm of Martinet, which produced over 3000 prints between 1796 and 1880, turned out some 200 on the Romantic ballet, very small engravings and slightly larger lithographs. And then there was Haguental, the super-pirate, who helped himself to the works of all the best English artists.

Austro-German prints, though interesting as documentation, are generally far less refined and attractive. Some 474 have also been catalogued by Edwin Binney III. Russian prints, rarely seen in Western Europe and the United States, are known mainly through reproductions in books, though often even these are adaptations from French, English and German originals. It is a matter of record, nevertheless, that during 1837, when Taglioni first appeared in St. Petersburg with "immense, immense, incredible success," 3000 prints of her were distributed and one wonders what could have become of such a quantity. There must also have been numberless engravings and lithographs of Russian ballerinas as well as of other visiting celebrities. A steady procession of Western dancers wended their way to St. Petersburg and were received with wild enthusiasm—Marius Petipa, Perrot, Saint-Léon, Grisi, Elssler, Grahn, Cerrito, Rosati, Ferraris, Adèle Grantzow and Yrca Matthias— and a serious effort of research remains to be done in tracking down the souvenir prints that may have survived. In the meanwhile, attention is drawn to two in the Harvard Theatre Collection: Taglioni's foot, shod in a ballet slipper, on *pointe* among the clouds, and an unusually beautiful colored lithograph of Grisi and Perrot in *The Naiad and the Fisherman* staged in the romantic moonlit setting of the Peterhof Pavilion gardens, 1851.

Finally, there is the American display of over 200 items, many copied from European sources and some pathetically crude. Technically the best and the most popular were fifty-two hand-colored ballet lithographs published at regular intervals after 1837 by Nathaniel Currier. They represent dancers who toured in the United States as well as some who never came here, and are often incorrectly titled.

A Selected Bibliography

Académie Royale de Musique: *Chroniques.*

Album de l'Opéra [various authors], Challamel, Paris, n.d.

Anonymous: *Les Adieux à Mlle Taglioni*, Paris, 1837.

——: *The Letters and Journal of Fanny Elssler*, New York, 1845.

Appleton, William W.: *Madame Vestris and the London Stage*, Columbia University Press, New York, 1974.

Arago, Jacques: *Mémoires d'un Petit Banc de l'Opéra*, Ebrard, Paris, 1844.

Baril, Jacques: *Dictionnaire de Danse*, Editions du Seuil, Paris, 1964.

Baron, A.: *Lettres et Entretiens sur la Danse*, Dondey-Dupré, Paris, 1824.

Beaumont, Cyril W.: *Complete Book of Ballets*, Grosset & Dunlap, New York, 1938.

——: *The Ballet Called Giselle*, C. W. Beaumont, London, 1944.

——: *Ballet Design: Past and Present*, C. W. Beaumont, London, 1946.

—— and Sitwell, Sacheverell: *The Romantic Ballet in Lithographs of the Time*, Faber and Faber, London, 1938.

Beetz, Wilhelm: *Das Wiener Opernhaus*, Panorama, Zurich, 1949.

Binney, Edwin, III: "A Century of Austro-German Dance Prints 1790–1890," in *Dance Perspectives*, New York, No. 47, Autumn 1971.

——: "Sixty Years of Italian Dance Prints 1815–1875," in *Dance Perspectives*, New York, No. 53, Spring 1973.

Blasis, Carlo: *Traité Elémentaire, Théorique et Pratique de l'Art de la Danse*, Beati & Tenenti, Milan, 1820.

——: *The Code of Terpsichore*, London, 1830.

——: *Notes Upon Dancing, Historical and Practical*, Delaporte, London, 1847.

Blessington, Lady Marguerite: *The Idler in Italy*, London, 1839.

——: *The Idler in France*, London, 1841.

Boigne, Charles de: *Petits Mémoires de l'Opéra*, Librairie Nouvelle, Paris, 1857.

Bournonville, August: *Mit Theaterliv*, Copenhagen, 1848, 1865, 1877.

——: *Lettres à la maison de son enfance*, Munksgaard, Copenhagen, 1969.

Bouteron, Marcel: *Danse et Musique Romantiques*, Goupy, Paris, 1927.

Brown, T. Allston: *A History of the New York Stage*, Dodd, Mead, New York, 1903.

Bunn, Alfred: *The Stage*, Bently, London, 1840.

Cambiasi, Pompeo: *La Scala 1778–1889*, Ricordi, Milan, 1888.

Cametti, Alberto: *Il Teatro di Tordinona poi di Apollo*, Tivoli, 1938.

Castil-Blaze, F.-H.-J.: *La Danse et les Ballets depuis Bacchus jusqu'à Mademoiselle Taglioni*, Poulin, Paris, 1832.

——: *L'Académie Impériale de Musique*, Paris, 1855.

Chaffee, George: "A Chart to the American Souvenir Lithographs of the Romantic Ballet 1825–1870," in *Dance Index*, New York, Vol. I, No. 2, February 1942.

——: "The Romantic Ballet in London: 1821–1858," in *Dance Index*, New York, Vol. II, Nos. 9, 10, 11, 12, September–December 1943.

——: "Three or Four Graces. A Centenary Salvo," in *Dance Index*, New York, Vol. III, Nos. 9, 10, 11, September–November 1944.

Delarue, Allison: *The Chevalier Henry Wikoff*, Princeton University Press, 1968.

Desarbres, Nérée: *Deux Siècles à l'Opéra*, Dentu, Paris, 1868.

Ehrhard, Auguste: *Une Vie de Danseuse: Fanny Elssler*, Paris, 1909.

Félix-Bouvier: *Une Danseuse de l'Opéra, La Bigottini*, Paris, 1909.

Fog, Dan: *The Royal Danish Ballet, 1760–1950, and August Bournonville*, Fog, Copenhagen, 1961.

Fourcaud: *Léontine Beaugrand*, Ollendorf, Paris, 1881.

Galerie des Artistes Dramatiques de Paris [various authors], Marchant, Paris, 1841.

Gautier, Théophile: *Portraits Contemporains*, Charpentier, Paris, 1874.

——: *A History of Romanticism*, Sproul, New York, 1902.

——: *Paris Besieged*, Sproul, New York, 1902.

——: *The Romantic Ballet as seen by Théophile Gautier*, translated and published by Cyril Beaumont, London, 1947.

——, Janin, Jules, and Chasles, Philarète: *Les Beautés de l'Opéra*, Soulié, Paris, 1845.

Guest, Ivor: *The Ballet of the Second Empire 1858–1870*, Adam and Charles Black, London, 1953.

——: *The Romantic Ballet in England*, Phoenix House, London, 1954.

——: *The Ballet of the Second Empire 1847–1858*, Adam and Charles Black, London, 1955.

——: *Fanny Cerrito*, Phoenix House, London, 1956.

——: *Victorian Ballet Girl*, Adam and Charles Black, London, 1957.

——: *The Romantic Ballet in Paris*, Wesleyan University Press, Middletown, Connecticut, 1966.

Hervey, Charles: *The Theatres of Paris*, John Mitchell, London, 1846.

Ireland, Joseph N.: *Records of the New York Stage*, T. H. Morell, New York, 1866.

Jullien, Adolphe: *Histoire du Costume au Théâtre*, Charpentier, Paris, 1880.

Kapp, Dr. Julius: *186 Jahre Staatsoper*, Atlantic, Berlin, 1928.

Kochno, Boris: *Le Ballet*, Hachette, Paris, 1954.

Kragh-Jacobsen, Svend, & Krogh, Torben: *Den Kongelige Dansk Ballet*, Copenhagen, 1953.

Levinson, André: *Marie Taglioni*, Beaumont, London, 1930.

Lifar, Serge: *Carlotta Grisi*, Lehmann, London, 1947.

[Linden, Elise]: *Fanny Elssler, Correspondence*, Ullstein, Berlin, 1921.

Lothar, Rudoph, & Stern, Julius: *50 Jahre Hoftheater, Geschichte beider Wiener Hoftheater*, Expedition, Vienna, 1900.

Lumley, Benjamin: *Reminiscences of the Opera*, Hurst & Blackett, London, 1864.

Maurice, Charles: *Histoire Anecdotique du Théâtre*, Plon, Paris, 1856.

Migel, Parmenia: *The Ballerinas, from the Court of Louis XIV to Pavlova*, Macmillan, New York, 1972.

Mille, Agnes de: *The Book of the Dance*, Golden Press, New York, 1963.

Moore, Lillian: "Prints on Pushcarts, The Dance Lithographs of Currier and Ives," in *Dance Perspectives*, New York, No. 15, 1962.

[Moore, Lillian]: *Russian Ballet Master, The Memoirs of Marius Petipa*, Adam and Charles Black, London, 1958.

Neiiendam, Robert: *Lucile Grahn: en Skaebne i Dansen*, Copenhagen, 1963.

Odell, George C. D.: *Annals of the New York Stage*, Columbia University Press, New York, 1928 ff.

Phelps, H. P.: *Players of a Century*, McDonough, Albany, 1880.

Pirchan, Emil: *Fanny Elssler*, Wilhelm Frick, Vienna, 1940.

Pougin, Arthur: *Acteurs et Actrices d'Autrefois*, Juven, Paris, n.d.

Reade, Brian: *Ballet Designs and Illustrations*, Victoria & Albert Museum, London, 1967.

Reyna, Ferdinando: *Des Origines du Ballet*, Tallone, Paris, 1955.

Rootzén, Kajsa: *Den Svenska Baletten*, Stockholm, 1945.

Roqueplan, Nestor: *Les Coulisses de l'Opéra*, Paris, 1855.

——: *La Vie Parisienne*, Lévy, Paris, 1882.

Royer, Alphonse: *Histoire de l'Opéra*, Bachelin-Deflorenne, Paris, 1875.

Sackville-West, Vita: *Pepita*, Hogarth Press, London, 1937.

Soria, Henri de: *Histoire Pittoresque de la Danse*, H. Noble, Paris, 1897.

Stowe, Harriet Beecher, *Sunny Memories of Foreign Lands*, London, 1854.

Swift, Mary Grace: *Belles and Beaux on Their Toes: Dancing Stars in Young America*, University Press of America, Washington, 1980.

Vaillat, Léandre: *Histoire de la Danse*, Plon, Paris, 1942.

——: *La Taglioni*, Michel, Paris, 1942.

Véron, Louis: *Mémoires d'un Bourgeois de Paris*, Librairie Nouvelle, Paris, 1856.

Vuillier, Gaston: *La Danse*, Hachette, Paris, 1898.

Wemyss, Francis Courtney: *Twenty-Six Years of the Life of an Actor and Manager*, New York, 1847.

Winter, Marian Hannah: *The Pre-Romantic Ballet*, Pitman, London, 1974.

Wyndham, Horace: *The Magnificent Montez*, London, 1935.

X. Y. Z.: *Le Nouvel Opéra*, Lévy, Paris, 1875.

Index

The letters A through H refer to the color plates following page 16. The List of Plates and Bibliography are not indexed.

Persons

Ballets

Opéra-Divertissements